The Postwar African American Novel

THE POSTWAR AFRICAN AMERICAN NOVEL

Protest and Discontent, 1945–1950

Stephanie Brown

University Press of Mississippi / Jackson

Margaret Walker Alexander Series in African American Studies

www.upress.state.ms.us

The University Press of Mississippi is a member of
the Association of American University Presses.

"'If I Can Only Get It Funny!': Chester Himes's Parodic Protest Novels" first appeared, in somewhat altered form, in *Invisible Suburbs: Recovering Protest Fiction in the 1950s United States*, edited by Josh Lukin (Jackson: University Press of Mississippi, 2008).

Copyright © 2011 by University Press of Mississippi
All rights reserved
Manufactured in the United States of America

First printing 2011

∞

Library of Congress Cataloging-in-Publication Data

Brown, Stephanie, 1970–
The postwar African American novel : protest and discontent, 1945–1950 / Stephanie Brown.
p. cm. — (Margaret Walker Alexander series in African American studies)
Includes bibliographical references and index.
ISBN 978-1-60473-973-2 (cloth : alk. paper) — ISBN 978-1-60473-974-9 (ebook) 1. American fiction—African American authors—History and criticism. 2. American fiction—20th century—History and criticism. 3. Protest literature, American—History and criticism. 4. African Americans in literature. 5. Discontent in literature. I. Title.
PS153.N5B677 2011
813'.5409896073—dc22   2010036027

British Library Cataloging-in-Publication Data available

To Stephen, Virginia, and Clara,
without whose help, patience and forbearance
this project could never have been completed.

Contents

3   Introduction

CHAPTER ONE
7   Beyond Protest: Retracing the Margins of the Postwar African American Novel

CHAPTER TWO
41   "If I Can Only Get It Funny!": Chester Himes's Parodic Protest Novels

CHAPTER THREE
67   Frank Yerby and the "Costume Drama" of Southern Historiography

CHAPTER FOUR
99   William Gardner Smith and the Cosmopolitan War Novel

CHAPTER FIVE
132   J. Saunders Redding and the African American Campus Novel

161   Conclusion

165   Notes

173   Works Cited

187   Index

The Postwar African American Novel

Introduction

A short article in a recent issue of the *Journal of Blacks in Higher Education* echoed what is likely to be common knowledge among English teachers: Of the many possible indicators of canonicity in African American literature, the roster of CliffsNotes titles is one of the most reliable ("Black Authors"). The author noted that of the 247 works available in 2001 from CliffsNotes, the 16 by black writers, ranging from Frederick Douglass's *Narrative of the Life of Frederick Douglass* to Ernest Gaines's *A Lesson before Dying*, undoubtedly make up the core of African American literary texts offered in college English classes. Of course, 16 books can give only the sketchiest representation of the literary output of a period of nearly 150 years. Perhaps it is inevitable, then, that only two novelists represent African American literature from 1940 until 1965 and that they are Richard Wright and Ralph Ellison.[1]

No one would suggest that redefining the African American literary canon is the responsibility of the editors of CliffsNotes; given that these guides are produced for the explicit purpose of supplying study aids for works that are regularly taught, these selections make perfect sense. Yet their choices, like those of the literature professors whose syllabi create the demand for CliffsNotes, mirror a wider and increasingly inexplicable lack of academic interest in a greater range of black writers of the 1940s and 1950s. This apathy is particularly surprising given the current emphasis on providing a more nuanced understanding of cultural production in the postwar years, an understanding that moves beyond the tendency to label works of the period as exclusively conservative and oppressive, or as, in Josh Lukin's felicitous phrase, just "an undifferentiated lump of *grisaille*" (1). Even as critics and historians reexamine and often explode assumptions about the postwar period both as a historical and cultural construct and as a literary and artistic era, a strange lacuna in African American criticism persists. As a result of this absence of inquiry, African

American literature produced during this period emerges, by default, as the space *between* Wright's *Native Son* and the Black Arts movement, a generally homogenous period of unremarkable social realist literary output epitomized by the Wrightian protest novel and punctuated only by the anomalous masterpiece of Ellison's *Invisible Man*. Despite periodic flares of critical interest (notably in the mid-1970s) in complicating the picture of postwar African American belles lettres with biographies and new editions of out-of-print works, subsequent generations of critics and scholars have, on the whole, done little to dislodge Wright and Ellison as the brightest stars in the firmament of canonical postwar African American novels, beside whom those relegated to serving as the era's lesser lights remain dim if not entirely obscured.

This book examines and dismantles the received wisdom that has led to this distorted image and works to restore to prominence some of Wright's and Ellison's overlooked but extraordinarily influential peers. I look closely at a brief moment in African American literary history—the period between the end of World War II and the solidification of the containment culture of the 1950s. It represents a defining moment in African American literature that is crucial to understand yet impossible to pin down. During this period, before the entrenchment of subsequent critical paradigms, we can see heated and unexpected negotiations among critics, writers, and editors concerning the appropriate form for the African American novel. This debate was multifaceted, engaging not only political, social, cultural, and artistic issues but also pragmatic questions of the literary marketplace and the limits (perceived and contested) of genre for African American novelists. To better understand the African American novel of then and now, I reconstruct the "imagined communities," to use Benedict Anderson's term, of black readers and writers of the postwar era by recovering the heated debates among authors, writers, and critics over the African American novel, debates that reflect far less consensus than has been generally understood.

By extension, this study also asks why we have come to embrace a revisionist and antipodean reading of the period as thoroughly dominated by Wright and Ellison and what investment we—critics and scholars—have in emphasizing their prominence at the expense of their then-promising contemporaries, among them such widely read novelists as Chester

Himes, Willard Motley, Ann Petry, Saunders Redding, William Gardner Smith, Dorothy West, and Frank Yerby, possibly the best-selling African American writer of all time. How can we begin to grapple with what Barbara Herrnstein Smith has dubbed the "contingencies of value" that have determined (and overdetermined) our evaluation of immediate postwar African American fiction? What effect has our consideration of the reception of specific novels had on our notions of the cultural work they did and might still do if these volumes were read today? What notions of genre and of a divide between "serious" and "popular" fiction obscure and obstruct our view of the period? What does it tell us that, for example, such very different contemporary novelists as Charles Johnson and Ernest Gaines share an insistence that they have been entirely uninfluenced by African American novels published before the late 1960s, which both authors regard as undistinguished?

Chapter 1 grapples with these issues, tracking the development of these paradigms while situating them within the vibrant broader critical conversation that emerges when we examine the reviews and analyses produced by African American scholars in the years in question. Many of these scholarly works refer to novels now long out of print, some of which form the core of this project. The novels discussed here are all understudied; some have simply been forgotten altogether. Yet as a group they represent a series of specialized (and highly marketable) genres, none of which was traditionally identified with the history of African American fiction. I begin my readings of individual authors in chapter 2 by considering Chester Himes's debut novel, *If He Hollers Let Him Go*, written during the war and published just as it was ending, to interrogate traditional assumptions about the book's generic classification as a "classic protest novel." Subsequent chapters address the largely forgotten work of a trio of now unfamiliar authors—Frank Yerby, William Gardner Smith, and J. Saunders Redding—all of whom were deeply engaged with the philosophical and aesthetic arguments surrounding the emphasis on the protest novel and chose instead to problematize and rework other genres. Yerby, whose work has long been considered valuable more as a curiosity in publishing history than as a serious contribution to the African American literary tradition, used the historical romance (which he called the "costume novel") to overturn the dominant historiographic modes of his era and rewrite the history of Reconstruction, while Smith appropriated the war novel to produce a sophisticated if idealistic exploration of his nascent cosmopolitanism. Finally, Redding, a longtime college professor, produced the first black academic novel, offering a scathing indictment of the black educational system even as he revised a generally satirical genre to allow for the critical difference the setting of such a work in a historically black college makes to the novel's purpose and its reception.

While no single case study can definitively establish an alternative view of the postwar black novel, the collective investigation of these works reveals a long-suppressed history of the literature, and the details revealed give shade and nuance to an image of the postwar black novel that has suffered from the broad strokes with which it has been delineated. A closer examination of a series of texts published between 1945 and 1950, combined with a reexamination of the critical climate and communities of readers at the time these works appeared, will help to redress this imbalance and contribute to an illumination of the contours of the ongoing critical discussion of the politics of theorizing African American literature.

CHAPTER ONE

Beyond Protest: Retracing the Margins of the Postwar African American Novel

To re-create the conditions of the production of the African American novel between 1945 and 1950, we must not only recover the lost voices of the time, we must pry open a space in the critical models available for theorizing postwar African American culture. Critical reassessments of this era have proliferated in the past twenty years, with the end of the Cold War providing cultural historians with both a sense of closure for a long-standing global narrative and a rich source of archival materials from the former Soviet Union and its satellites. Early contributions to the field include Lary May's pioneering collection, *Recasting America: Culture and Politics in the Age of Cold War* (1989), Stephen J. Whitfield's *The Culture of the Cold War* (1990), and W. T. Lhamon's cultural history, *Deliberate Speed: The Origins of a Cultural Style in the American 1950s* (1990). Often, however, the focus has been on the work of white writers, while black musicians and (more rarely) visual artists have stood in for the cultural production of African Americans more generally. Ralph Ellison provides the single exception, yet even Ellison criticism is problematic: the durable comparison between the aesthetic of *Invisible Man* and that of a symphonic jazz composition, for example, blurs the boundaries between music and writing, managing the oxymoronic feat of marginalizing the canonical. Alan Nadel's *Containment Culture: American Narrative, Postmodernism, and the Atomic Age* (2002) offers a refreshing shift from Ellison to John A. Williams and Alice Walker as representative Cold War African American novelists, but the fact that the works he discusses date from the mid-1960s and mid-1970s, respectively, again underscores the absence of attention to black writing of the late 1940s and 1950s.

Instead of nuance, we have received a tidy narrative. The critical truism is that with the publication of *Native Son* in 1940, "America was aroused out of her contumelious indifference" to black writers (Chandler 28). Wright's work galvanized readers with a new genre, the gritty social realist novel, which redefined African American literature and accordingly provided a template for "authentic" work by black writers for the next twenty years. Jeff Karem's *The Romance of Authenticity: The Cultural Politics of Regional and Ethnic Literatures* (2004) offers a useful analysis of the shift that *Native Son* is presumed to have inaugurated and encapsulated. As scholars such as J. Martin Favor have established, "authenticity" in African American writing before 1940, even when it was produced in the urban north, was overwhelmingly identified with a "folk" culture rooted in the rural South. That assumption, Karem notes, limited Wright even as it paradoxically established his credibility as a black urban observer; although *Native Son* defied readers' expectations for another regional portrait of black life in the mold of Wright's *Uncle Tom's Children*, most were willing to trust Wright's knowledge of black life because of his southern provenance.

Wright's investment in both the conventions of realism and leftist politics also clearly allowed a line of influence to be drawn between *Native Son* and subsequent literature and art produced by African Americans. Literary historian Stacy I. Morgan offers a detailed and subtle treatment of the period that is representative of a growing body of critical work focusing on the African American Left in the 1940s and 1950s. In *Rethinking Social Realism: African American Art and Literature, 1930–1953* (2004), Morgan identifies the 1940s and early 1950s as the high-water mark of social realism for African American "cultural workers." Although contemporary literary scholars usually identify social realism with the Great Depression, according to Morgan, "the careers of African American cultural workers tell a different story, one that extends for at least a full decade beyond the bounds of conventional periodizations.... [M]any of the more striking works of social realism produced by African Americans date from the 1940s and early 1950s" (21).

Morgan's thesis reflects the substantial body of influential work produced in recent years by scholars operating at the intersection of critical race theory and cultural histories of the U.S. Left, such as Bill V. Mullen, James Smethurst, and Alan Wald. Actively seeking to combine Mary Helen Washington's well-known 1997 question, "What happens to American Studies if you put African American Studies at the center?" with Cary Nelson's call to "put the Left at the center . . . of the story or stories we tell about the American literary heritage" (771), these critics have posited the continuous presence of African American leftist engagement, both in and beyond the literary realm, in the mid–twentieth century. As Mullen and Smethurst write, "Revisionist cultural archaeologists searching for the remains of a buried radical past too often limit their efforts to the Red Decade of the 1930s and the countercultural 1960s. . . . What unites [recent work in the field] is a willingness to think about Left continuity as well as rupture and conflict. It is also marked by a much greater interest in race and ethnicity" (3). Their painstaking reconstructions of black cultural life in the late 1940s and early 1950s provide not only a wealth of newly excavated archival materials but also invaluable methodological and theoretical models to which this study is indebted.

Yet while this antiracist leftist scholarship offers fascinating readings (and startling recoveries) of modernist texts in several genres (most notably poetry and the short story but also drama, nonfiction and visual art), its focus has done little to alter the persistent view of postwar African American novels, unarguably the most influential fictional mode of the period both critically and commercially, as dominated by social realism. Indeed, even when seeming to propose other models for the works examined, critics almost reflexively emphasize the works' political engagement when offering their ultimate assessments of value. For example, Alan Wald's informative introduction to Lloyd Brown's *Iron City*, published in 1951 and reissued in 1994 after having been "consciously erased from U.S. cultural memory by the press and ersatz literary histories" (ix), leaves the impression that Brown's novel is noteworthy for its unusual textual strategies, implying that *Iron City* is representative of a tradition that has been repressed and is thus in need of recovery. Yet the description of the novel places it squarely within a recognizable definition of social realist fiction: "Brown's aim in *Iron City*," Wald writes, "is to depict strategies of defiance through representative protagonists. . . . Moreover, from a literary point of view, the behavior of these protagonists is intended to express the authentic patterns of Black life and culture" (viii).[1] Similarly, James C. Hall's afterword to the 1998 reprint of William Demby's novel, *Beetlecreek* (1950), despite usefully identifying the early 1950s as a "watershed" in African American literature not merely because of *Invisible Man* but also because of a "diverse and vital" range of texts, nevertheless undercuts *Beetlecreek*'s originality in contrasting it with Demby's later, more recognizably (post) modernist work from the 1960s on. Although Hall writes that *Beetlecreek*, with its "existential seriousness" and simultaneous leftist critiques of emergent McCarthyism and postwar American materialism, offers "difficulties of categorization [that] might lead to [Demby's] falling through the literary critical cracks," Hall nevertheless strongly emphasizes aspects of the novel that point toward its inclusion among its social realist contemporaries. Hall notes, for example, that *Beetlecreek*'s inversion of the familiar tropes of protest fiction (the victim is a socially awkward white man falsely accused of pedophilia and subjected to vigilante violence; the mob is made up of young black men who style themselves "Nightriders" in an obvious imitation of the Ku Klux Klan) has been incorrectly interpreted as a marker of a race-transcendent "universality." But "the critical response that asserts universality without significant context suggests a desire on the part of white critics (and some black ones too) to escape history. . . . [T]o imagine the novel's moral economy as not racialized is to engage in an act of willful disavowal" (Hall 233). While Hall is right to problematize the approach of critics who elide the presence of race in the text, his alternative reading of the book as "rooted" in its time and place and "relentless" in its realistic description of prejudice nevertheless fits fairly neatly into existing models for black protest fiction.

The characterization of the African American novel of the period as dominated by social realism takes care to account for the apparent exception, Ellison's *Invisible Man*, begun in 1946 and hailed (or derided) in 1952 as a modernist triumph. The author's famous, largely unchallenged dictum provides a handy classification: in claiming that Wright was not his literary ancestor but merely a "relative," Ellison neatly places himself outside the direct line of literary inheritance presumed to encompass his "minor" contemporaries. Ellison's disavowal of *Native Son* may be linked to what Barbara Foley establishes, through a comprehensive reading of the successive drafts of *Invisible Man*, as his desire to dissociate himself from his past involvement with the organized Left by the time of the book's publication, an "act of purposive self-disappearing" that Foley argues allowed the book to "participat[e] fully in the discourse of anticommunism pervading the moments of its reception in 1952 and its garnering of the National Book Award the following year" ("From Communism" 164). A variant on this depiction of *Native Son*'s relationship to *Invisible Man* positions Ellison's work as thematically responsive to Wright but so much more technically sophisticated that it transcends derivative "protest fiction." For example, in *Politics in the African American Novel* (1991), Richard Kostelantz argues that "Ellison's narrator undergoes so many of the same experiences that touch Wright's protagonists that *Invisible Man* becomes an implicit commentary on a predecessor's oeuvre." One of the "crucial differences," Kostelantz notes, is that Ellison requires only one novel to respond to all of Wright's work because "in scope as well as detail, [Ellison] is writing African American literature." Finally, according to Kostelantz, James Weldon Johnson, W. E. B. Du Bois, and Wright lack Ellison's "technical capacity" (108–9).

The progression from *Native Son*'s celebrated role as the progenitor of the black protest novel (as black social realism came quickly to be known) to the dismissal and obscurity of Wright's later work and the meteoric trajectory of *Invisible Man*, followed by decades of unfulfilled anticipation of Ellison's second novel, is a critical narrative that was tailor-made to fit the expectations of the largely white postwar literary critical establishment. Wright's success allowed him to promote and sometimes subsidize the work of new and aspiring black writers, lending credence to the theory of his influence over a generation of African American novels; his voluntary expatriation to Paris in 1946 then further highlighted the perceived divide between his early "authentic" works (*Native Son* and the autobiographical *Black Boy*) and his later "minor" fiction. At the same time, *Native Son*'s publication date and subject matter enabled the novel's positioning as a product of a prewar sensibility relevant in an era of postwar progress and abundance only to an African American minority. By establishing Ellison as the exception that proved the rule, critics working within New Critical paradigms privileging self-contained and self-conscious models for fiction and publishers keen to maintain discrete genres could position *Invisible Man* as a brilliant modernist outlier while retaining the dominant narrative of the "authentic" postwar African American novel as racial protest presented in the social realist model.

Little has changed in the intervening six decades, in part because of the tendency to periodize black literature into peaks and valleys, a narrative that emphasizes the importance of discrete schools, movements, and "renaissances" but systematically overlooks work that falls chronologically or thematically outside fairly rigidly defined boundaries. In "Harlem on Our Minds" (1997), Henry Louis Gates Jr., for example, divides twentieth-century African American letters into four distinct cultural renaissances. The first took place around the turn of the century and lasted until about 1910; the second, which encompassed the 1920s and, some argue, stretched into the 1930s, was what was then called the "New Negro" movement but is now known simply as "the" Harlem Renaissance; the third was the Black Arts movement of the late 1960s and early 1970s; and the fourth began in 1987 and remained in progress a decade later (2–4). Conspicuously absent in this chronological landscape, of course, is a substantial chunk of the century. Something similar happens in Bernard W. Bell's *The Contemporary African American Novel* (2004), in which only one out of eight chapters is devoted to the African American novel before 1962; appropriately labeled "Mapping the Peaks and Valleys," this chapter subdivides the period under discussion here into two sections, one dominated by Wright and the other demarcated by the appearance of *Invisible Man*. Bell offers *Invisible Man* as the decisive break that begins a movement "beyond naturalism" and toward what he calls the "rediscovery of myth, legend and ritual" (128) in the African American novel; other publications between 1940 and 1952 clearly constitute one of the valleys to which the chapter title alludes. The titles of similar studies suggest the pervasiveness of the trend, from Edward Margolies's *Native Sons: A Critical Study of Twentieth Century Negro Authors* (1968) to a collection edited by Herbert Hill, *Anger, and Beyond* (1966), to Noel Schraufnagel's *From Apology to Protest* (1973), which compares the impact of *Native Son* on African American fiction to that of Samuel Richardson's *Pamela* (1740) on the modern English novel.

In short, when it is approached from the vantage point of the classificatory rubric, the period from 1940 to at least 1952 is too easily labeled the golden age of "protest fiction," written by imitators of Wright, and little else. Objections to the presumed inevitability of the peaks-and-valleys model are occasionally voiced but usually remain well-intentioned general injunctions. Daylanne English has already taken Gates to task for reproducing a critical paradigm by which Wright "stands metonymically" for the era. Noting Gates's lack of emphasis on the decades between the Harlem Renaissance and the Black Arts movement, English observes that "there is a contemporary academic selection process at work whereby the Harlem Renaissance often emerges as the most compelling moment in African American history, one that (not coincidentally) lends itself particularly well to generalization" (808). She also points out that a number of other important writers of the 1940s and 1950s "merit far more scholarly attention than they have received to date" (808). However, she does not provide this scholarly attention; the remainder of her article focuses on the 1920s. Craig Hansen Werner similarly observes the tendency but fails to provide redress. His important study, *Playing the Changes: From Afro-Modernism to the Jazz Impulse* (1994), notes that even within the period to which English alludes, further internal periodization has led to an inevitable pre- and post-Ellison divide, with Wright serving as a touchstone for the 1940s while "criticism of African American literature of the fifties frequently posited a simple reaction against Wright" (243). This bifurcation, which again emphasizes the centrality of the two figures, "established an interpretive framework—reflected in both academic criticism and the mass media—that continues to undervalue the work of artists who cannot be reduced to familiar categories" (187). Yet the majority of the undervalued writers in Werner's study (which focuses more on poetry than on any other genre) wrote well before or well after the 1940s.[2]

One might point out that this tendency is neither new nor objectionable—literary history has generally been defined in this way, and literary production is periodized for a variety of reasons ranging from a desire for historical coherence to a need for more efficient marketing. The cohesiveness afforded by the emphasis on literary movements spearheaded by remarkable individuals or small clusters of individuals is especially critical for marginalized groups, who have historically been forced to demonstrate the value and validity of their work in the face of overt and covert opposition from mainstream cultural arbiters and for whom establishing the narrative of a clearly delineated tradition carries additional urgency. Thus, labeling the postwar period in African American literature a relative wasteland throws both the avant-garde glamour of the Harlem Renaissance and the politically engaged brilliance of the Black Arts movement into sharper relief; it also clarifies their specific significance for contemporary writers and to contemporary debates. Moreover, at least one critic had already adopted the peaks-and-valleys model by the mid-1950s. In 1950, Alain Locke wrote eloquently of the "cultural maturity" of the African American novel, which he likened to an adolescent who has finally grown up; yet three years later, in a survey of black fiction of the preceding year, tellingly titled "From *Native Son* to *Invisible Man*," he anticipated future generations of scholars by announcing that "there have been in my judgment three points of peak development in Negro fiction by Negro writers. In 1923, from a relatively low plateau of previous problem fiction, Jean Toomer's *Cane* rose to unprecedented heights. . . . In 1940, Richard Wright's skillful sociological realism turned a hard but brilliant searchlight on Negro urban life in Chicago . . . and has remained all these intervening years the Negro novelist's strongest bid for fiction of the first magnitude. [Now] 1952 is the significant year of Ellison's *Invisible Man*" (34). For Locke, *Invisible Man*'s "distinctive and most original tone and flavor" derive from Ellison's mastery of modernist symbolism and the novel's "real and sustained irony" (35); Locke subsequently draws an implicit contrast between Ellison's triumph and other novels published in the same year by "tractarian authors" offering "pasteboard pillar[s] for propagandist indictments of society" and the "damaging . . . notion that the Negro character is foredoomed to a defeatist end" (37–38).

Yet however recognizable today's critics may find Locke's view, it was anomalous at that time and is now inevitably reductive. Black writers of the postwar era did not see themselves as providing a backdrop for other, more interesting, authors. Rather than seeing their literature as existing in a lull between innovations in the field, postwar authors and scholars enjoyed a heady sense of possibility, seeing African American literature as becoming more sophisticated in a process more akin to a steady curve upward. When we look at what critics of the 1940s and 1950s were saying, a new picture emerges. Looking back over previous decades, black critics were less likely to see heights from which their work had fallen than to see the foundations of their superior art and judgment. Critic Hugh Gloster illustrates this point of view in the introduction to his survey of twentieth-century African American literature, *Negro Voices in American Fiction* (1948). As he considers the prewar fiction with which his study is largely concerned, he describes the remarkable diversity of works that has influenced his approach, which privileges no particular genre. Although he notes that many of the prewar texts he has assembled are "frequently inferior examples of their form" (ix), Gloster concludes that African American fiction in the immediate aftermath of World War II is on the verge of maturing into unprecedented greatness, having put behind it the technical weaknesses and unbecoming political stridency of its youth. In the postwar period, Gloster writes, "we may predict that the Negro writer will obtain full membership in the American literary fraternity" (256).

This notion of prewar black fiction as providing green and callow versions of what could and would now be produced was echoed again and again by Gloster's contemporaries. For example, the contributors to a 1950 symposium issue of *Phylon*, a group that included academics from the fields of literature, history, and sociology as well as novelists, poets, and journalists and thus represents a wide range of perspectives, articulate a clear vision of an African American literature that had evolved dramatically, noting repeatedly that the African American novel is not only technically better than ever but also more varied and better representative of what the contributors argue are the authentic experiences of black people and of blackness itself. In the words of one participant, N. P. Tillman, "The market no longer demands a specific type of story from a Negro author, so that he has a wide choice of material and approach. . . . This freeing of the writer from narrow limitations is resulting in a broadening of his point of view and, indeed, in his seeing the Negro in a better perspective" (387). Another contributor, Thomas D. Jarrett, whose essay, "Toward Unfettered Creativity: A Note on the Negro Novelist's Coming of Age," makes arguments representative of the issue as a whole, writes that "Negro novelists, day by day, are evincing greater potentialities, employing new themes and new techniques and, above all . . . are giving more attention to literary values" (317). Rather than rallying writers to the social protest form, the critics argued passionately and eloquently that an emphasis on multiple varieties of authentic black experience liberated rather than confined black literature. Indeed, these authors argued that because an understanding of the multiple particularities of black experience might enable black writers at last to address universal themes. Charles H. Nichols's contribution, "The Forties: A Decade of Growth," argues that black literature of the preceding decade had reached new heights by leaving behind stereotype: "In his literary efforts, the Negro is coming of age—though, happily, not as a Negro (whatever the racial tag implies)" (377). Nichols, who sees the future of black writing in figures such as Motley and Yerby, emphasizes the centrality of what he repeatedly calls "universal theme" in the works of new black writers: "The racial pride, the Quixotic radicalisms, the propaganda, the adolescent sense of emancipation and defiance . . . have given way to a deeper, subtler tone, a more universal quality, and a more impressive technique" (379–80).

Even when Wright is acknowledged as the impetus behind the "growth" to which Nichols refers, his contribution is recast not as a work of protest fiction dealing with a historically and socially specific subject but rather as a novel notable for its "universality." In the words of G. Lewis Chandler, in "Coming of Age: A Note on Negro American Novelists" (1948), *Native Son* "despite its obvious weaknesses" (which Chandler felt included its "inartistic features") and its "equally obvious propaganda . . . has more than enough breadth to include all exploited peoples" (28). William Gardner Smith notes in "The Negro Writer: Pitfalls and Compensations" (1950) that, like their white counterparts, his contemporaries are "under tremendous pressure to write about the topical and the transient"; nevertheless, he insists, the black writer must resist the urge to comply and instead remember that "novels which last through all time are concerned with universal themes" (299). In asserting that black writers are better equipped than their white peers to take on the burden of redeeming American literature from "superficiality and esoterica," Smith does not locate their difference in an African heritage but suggests that blacks share a perspective with Europeans:

> Emotional depth, perception of real problems and real conflicts is extremely rare in American literature, as in American society generally. . . . America's is a superficial civilization: it is soda-pop land, the civilization of television sets and silk stockings and murder mysteries . . . . It is difficult, in such an environment, to bring forth works with the emotional force of, say, *Crime and Punishment*. . . . The Europeans

would understand it. For what man or woman who has seen a lynching, or been close to the furnaces of Dachau, can really seriously concern himself with the insipid and shallow love affair between Susie Bell and Jerry? (301)

Linking the victims of racist ideologies worldwide, then, Smith sees African American literature as possessing an inherent cosmopolitanism based on its writers' marginalized status, allowing African American writers to posit race as an organizing category of identification for oppressed peoples everywhere.

A hierarchy of black writers thus was created out of two definitions: "racialistic literature," which, as Sigmund Ro notes, postwar black writers and critics condemned by associating it with "an adolescent and immature past," and the preferred "racial art" (227). What "racial art" meant in practice was open to debate, and the inconclusive resolution of that discussion is a second factor shaping the image of postwar black fiction that we recognize today. Little, it seemed, could be agreed upon, apart from the fact that Richard Wright needed to be at the center of any conversation about "authenticity" and race in literature. In a much cited (and subsequently much anthologized) 1937 essay, Wright outlined the "Blueprint for Negro Writing":

> Reduced to its simplest and most general terms, theme [for black writers] will rise from understanding the meaning of their being transplanted from a "savage" to a "civilized" culture in all of its social, political, economic and emotional implications. It means that Negro writers must have in their consciousness the foreshortened picture of the *whole*, nourishing culture from which they were torn in Africa, and of the long, complex (and, for the most part, unconscious) struggle to regain in some form and under alien conditions of life a *whole* culture again. It is not only this picture they must have, but also a knowledge of the social and emotional milieu that gives it tone and solidity of detail. Theme for Negro writers will emerge when they have begun to feel the meaning of the history of their race as though they in one lifetime had lived it themselves throughout all the long centuries. (104–5)

Here it seems that the black writer's task is defined through a combination of race identification, choice of subject matter, and what can only be called a somewhat mystical relationship between style and self. For others, the black author's position was not a matter of choice or degree but rather a "natural" all-or-nothing proposition. "Of course, writing by Negroes is different," affirmed novelist, critic, and literary historian J. Saunders Redding in 1949, one year before the publication of his novel, *Stranger and Alone*; in a formulation to which he would return in subsequent essays and speeches, Redding argued forcefully that "to leave unsounded the profoundest depths of the peculiar experiences of [one's] Negroness," to deny that difference in quest of a "nonracial aesthetic tradition," is to choose "apostasy" ("Negro Writer and American Literature" 8–9). For Redding, black writers of the postwar era had not merely an opportunity but an obligation to communicate their racial difference literarily. Redding's extensive corpus of literary criticism makes no secret of his distaste for African American writers who seek to write themselves into a "nonracial aesthetic tradition" that has what he described as obvious "pathological overtones." Though some black writers whose work focused on technical innovation rather than race-conscious content developed "an amazing virtuosity," comments Redding with typical astringency, "they were definitely—as the saying goes—off" (9).

Yet although he condemned the apostasy of the "nonracial," Redding recognized the particular hazards and difficulties facing African American writers. In a passage from *On Being Negro in America* (1951), he pleads for stylistic freedom: "I hope this piece will stand as the epilogue to whatever contributions I have made to the 'literature of race.' I want to get on to other things.... The obligations imposed on the average educated or talented Negro (if this sounds immodest, it must) are vast and become at last onerous. I am tired of giving up my creative initiative to these demands" (26). Even in recognition of these aesthetic limits, he continues to argue for the importance of recognizing the particularity of the black experience within the broader sphere of American literature. At the inaugural Conference of Negro Writers, held in 1959, he said that the uniqueness of black identity was undeniable ("The American Negro writer is not just an American with a dark skin") and was a necessary component of a national scene that was in constant flux: "There is no American national character.

There is only an American situation, and within this situation these [black] writers sought to find themselves" ("Negro Writer and His Relationship" 3, 7).

Calls by black critics for "authenticity" in black postwar writing were heartily seconded by white critics who sought to cast black writers in the role of interpreters for white readers of the experiences of racial minorities rendered "unknowable" by de facto and de jure segregation. Such communication between the races was the avowed objective, for example, of the essay collection *What the Negro Wants* (1944), edited by white University of North Carolina Press director William Terry Crouch and featuring essays by fourteen black leaders chosen for their diverse approaches and views, as well as of white novelist Bucklin Moon's anthology, *Primer for White Folks* (1945): "In so far as space permits, [this collection] is an attempt to present a general picture of the Negro—his backgrounds, his relationships with whites, his everyday denial of first-class citizenship, and what he really wants in this American life" (xi). The need for interpretation, it was argued, received additional urgency from World War II, as victory over the Axis powers was deemed impossible if the United States, black and white, could not present a united front to the world. As Sterling Brown acerbically notes in a contribution to Moon's *Primer*, many whites did not interpret this imperative as a call for racial equality or the extension of democratic rights to all citizens; rather, they saw the Nazi threat as a justification for labeling "dissatisfaction with Jim Crow ... tantamount to subversiveness" (373). In support of his argument, Brown reproduces verbatim a sign he saw "printed under a large red V on a bus in Charleston, South Carolina": "Victory Demands Your Co-operation. If the peoples of this country's races do not pull together, Victory is lost. We, therefore, respectfully direct your attention to the laws and customs of the state in regard to segregation. Your co-operation in carrying them out will make the war shorter and Victory sooner. Avoid friction. Be patriotic. White passengers will be seated from front to rear; colored passengers from rear to front" (373). Similarly, a white union organizer in Chester Himes's *If He Hollers Let Him Go* (1945) shouts out what he considers "the trouble with you colored people": "You forget we're in a war. This isn't any time for private gripes.... [I]n order to beat fascism we got to have unity." Recognizing the irony inherent in this exhortation (the organizer uses his rationale as an excuse not to defend his black coworkers), Himes's protagonist replies, "Let the white people get some goddamn unity" (114).

Nevertheless, the war provided several excellent arguments for civil rights activists of the era. Blacks were crucial to the war effort, both as soldiers and in industry; furthermore, the ideology of freedom and democracy for which the United States was allegedly fighting was meaningless if it was mere hypocritical posturing. Finally, in a modern world in which "no spot on the globe is more than sixty hours away by aeroplane," the civil rights struggle in the United States would inevitably find analogues in the struggles of colonized people in other parts of the world (Logan v). "Events abroad," wrote African American journalist Roi Ottley, "have lifted the 'Negro problem' out of its limited orbit of a strictly domestic issue. Today, more and more, race and color questions are being thrown into the public scene" (v).

Not every observer, of course, believed that writing by or about African Americans could demystify black experience. For example, in the introduction to her memoir, *Color Blind: The White Woman Looks at the Negro* (1946), Margaret Halsey emphasizes that while "most writing on the race problem [is either] passionate fiction about race clashes, lynchings and various forms of violence and degradation or ... passionless non-fiction, loaded to the gunwales with statistics about wages and graphs about venereal disease," neither form is adequate to the task of fostering communal understanding. Halsey ultimately says she can only present her own perspective (as the former director of a servicemen's canteen that served both black and white soldiers), and even that is limited:

> I have gone on at great length about my own feelings when playing hostess to a Negro girl, but I have said nothing about her own feelings. That is because I do not know what they were. Negroes do not tell white people how they feel, and if they did, it would not ring a bell with us.... White people who say they "understand" the Negro merely mean that they have seen a lot of Negroes around; this does not imply a mastery of their psychology any more than living next door to Einstein implies a mastery of the theory of relativity. (8–9)

Halsey's misgivings notwithstanding, many observers had faith in the black artist's ability to succeed in speaking truth to white America where the sociologist might fail. In particular, the African American novel labored under a heavy representational imperative. In the conclusion to *The Negro Novelist: 1940–1950* (1953), critic Carl Milton Hughes observes,

> Even though Negro novels are defective, they are not without positive virtues. The most striking quality about them is their authentic interpretation of Negro life and the Negro world from experiences inside the restricted and isolated Negro world.... Realistically drawn pictures of the Negro life in American society are actually shocking because of the deviation from publicized and ordinary patterns of American life in the sense of standardized living. Sections of novels dealing with pertinent issues and positing demands of the Negro for a larger life become brochures of Negro life in the American cultural pattern. (267)

Hughes thus sees African American fiction as synonymous with the black social realist novel, whose contours in turn overlap almost perfectly with those of the "novel of protest." This protest novel is to Hughes and a significant number of his contemporaries the only real postwar African American literary form; yet, as Hughes makes clear, it is curiously stunted and incomplete: "Varied as it is and inclusive of American interests, Negro writing concentrates on one weakness of American society"— the "unhappy fact" of the inequality of races—"rather than its virtues.... Variations on the same theme are hardly conducive to producing a great literature" (250–51).

Like these black critics, Hughes casts the African American novel as a primitive form of the genre, a fictional analogy to the earlier, necessary stage of development through which Freud describes all individuals as passing: Hughes considers the genre not yet fully mature, not yet ready to take its place among the more technically sophisticated and intellectually demanding novels of white postwar writers and their "muckraking" and "proletarian" fiction. After all, he notes without irony, "it is only in a positive affirmation of American democratic heritage that any American author can point the way of truth" (266). Unlike the participants in the *Phylon* symposium, however, Hughes does not view African American fiction as having progressed beyond this "immature" phase; indeed, for Hughes, the African American novel is the perpetually rebellious teenager (or intellectually compromised communist) of the American literary family. Although Hughes's unusually naive boosterism sets him apart from critics who take a dimmer view of the "truth" behind mainstream postwar writing, his identification of Wright as the major figure behind the emergence of the obsolete "novel of protest" as the dominant mode in African American literature is entirely consistent with their views. Positioning Wright as the head of a "school" of protest fiction writers identifies him as the first black naturalist, confirming the thesis that African American writers were, no matter what they believed, stylistically speaking generally behind the curve set by white writers.

If the insistence that fiction by black writers was exclusively protest fiction meant that it could never be considered at the vanguard in a technical sense, African American writers could perhaps have taken some consolation in the knowledge that their efforts were being cast in some quarters as thematically or spiritually representative of the ur-American novel had it not been for the fact that the reasons for this perception reflected less the literature itself than the ideological climate surrounding it. The tendency to collapse all African American literary production into the model of the racially "authentic" novel of social protest would become more and more marked over the two decades following World War II, even as it grew to be a less and less justifiable representation of the books African Americans were writing and reading. Although, for example, beginning in the late 1940s, novels by black writers about white characters on what were considered racially "neutral" themes (books that are, by and large, not what their authors are remembered for today) began to emerge with great regularity, this trend was ultimately ignored or recuperated back into the model of postwar black literature that argued for the "protest model" and the supremacy of Wright. For example, following her success with *The Street* (1946), Ann Petry published *A Country Place* (1947); indeed, Arna Bontemps so identified her with this latter work that he grouped her with Motley and Yerby as one of the new black writers who readers neither "knew nor cared" were black (4). Similarly, Zora Neale Hurston (breaking what she called "that old silly rule about Negroes not writing about white people" [qtd. in Hemenway 308]) wrote *Seraph on the Suwanee* (1948), William Gardner Smith published *Anger at Innocence* (1950), and Chester Himes came out with *Cast the First Stone* (1952), set in an all-white prison.

The fact that the model offered no space for black writing that was not "protest fiction" helps to explain Robert Bone's 1958 dismissal of what he considered the brief postwar vogue for "raceless" fiction as the flip side of the protest novel: "Both," he writes, "are propaganda novels.... All that has happened is that the Negro's propaganda needs have changed" (160). In other words, like the psychoanalysand who demonstrates his complex by denying its symptoms, the postwar black author who rejected the tenets of Wright's prescription for "Negro writing" merely illustrated the sway they held over him. The fact that Bone discusses these novels despite his misgivings about their value or utility for advancing the cause of black literature marks a substantial difference between his treatment of postwar black literature and subsequent renderings of the era that would simply erase "raceless" fiction from the radar screen in favor of the protest model that allegedly insisted that black writing hew to a specific perspective, if not format, to maintain its authenticity. As critic Madelyn Jablon puts it, because of this treatment of literature by African Americans as distinct from white literature, "an aversion to formal innovation became rooted in the sociohistorical approach to African American literature. Within this context, black writers who demonstrated an interest in artistic concerns such as those suggested by literary self-consciousness or metafiction were criticized for undercutting the most important justification for the study of black literature: content that expressed the need for political reform" (16).

Why was *authenticity* such an important watchword for black literature of the postwar period, and how did writing an "authentically black" novel qualify an author as quintessentially American? In large part, this emphasis on the centrality of African American literature to the postwar American literary establishment's self-image was the result of seeing the African American individual as in many ways the most uncorrupted, undiluted American of all. Ironically, the member of American society most rigorously denied representation emerges in the discourse surrounding the definition of authentically black cultural production as its most representative figure. As Edward Margolies wrote in 1965 of American literature's postwar "native sons,"

> The works of Negro writers are more inherently "American" than those of their white counterparts, just as the Negro is himself more

a product of the American environment than most others.... Th[e] swift and brutal severance of all interpersonal and cultural relationships [that resulted from slavery] had an unimaginably destructive impact on the African's personality, and the deleterious results of this deindividualization—extended and aggravated by three hundred years of slavery and oppression—remain today as a burning scar on the personality formation of most Negro Americans.

Yet the Negro has managed to survive, mainly by reconstructing his personality around the system of values he discovered in his new country. Undoubtedly he is the only American who has had to rely so exclusively on the American environment in order to recreate his identity. This almost unadulterated Americanness of the Negro is, of course, reflected in his literature—the Negro author in his quest for expression stands as an intensified image of the total American search for self. (20)

At the same time that they are seen as quintessentially American (as Margaret Just Butcher wrote in *The Negro in American Culture* [1956], "The American Negro's values, ideals, and objectives are integrally and unreservedly American" [285]), African Americans come to embody a postwar white American desire for the outsider as insider—what Margolies calls "the most estranged and alienated of all Americans."[3] Black author Julian Mayfield echoed this assessment in 1960, arguing that "the advantage of the Negro writer, the factor that may keep his work above the vacuity of the mainstream, is that for him the façade of the American way of life is always transparent. He sings the national anthem *sotto voce* and has trouble reconciling the 'dream' to the reality he knows" (33). Thus, in a Cold War–era society desperate to define the qualities that made America unique (and therefore better than its communist rivals) yet simultaneously anxious to allay its fears that Americans were losing their uniqueness in the lonely crowd, defining the authentic representation of blackness in literature gains importance. However, the interpretation of this responsibility carried different ramifications for black and white critics. In this context, postwar African American scholars' emphasis on the increased "subtlety and sophistication" of theme and technique they perceived in black fiction of the late 1940s was lost. Instead, as the postwar era wore on, the critical consensus grew that the purpose of African American literature is not to be literary but rather to bear witness to an experiential blackness positioned as the repository of all that technological advances and material gain have stripped from white American men in the name of progress and the Cold War. The true African American experience, unvarnished and raw as it must be, offers postwar America's only hope of redemption.

As middle-class white American intellectuals of this period began increasingly to see themselves as victims of a postwar society that was, in Warren Susman's phrase, "spoiled by success," the African American "experience" began to be cast as simultaneously oppositional and inscrutable to white culture, a locus of urban authenticity in an increasingly standardized, corporatized, and suburban postwar United States. By the late 1940s, questions of what constituted the authentic had gained new resonance. A constellation of factors, some if not most of them unique to the decade immediately following World War II, combined to make the period cling desperately to notions of the real. In his perceptive essay, "Hip and the Long Front of Color" (1989), Andrew Ross speaks of a Cold War desire to rediscover "useful history," grounded in local and vernacular practices, overwhelmingly identified with both a racialized Other and/or a working class romanticized to the point of unrecognizability. Even as the era rejoiced in its technological advances and standardization of the trappings of middle-class affluence (poverty would not be "discovered" until 1962, with the advent of Michael Harrington's *The Other America*, and few questioned the general belief in the accumulation of household accoutrements, to which Richard Nixon alluded in his famous 1959 "kitchen debate" with Khrushchev, as synecdoche and symbol of the triumph of capitalism in the West), concerns about the homogenization and superficiality of American culture preoccupied more than a suspicious and alienated few. Fears of a creeping sameness identified closely with modern advances had long characterized a distinct strain of American literature, from at least post–Civil War local colorism to modernism. In his exhaustive exploration of this shift from a nineteenth-century aesthetic of imitation to the twentieth-century fascination with the authentic, Miles Orvell argues that the change was inevitable, the "logical conclusion of the modernist drive to produce 'Not "realism" but Reality itself'" (240). For Orvell, that shift is best represented in James Agee and Walker Evans's compendium of

Depression-era observations, *Let Us Now Praise Famous Men* (1941). Agee and Evans's work, characterized both by the obsessively documentarian impulse of the proletarian literature of the 1930s and by incessant doubts about the possibility of even radically reinvented language communicating the real, also might be considered to mark this shift from a literature of observation to one of immersion.

Rather than abating, the quest for the "authentic" intensified dramatically after World War II even as it became imbricated in increasingly problematic discourses of race. Television was a major contributing factor in this new suspicion of representation. At the same time that the new medium broadcast the ideal family and diminished previously broad differences in accent, it allowed for the division of the lives of others into short, discrete segments, bringing previously exotic realities into the living room and effecting a radical change in the ways in which viewers experienced media. Film had for many years offered this opportunity to usurp another person's reality, yet television was qualitatively different, partly in its emphasis on the molding of the everyday into set patterns, partly in its ubiquity. After the war, the number of television sets per capita soared, and by 1952, a year after Jack Kerouac wrote *On the Road*, American homes nationwide totaled more than a million TVs. Television enabled viewers to naturalize the process of suturing themselves into the subject positions demanded of them in a way film did not; because watching television was less an event than was going to the movies, the idea of "borrowing" a variety of realities, each for thirty minutes at a time, while sitting in one's own living room became deceptively mundane, blurring the boundaries between viewer and object far more effectively than film had ever done. As W. T. Lhamon Jr. notes, during the 1950s, the Hollywood film responded to the threat of television by "paring down" to its unique strength, the spectacle, "stressing its gigantism and its capacity to bring off special effects" (24). The influence of television on quotidian perceptions was interpreted as pernicious by some (see Robin R. Means Coleman's discussion of contemporary condemnations of Amos 'n' Andy in *African American Viewers and the Black Situation Comedy* [1998]) and as an opportunity for cultural legitimization by others (see Donald Weber's account of the mainstreaming of Jewish culture in *The Goldbergs* in "Memory and Repression in Early Ethnic Television" [1997]). Television clearly was widely regarded, in the 1951 words of *Pittsburgh Courier* columnist J. Bibb, as "destined to become a dynamic and far-reaching method of propaganda" (qtd. in Coleman 64).

Two brief and widely known examples illustrate this trend. *On the Road*, researched and set in the late 1940s and articulating the desire to discover "the real America" before it was lost altogether in an ever-widening sea of simulacra, offers a useful indicator of members of the intelligentsia's prevailing postwar attitudes toward racial authenticity. The book's protagonist, Sal Paradise, is looking not merely for authentic places but also for people whose authenticity, relentlessly figured as racial or ethnic difference, stands in contrast to his own lack thereof:

> At lilac evening I walked with every muscle aching among the lights of 27th and Welton in the Denver colored section, wishing I were a Negro, feeling that the best the white world had offered was not enough ecstasy for me, not enough life, joy, kicks, darkness, music, not enough night.... I wished I were ... anything but what I was so drearily, a "white man" disillusioned.... I was only myself, Sal Paradise, sad, strolling in this violet dark, this unbearably sweet night, wishing I could exchange words with the happy, true-hearted, ecstatic Negroes of America. (180)

Sal's giddy depiction of "ecstatic" black life, of which this passage is just one of many examples, is based entirely on his perceptions as an outsider, since, as he readily admits, he cannot even talk to the blacks he meets, let alone really get to know them.[4] His portrait of African American life is an amalgam of his interests, "joy, kicks, darkness [and] music," specifically jazz, which throughout the book is figured as the natural performative offshoot of the black identity. Sal sees African Americans as "natural" masters of the jazz idiom he is struggling to learn. Kerouac's contemporary, Norman Mailer, perhaps still more explicitly identifies African Americans with this kind of instinctual, authentic artistry. For Mailer as for Kerouac, the survivalist modus operandi of the African American living in a racist America provides a blueprint for the redemption of the "white man disillusioned," if only he will recognize it. "For Hip," Mailer pronounces in the hugely influential and widely read essay "The White Negro" (1957), "is the sophistication of the wise primitive in a giant jungle, and so its appeal is still beyond the civilized man" (343). In the same essay in which he discussed Kerouac, Baldwin demystified Mailer's romance with his constructed image of blackness while reinscribing some of its beliefs. In "The Black Boy Looks at the White Boy" (1961), Baldwin writes that "Negro jazz musicians, among whom we sometimes found ourselves, who really liked Norman, did not for an instant consider him remotely 'hip.'... They thought he was a real sweet little ofay cat, but a little frantic" (qtd. in Dearborn 121). Mailer designates black experience coterminous (when not synonymous) with a specifically sexualized primitivism communicated, again, in the jazz idiom that is the black artist's "natural" mode of expression:

> Knowing in the cells of his existence that life was war, nothing but war, the Negro (all exceptions admitted) could rarely afford the sophisticated inhibitions of civilization, and so he kept for his survival the art of the primitive, he lived in the enormous present, he subsisted for his Saturday night kicks, relinquishing the pleasures of the mind for the more obligatory pleasures of the body, and in his music he gave voice to the character and quality of his existence, to his rage and the infinite variations of joy, lust, languor, growl, cramp, pinch, scream and despair of his orgasm. (341)

In 1946, Halsey had described the same phenomenon, arguing that "in order to get the Negro's labor cheaply, we have forced a primitive life upon him [and thus] he probably has fewer inhibitions than the white American" (113). Halsey even anticipates Mailer's use of combat metaphors, noting that

> no white person... can understand what it means to be a Negro living in the United States of America, any more than a non-combatant can understand what it means to be in action. The constant danger which enshadows the Negro American all his life... is something that cannot be conveyed to those who have not lived through it, any more than the feelings and sensations of being in combat can be shared with those to whom it did not happen. (116)

Halsey's and Mailer's essays, written a little over a decade apart, reach very different conclusions. For Halsey, forcing African Americans through segregation, intolerance, and violence into a life "in the enormous present" is obviously wrong; to Mailer, such a characterization of black life is not only accurate but culturally valuable. To be white is to be, with rare exceptions, "square," to value what Kerouac describes as "white ambitions." In this formulation, blacks are spared the fate of the corporate man, allowed no access to David Riesman's "lonely crowd." At the same time, however, they are also, perhaps unremarkably, denied the burdensome intellectual capacity that presupposed the development and fulfillment of "white ambitions." Instead, what might seem to be intellectual engagement by blacks was, Mailer revealed, merely the performance of intellectual engagement, played by ear:

> I remember once hearing a Negro friend have an intellectual discussion for half an hour with a white girl who was a few years out of college. The Negro literally could not read or write, but . . . as the girl spoke, he would detect the particular formal uncertainties in her argument, and . . . would respond to one or another facet of her doubts. . . . Of course, he was not learning anything about the merits and demerits of the argument, but he was learning a great deal about a type of girl he had never met before, and that was what he wanted. Being unable to read or write, he could hardly be interested in ideas nearly so much as in lifesmanship. (350)

Mailer's "Negro friend" is a natural artist, able to perform as an "intellectual" without even the ability to read in the same way that the jazz musicians Kerouac extols in *On the Road* can play brilliant music despite their lack of formal training. In both cases, the untutored, "spontaneous" quality of their skill arises from their experience as blacks in a white world that forces them to express their oppression as art. An overlap exists between black life and black art, between autobiography and "protest fiction." There is no particularly great logical gap between Mailer's insistence on the African American as a specialist in "lifesmanship" and Hughes's belief that the African American novel is valuable primarily for what it communicates about authentic African Americanness. Again, the black writer can take as his subject only the writing of black life, a topic whose central thrust is always predetermined by its emphasis on "protest." Mailer's insistence that black existence can be "war nothing but war" suggests the essential homogeneity of black experience as resistance. The major literary vehicle for the communication of this crucial authenticity was the African American protest novel, itself understood to be an unsophisticated (and thus more real) version of the novel form itself; jazz was the other.

Given the intersection of these critical assumptions, the positioning of *Invisible Man* as the exception that proves the rule is more complicated than it may initially seem. *Invisible Man*'s absolute canonical centrality stems from its flexibility—it is a modernist masterpiece that fits neatly into the New Critical paradigm dominant at this time—as, for example, Nadel's treatment of Ellison's extensive use of allusion and intertextuality makes abundantly clear. *Invisible Man*'s technical audacity links it both to works of high modernism and to jazz, a linkage devoutly sought and probably deeply envied by the Beat writers of the same era. Yet while Kerouac's voyage of self-discovery as a "white man disillusioned" in Cold War America invited derision from black readers, Ellison's "performance" of his masterpiece was cast as a "natural" act of artistry, and the fact that the author was also a jazz musician made the comparison even more self-evident. For all the protestations Ellison would make over his long career about his lengthy apprenticeship with major Western writers, the singularity of his novel nevertheless also allows it to be cast not as the pinnacle of workmanlike scholarly craftsmanship but rather as a kind of one-off, the singular work of a prodigy who would never repeat himself and whose work could not be equaled by any of his contemporaries. Thus, the critical response to Wright and to Ellison is widely dissimilar yet oddly familiar. While Wright writes "what he knows"—that is, from his experience as a black man—Ellison writes with a natural gift that also springs somewhat magically from his essentialized blackness. Furthermore, because his novel is not only technically brilliant but also politically charged, it partakes of the conflation of the protest form and the postwar African American novel that defines the genre.

The strictures of the protest novel form clearly confine and constrain the "experience" whose representation it purports to enable and ultimately only reifies the black identity most useful for white intellectuals seeking a space in which to articulate their dissatisfaction with their postwar whiteness. In this formulation, the protest novel sought not artistic innovation or philosophical complexity but simply the expression of the "black experience," meaning that it could be overwhelmingly considered to share discursive space with what Barbara Foley in *Telling the Truth: The Theory and Practice of Documentary Fiction* (1986) terms "the Afro-American documentary novel." Foley's book is concerned with African American fiction only insofar as it contributes to her theory of the development of the documentary novel. She divides this development into several phases, each roughly identifiable with a century. She begins in the eighteenth century with the pseudofactual novel, in which, she argues, improbable events could readily occur, since the narrative insisted on its own truth value. The nineteenth century saw the rise of the realist historical novel, in which, paradoxically, the fact that the text agreed to its own fictiveness meant that characters had to be believable representative types rather than real people and events had to be plausible. Finally, Foley outlines the twentieth-century modernist "splitting" of the documentary novel into the metahistorical novel and the fictional autobiography. The African American novel, Foley argues, both fits into her scheme and revises it substantially because of its subversion of "bourgeois hegemony" through the "powerful historicizing of the referent" (234). The African American protagonist, according to Foley, enjoys no privileged status in the mind of the reader; thus, she or he does not reinforce an interpretation of reality shared by reader, author, and character but rather asserts difference, pointing to contradictions in the referent and challenging the accepted "representation" of reality. However, Foley substantially undermines her argument by adopting a naive stance toward the extratextual authenticity of the lived experience of the writers she discusses. In a note to her chapter treating black writers, she justifies her inclusion of several white writers of black documentary fiction, including Harriet Beecher Stowe, adding, "I do not mean to imply that they become honorary Afro-Americans because of this fact" (234), implicitly drawing a color line between "real" writers of black documentary fiction and pretenders. Discussing Ernest Gaines, Foley for the first time invokes biographical data to bolster her claims of the truth value of the words of Miss Jane Pittman, noting that "the novel owes much to Gaines's own childhood on a Southern plantation during the Depression when he listened to lengthy stories about slavery told by elders of his grandparents' generation" (263).

Foley is one of the few observers who has questioned the assumed relationship between the midcentury African American novel and the realist novel, which in Foley's words "purports to represent reality by means of agreed-upon fictionality, while grafting onto its fictive pact some kind of additional claim to validation" (25). However, if we take Carl Milton Hughes's work as representative, critics "assumed the necessary connection between an acceptance of realistic methods and social progress in the realm of race," in the words of Kenneth Warren (4). The black literary tradition was privileged as a better articulation of authenticity than any other because it allegedly was the most "truthful." While blacks lacked the ability to communicate honestly and still gain distinction in most other arenas of life, artistic expression was privileged as a site in which resistance and difference might be tolerated and even rewarded. As Warren notes,

> The discussion and analysis of literature and culture has been central to ventriloquizing a black collective state of mind.... From such efforts as Robert Park's "Negro Race Consciousness as Reflected in Race Literature" (1923) and William T. Fontaine's "The Mind and Thought of the Negro of the United States as Revealed in Imaginative Literature" (1942), students of "the Negro" have remarked on the relative paucity of an intellectual archive through which to understand "the race," and in response have suggested that imaginative literature can step in to fill the void.... As scholars like Fontaine and Park assert, the inclination of the race just happens to be toward the literary. In Park's words, "The Negro has always produced poetry of some sort. It has not always been good poetry, but it has always been a faithful reflection of his inner life. Expression is, perhaps, his métier, his vocation" (285). Although no respectable scholar holds to the obvious racialism of Park's account, and most, like Gates, have protested the naïve sociological presumption that literature merely reflects external reality, what has remained true of much African Americanist inquiry has been the claim that expressive forms remain more crucial to a consideration of the conditions of black peoples than they do to considerations of other social groups. ("End(s)" 644)

In this context, it is not difficult to see why many vocal participants in the debate over the purpose of black writing accepted a connection between realistic methods and social progress. As critics, we must ask what "realistic" representation means in the context of postwar African American writing. Does it imply the superimposition of coherent form on incoherent societal fragmentation, as is now a critical commonplace with regard to the nineteenth-century novel? Or does it simply give the "gothic horror" of black life short shrift by restricting it to what can be conveyed through "mere" realism and letting (white) readers off the interpretive hook, as Leslie Fiedler suggested in 1960 in comparing Wright unfavorably to Ellison and as Henry Louis Gates Jr. has echoed more recently in positive assessments of Toni Morrison's work ("Harlem")? Does "realistic" representation offer a new kind of exploitation of the experientially based blackness it privileges and purports to accord recognition, providing instead a cognitive framework for the reader's sentimental identification? This book answers that question by examining the responses to the imperative to work within constraints set by a white publishing establishment that privileged (and indeed continues to privilege) some representations of blackness over others. How did writers respond to the call to produce texts about blackness but not (necessarily) for black readers? What can a careful reconsideration of a few of the "forgotten" texts of the period tell us about both readerly expectations and writerly subversions of these constructed concepts of black authenticity?

A closer look at the fiction and criticism produced and read at that time produces a radically different picture of postwar African American letters. The postwar era was hardly univocal, with a number of prominent critics and writers (many of whom have now sunk into noncanonical oblivion) openly contesting not only Wright's "blueprint" but also the critical ethos that his essay implies. Furthermore, readers of the period established their own criteria for black writing. Literary history, like military history, is written by the dominant forces in the field. This project considers what happens when we leave behind the maxims of a largely white critical establishment and turn instead to the everyday practices of a black reading public, gleaned from a consideration of black literary journals as well as book reviews in publications aimed at a black readership. This book seeks to recover the hopes, fears, anxieties, tensions, and aspirations of a brief moment in African American history—the years between the end of World War II and the beginning of the decade now overdetermined as "the Fifties," synonymous with a containment culture created by events that Nadel identifies as taking "the form not only of the Korean War but also of lengthy, well-publicized trials of spies and subversives [and] apparent in the form of ubiquitous loyalty oaths, Senate (McCarthy) and House Un-American Activities Committee (HUAC) hearings, in Hollywood and academic purges, in extensive 'anti-communist' legislation" (74). Although containment culture was nascent, the period between 1945 and 1950 nevertheless offered a more flexible environment in which the debate regarding the purpose and future of the African American novel could remain in flux. James Smethurst notes that "commentators often have characterized the immediate post–World War II era of African American letters and culture generally as cautiously optimistic, save for some lingering anxiety over potential nuclear Armageddon and McCarthyism" (208). Like Smethurst, I disagree with this view, which implies that African American writers had, perhaps with willful naïveté, set aside their concerns about the impact of race prejudice on the terms of their cultural production so that they could focus on issues perceived as "universal." A clear shift in the tone and emphases of the critical conversation occurred after 1945, but Smethurst oversimplifies that conversation.

A deeper analysis has been delayed in part by certain insidious assumptions. For example, observers have long taken for granted the idea that when the presumed reader was white, many black writers were forced to tailor their textual strategies accordingly. Adherents of this assumption, informed in some measure by ideological imperatives that conflate literacy and whiteness, have included Sterling Brown, who wrote in 1941 that "the number of Negroes reading books in the field of their special interest is certainly not high. The number of those who buy books about Negro life by Negro authors is certainly low." Furthermore,

> with a small proportion of a small middle class able to afford books, a smaller proportion of readers, and a smaller proportion still of book-buyers, the likelihood of a Negro audience for books by Negro authors is not promising. There is, on the part of many a dislike for books about Negroes and books by Negroes ... based upon a caste-ridden

disdain of Negro life and character, an anguish at being identified with an ignorant and exploited people to whom many "upper class" Negroes are completely unsympathetic. (145)

Brown's remarks echo the perspective of white publishers of the era, who argued that the book-buying public was overwhelmingly white and that black texts, however defined, thus were exotic.[5] While refugees from the white middle class might embrace their conception of black authenticity, Brown argues that middle-class blacks emphatically did not. One of Brown's major concerns is the development of a black readership competent to understand black texts; he believes that white readers lacked the motivation and ability to do so. Brown goes on to state baldly that a "complete picture" of black life is not possible in an environment dominated by white publishers and readers, as white conceptions of black life are restricted; nevertheless, "the Negro must also work within the present publishing framework. If prejudice does exist, denying complete and honest treatment of Negro life and character, and of course it does, the individual Negro writer must act as far as possible as if it did not exist. He cannot afford" not to do so (146). Houston Baker echoes Brown's frankness, writing that although some critics charge that capitalist imperatives have undermined black cultural authenticity, "making black expressiveness a commodity ... is a crucial move in a repertoire of black survival motions in the United States" (196). For that matter, forty years after Brown wrote this essay, he had not revised his view; in a 1980 interview, he told John Edgar Tidwell and John S. Wright that the lack of an adequate reading audience "is true. I've heard from any number of people that they're glad my book is out, but they ain't never said they're going to buy it. 'Can I get it at the library?' is what they say" ("Steady" 815).

In a logical contortion well suited to the exigencies of the consumerist society only a few years away, Brown neatly argues that popularity—that is, commodification of white constructions of black authenticity—would create a space for the subsequent articulation rather than vitiation of "true" authenticity, whatever that might be. Almost two decades later, black playwright William Branch suggests that Brown's point is well taken, noting that "whether we decide to be American writers who are Negro, or American Negroes who are writers ... we nevertheless all agree that we want to be *selling* writers. Our books and stories and essays in manuscript collecting dust on a shelf are of little value to anyone" (46). Branch exhibits a canny understanding of the potential niche market available for black writers among white readers anxious to reject their own conformist culture as well, commenting that black writers ought not to "deny their own cultural riches in their eagerness to 'be like everyone else,' especially when 'everybody else' is not necessarily to be admired, whether in the majority or not" (48).

The substantial market for fiction by African American writers that exists today is not the result of a sudden flood of previously nonexistent black readers onto the market but rather the culmination of decades of a steadily increasing audience, black and white, for black fiction. In 1950, observed Tillman, "the American reading public accepts a book by a Negro now on much the same basis as it receives a book by a white author. Consequently, the Negro writer has a more direct line to the publisher than ever before, for the primary aim of the publisher is to feed the demands of the book buyers" (387). At the same time, the specifically African American audience whose absence Brown laments was growing, and its tastes helped to shape the debate surrounding the production of black literature. While Langston Hughes pointed at midcentury to the increasing number of black-owned "first-rate bookstores" in major cities, emphasizing the effect of an educated black elite on public taste, journalist and *Ebony* magazine editor Era Bell Thompson wrote that the number of African American consumers of all types of black fiction was constantly growing:

> Merchandisers, already vying for the newly discovered Negro buying market, were made even more aware of black dollar potentialities when the colored Associated Publishers, Inc. . . . told the story of fourteen million Americans with an eleven billion dollar annual income—an untapped market right at their own doorstep which requires no foreign language, no special package labeling, and which annually buys more than the total value of United States domestic exports below the Rio Grande. . . . What does all this mean to the Negro writer? It means more markets and also greater competition. (304–5)

Moreover, if the road to making African American fiction saleable is to work within the constraints of the protest novel genre and to fulfill the expectations of a largely white reading public, as Brown seems to argue, the question arises of why even a cursory examination of book sales reveals that far and away the most popular black writers of the era were Willard Motley and Frank Yerby. Tillman is undoubtedly thinking of their work when he argues for the parity of reception for black and white postwar writers. Motley's novels are identifiably social realist in orientation but explicitly avoid categorization as African American protest fiction by employing a (sometimes improbably wide and almost always suspiciously harmonious) panoply of ethnicities and races to illustrate their somewhat naïve contention that people are just people. Motley was more insistent than any of his peers that he did not wish to be known exclusively as a black writer. He repeatedly expressed his hope that his work would be deemed "universal" and, according to his biographer Robert Fleming, fought with his publishers to maintain a "raceless" identity on his book jackets. (He lost.) The product of a middle-class upbringing in the only black family in a white Chicago neighborhood, he embarked on lengthy periods of research in neighboring slums, deliberately seeking out members of a variety of ethnic groups and mining current events, such as the 1941 execution of Bernard Sawicki, in search of material. In an article written for the *Chicago Sun-Times* in the middle of 1963's grim parade of race-motivated crimes and tragedies, Motley recalled "feeling that I could not write or learn about man in the narrow boundaries of my neighborhood where a Pole was a 'polack' and an Italian was a 'dago,' where no new thoughts were moved in, [and moving] to the slums of Chicago [where] I found my childhood belief to be true: people are just people" ("Let" 2). Motley's best seller, *Knock on Any Door* (1947), tells the story of an impoverished Italian American youth sentenced to die for killing a brutal policeman. Though the novel would later be called "*Native Son* in whiteface," Motley was then more regularly compared to James T. Farrell or Nelson Algren. Sales of the book were such that a well-received film version was made in 1949, directed by Nicholas Ray and starring Humphrey Bogart and John Derek. Yerby enjoyed an astonishing career producing historical romances populated largely with nonblack characters, beginning with the 1946 *The Foxes of Harrow*, which sold five hundred thousand copies in two months and a million copies in its first year. In 1947, his second novel, *The Vixens*, was similarly successful. He subsequently produced a novel a year, beginning with *The Golden Hawk* in 1948.

As even very brief descriptions of their work make clear, the two writers have little in common apart from the fact that despite their astonishing popularity, their names have until very recently been almost entirely absent from scholarly inquiry. We need to reevaluate Bone's comment that these novels merely reflect the "wave of assimilationist sentiment" that he sees as a "direct response to a new era of race relations ushered in by the war" (160). This presumption demands reconsideration not only in the light of the emphasis of subsequent critical race theorists on deconstructing reified ideas of racial "authenticity" but also because we need to ask how such observations contribute to ossifying critical commonplaces still taken for granted fifty years after the fact. Furthermore, we must take issue with dichotomies that collapse differences among a panoply of writers to force their multivalent work into two conveniently linked categories.

Hughes's and Bone's comments may be characteristic of what we now perceive to be mainstream postwar evaluations of the state of African American fiction, but this retrospective critical hegemony can be maintained only by overlooking dissenting voices, of which there were many. In contrast to Hughes's view of African American novels as immature, other critics in the late 1940s suggested that writing by African Americans had come of age, largely by repudiating the ideas set forth by Wright. Yerby, for example, finds an early defender in Rebecca Chalmers Barton, who in her groundbreaking study of African American autobiography, *Witnesses for Freedom* (1948), emphasizes not the sameness but the extraordinary diversity of African American writers of the 1940s. Though she admits that "an indictment of white behavior runs, like a scarlet thread, through all their pages," she insists that "individuality" is the most important feature of the many texts she discusses, and she points to Yerby as an example of an important new black writer despite the fact that he had at that time published only two novels, both nineteenth-century historical romances (280). As chapter 3 demonstrates through its examination of the manuscript versions of Yerby's second novel, Yerby's fiction was more individual than Barton could possibly know.

This insistence on universality does not translate into the production of "raceless" fiction for all critics of the time, of course; in his self-consciously titled essay, "A Blueprint for Negro Authors" (1950), black literary critic and scholar Nick Aaron Ford offers his own updated gloss on Wright's admonitions, advising novelists not to abandon race as a theme but to subordinate it to the more pressing need for "good craftsmanship." The evolution of Ford's views illustrates the development of ideas within the field of African American literary studies generally in the 1930s and 1940s. In *The Contemporary Negro Novel: A Study in Race Relations* (1936), Ford argues that the political imperative underlying black writing makes it crucial for black writers to write their own stories as "authentically" as possible, for "in spite of the faithful representation and sympathetic treatment of the race by [white] authors, they cannot think the thoughts of their characters, nor can they see the world through their eyes" (14). By the end of the next decade, however, Ford had concluded that "there is widespread dissatisfaction not only with the failure of [African American] authors to achieve a maturity of artistic technique, but also with the limited goals some of them have seemingly set for themselves" ("Blueprint" 374).

Nevertheless, Ford's choice of black contenders for the title of "first-rate American novelist" includes only one figure who might today be considered remotely canonical. Ford identifies Yerby and Motley as Wright's equals and suggests that "if they continue to improve ... William Attaway, Ann Petry, Arna Bontemps, William Gardner Smith, and J. Saunders Redding" will join the list "in the near future" (374). Finally, in a lengthy essay, "The Race Consciousness of the American Negro Author: Toward a Reexamination of an Orthodox Critical Concept" (1949), John S. Lash insists that although many black critics liked to think that African American writers lived in an "Ebony tower," what was called "race consciousness" in fiction was really a construction largely "determined by racist configurations" (34). Echoing Brown's cynical assessment of the artificiality of "authentic" black writing, Lash ends his essay by remarking that "race consciousness . . . is in fact an attitude, a technique of writing, a genre of literature which is not necessarily in actual practice Negroid. It is rather subject to exploitation by any writer who chooses to follow its ritual and chant its liturgy" (34).

Far from consisting of *Native Son, Invisible Man*, and an undifferentiated mass of predictable protest fiction, the African American novel in the immediate postwar period took varied forms and was open to vibrant, earnest debate, a fact that has been obscured by subsequent critical renderings of the era. A topography of African American literary history that flattens the period in question to better emphasize those before and after it may make for a convenient critical shorthand but ultimately does the field a disservice, limiting our ability to see continuities and contiguities. As the nature of the series of questions with which I began suggests, clarity is to be found only in and through careful examination of individual texts whose publication dates make them rough contemporaries but whose textual strategies and generic choices illustrate the enormous range of options black writers of the late 1940s believed were available.

CHAPTER TWO

"If I Can Only Get It Funny!": Chester Himes's Parodic Protest Novels

Of all of the African American writers working in the 1940s, possibly none had a more contentious relationship with the genre of the African American protest novel than Chester Himes, whose *If He Hollers Let Him Go* debuted in the autumn of 1945, just as Americans, black and white, were coming to terms with the fact that World War II had finally ended. *If He Hollers Let Him Go*, which describes the racism and discriminatory practices that lingered in the wartime defense industry despite its integration by presidential order in 1941,[1] hewed sufficiently close to critical expectations for black protest fiction at the time to be considered by reviewers noteworthy only for its vehemence; Himes recalled that one critic deemed the novel a "series of epithets punctuated by spit" (*Quality* 77). The critical assessment of his first novel set the tone for the reception of Himes's subsequent works, which have routinely been dubbed second-rate protest fiction. The perception that Himes's major novels are indebted to Richard Wright both for their subject matter and for their style remains dominant today. As Darryl Dickson-Carr observes, "Himes's landmark novels ... could not reasonably qualify as satire so much as social document fiction; he is closer to Richard Wright than to Rudolph Fisher" (88).[2]

Deemed imitative of but inferior to *Native Son*, *If He Hollers Let Him Go* was occasionally lauded but more often damned with faint praise. Robert Bone, summing up the general response, found the novel "Wrightian to the core" but nevertheless "an impressive failure" (173). However, a closer examination of *If He Hollers Let Him Go* reveals its ambivalence toward and critique of the conventions of protest fiction as Himes clearly understood them. Even as *If He Hollers Let Him Go* fulfills the expectations of readers of African American social realist fiction, the novel draws attention to its construction within the nexus of established and emerging discourses surrounding the production of the African American novel. The result is a text that simultaneously embraces and resists the protest genre, imitating but also questioning and subverting its core themes, strategies, and assumptions. Of all the critics who reviewed *If He Hollers Let Him Go*, only J. Saunders Redding picked up on the ambivalence of Himes's text toward the conventions of the protest novel. Though even Redding misinterprets Himes's strategy as a weakness, this intuitive reading foregrounds the disjuncture between the reader's expectations and those of the genre. Noting that the plot seemed "false," Redding argues at length that the events in the narrative seemed "phony" because "there is nothing inexorable or inevitable or completely logical in the way things happen, or even in what happens"; consequently, the author seems to have chosen "the particular sequence of events for reasons not quite clear" ("Second," June 1, 1946). Redding's inability to recognize Himes's narrative choices as markers of his intervention in the generic paradigms he sought to escape rather than as merely examples of bad writing offers insight into the power of the protest genre to mold the expectations of even the most skeptical and sensitive postwar reader of black fiction.

Rather than a failed Wright imitator, however, Himes was an author who recognized the limits the growing imperative to write in the protest genre placed on black writers' aesthetic and political expression. In form as well as content, Himes illustrates generic constraint as well as discriminatory practices, protesting, in effect, the protest form itself. Specifically, *If He Hollers Let Him Go* uses black humor and metatextual strategies unmistakably to suggest a parodic reworking of a genre whose limitations, both as fiction and as political protest, Himes foregrounds mercilessly. Eschewing the third-person narration nearly ubiquitous in social realism, Himes models his slangy, heavily ironic first-person narration on the voices of the protagonists of the hard-boiled detective fiction of the 1930s. This approach allows his narrator to observe and offer mordant commentary on the narrative trap in which he finds himself as the novel's plot signals its inexorable devolution into that of a classic protest novel, a narrative trajectory that the protagonist, like the reader, can predict but is powerless to stop. Furthermore, Himes suggests, the protest novel is not only compromised artistically but also ineffectual politically, since its narrative formula is sufficiently predictable to have little impact on the reader beyond evoking recognition of the inescapability of its tragic nature. Thus, the genre allows for what critic Doris Sommer has termed the "facile conflations of understanding with identification between reader and text" (25) that result when a reader's horizons of expectation are met and confirmed by an alien text's accommodation of difference.

If He Hollers Let Him Go certainly calls into question the ability of black protest fiction to shock an American public already steeling itself to bear with equanimity the horrors of war and historically unwilling to acknowledge the depth and breadth of its "race problem." In his preface to *Native Son*, Wright relates that his motivation for writing the novel stems from his disgust that his first book, *Uncle Tom's Children*, had evoked what he saw as a sentimental response; after Eleanor Roosevelt sent him a letter congratulating him on his achievement, Wright realized his "awfully naïve mistake. . . . I had written a book which even bankers' daughters could weep and feel good about. I swore to myself that if I ever wrote another book, no one would weep over it" ("How Bigger" 454). Himes recognized Wright's "naïve mistake" but glossed the typical white reader's response somewhat less sympathetically. In a 1963 letter to fellow novelist John A. Williams, Himes, by then an expatriate, expressed his view that literature by and about African Americans had done little to ameliorate the problem of racism: "It always strikes me as funny (in a strange way) that white people [reading African American literature] can take problems of race so seriously, guiltily, when they make these problems themselves and keep on making them. It's like a man taking a rifle and shooting his toes off one by one and crying because it hurts" (Williams and Williams 38). *If He Hollers Let Him Go* cavalierly dismisses the effectiveness of the brutality of *Native Son* by demonstrating the ease with which its initially disruptive narrative can be recuperated back into broader discourses supportive of racial hegemony: "You couldn't pick a better person than Bigger Thomas to prove the point" of the oppressed status of African Americans, drily observes Himes's protagonist. "But after you prove it, then what? Most white people I know are quite proud of having made Negroes into Bigger Thomases" (88).

Just as Himes's understanding of the protest novel's form as inadequate literarily and politically is apparent, so too is his awareness of the trap laid by the identification of the African American protest narrative with the identity of the African American individual. Although Himes sometimes dismissed his earlier fiction as "the classic Negro novels, in which a black protagonist protested after being a victim of severe racism" (Flontina Miller qtd. in Fabre and Skinner 117) and usually claimed to have changed his philosophy of writing only in the mid-1950s, when he decided that the protest novel "had accomplished as much as it could during the life of Richard Wright and . . . a new approach was needed" (117), his discomfort with the genre began much earlier. *If He Hollers Let Him Go* marks the beginning of Himes's engagement with what he, like the other writers treated in this volume, considered the dangers of self-imposed generic restrictions on narratives for both black writers and readers.

Himes recognized that preexisting narratives structure lived experience long before postmodern theory postulated the reliance of a performative self on language. He thus challenges the reader's complicity in the notions that some narratives are better suited to particular selves than others and that the black novel bears the particularly heavy burden of interpreting "blackness" textually. For Himes, the focus of such texts can easily become, as Joel Williamson puts it, "not whether to be or not to be . . . but of how to be" black (164), a task Himes found unwelcome, unnecessary, even dangerous. Although he considered "Dick" Wright a good friend and *Native Son* a "great book," Himes also remarked in a 1972 interview that if he were asked to assemble a list of required reading for "a ghetto kid in Cleveland," he would not include that novel. Questioned further, Himes clarified that he did not know "if it would affect a ghetto kid's mind the right way. . . . I think it would have an adverse effect" (Fabre 109). In the same interview, Himes articulated his position on the role of literature in social change: "If the problems of the ghetto can't be solved by inspirational writings, then they can only be solved by outright revolutionary books" (109); *Native Son*, he felt, was neither inspirational nor revolutionary. Books, he argued, can be "outright revolutionary" only when both form and content simultaneously stir the status quo; thus, Himes's reading list for the theoretical ghetto kid would privilege William Faulkner's *Light in August* because it deploys the formal innovations of modernism in revealing that "the whole business of racism [is] quite absurd" (109).

If He Hollers Let Him Go, then, functions as a bridge between *Native Son* and the novels of the latter half of the decade, including those by Frank Yerby, William Gardner Smith, and Saunders Redding, that move beyond the protest novel actively to interrogate intersections of race and genre. However, if its critique of the protest genre is to be fully comprehensible, *If He Hollers Let Him Go* needs to be read not only as a reluctant participant in the genre's conventions but also through the lens of Himes's later work, *The End of a Primitive* (1956), which still more explicitly attacks the critical myopia that leads to the exclusive identification of "authentic" postwar African American fiction with social protest. By manipulating (and sometimes eschewing altogether) the conventions of realism even as it presents a story of the murderous effects of racist absurdity on the life and work of a black writer clearly modeled on Himes, *The End of a Primitive* does violence to the readerly expectations presupposed by the protest genre while, in the words of novelist John A. Williams, "attacking the sensitivities on all levels" (qtd. in Fabre and Skinner 67). My discussion of Himes thus closes with a brief consideration of this disturbing and stylistically challenging later novel, which has until now garnered virtually no critical attention, to shed more light on Himes's heretofore unrecognized objectives in *If He Hollers Let Him Go*.

If He Hollers Let Him Go is the story of Bob Jones, an African American shipyard worker in wartime Los Angeles whose apparently upwardly mobile life unravels over the course of a single workweek. At the novel's outset, Jones has a steady job, which offers the bonus of a draft deferment, as the "leaderman" of an all-black crew as well as a beautiful, wealthy, and cultured fiancée. Describing himself as "taller than the average man, six feet two, broad-shouldered, and conceited," Jones initially believes that "race was a handicap, sure.... But hell, I didn't have to marry it" (3). However, his life spirals out of control as he feels the pressures of prejudice begin suddenly to impact his professional and personal life, driving him toward imminent disaster. Verbally insulted by a white female coworker, Jones responds in kind and is demoted; threatened and physically assaulted by a white mob after winning a game of craps, he stalks one of the men responsible, vowing to kill him. As these events merge with a broader pattern of discriminatory treatment and his sometimes paranoid assessments of his surroundings, Jones finds himself unable to function: "My nerves are on edge," he tells his fiancée, Alice. "I keep expecting trouble every minute. Everything's going wrong all at once—it's pressing me too hard. Goddamnit! You! And the job! And just living in the world—" (95). Jones ultimately carries out none of his threats; nevertheless, he finds himself accused of attempted rape by the woman who originally caused his demotion, Madge. He is subsequently beaten severely by his white male coworkers, jailed, and finally forced out of his job and into active duty in the army as a condition for the dismissal of the trumped-up charges against him.

Like his contemporaries, Himes viewed World War II as an inevitable turning point in race relations; however, his vision of the coming changes was far less optimistic than those espoused by others. The war provides Bob Jones with a substantial salary (he refers repeatedly to his expensive new car and clothing as well as to costly restaurant meals and nightclubs) but also unleashes a "tight, crazy feeling of race as thick in the street as gas fumes" (*If He Hollers* 4) when Pearl Harbor provides new excuses for racism: "I was the same color as the Japanese and I couldn't tell the difference," Jones says, alluding to the conflation of all nonwhites into a single, undifferentiated group by jingoistic whites quick to identify minorities as threats to homeland security. "'A yeller-bellied Jap' coulda meant me too" (4). In "Democracy Is for the Unafraid," an essay that appeared in Bucklin Moon's *Primer for White Folks* just months before the release of *If He Hollers Let Him Go*, Himes foresaw the war resulting neither in genuine racial tolerance nor in a détente between blacks and whites. Rather, he wrote, "what I fear is happening in America today [is that] the cowardice of a relatively small percentage of white Americans is seeping into the consciousness of the majority and making them all afraid of the darker races" (480). Making an explicit link between fascism abroad and domestic racism ("Are we seeking the defeat of our 'Aryan' enemies or the winning of them?" [480]), Himes diagnosed the wartime climate as stemming not from a legitimate horror of Nazism but from an irrational fear of racial difference:

> Fear may easily become the greatest tragedy of this historical period. For the eventual peace of the world and the continuation of progress

depend on the white man's ability to live in equality, integrity and courage in a civilization where he is outnumbered by peoples of other races. *It is imperative that he be unafraid.* For if, because of his fear, he finds himself unable to live as a neighbor and equal competitor with other races, there will be no peace and little progress.... We have also to understand that in the growing weakness of the white race in America, as demonstrated by its present fear-driven actions, dictatorship may come to the United States before we know what true democracy is like. (480–81)

Given that this essay appeared just before the publication of *If He Hollers Let Him Go*, it perhaps follows that Himes's attempt to delineate Bob Jones's inner life would be read, like Moon's *Primer*, as an effort to acquaint a white readership with the unseen psychological effects of racism on blacks. Indeed, this was not an unreasonable assumption; though Himes's fiction moved further and further from psychological realism over the course of his career, he nevertheless articulated on numerous occasions an unfulfilled desire to write "a novel that just drains a [black] person's subconscious of all his attitudes and reactions to everything" (qtd. in Fabre and Skinner 67). Yet contemporary reviewers saw nothing else, praising the book for being "effective in defining sharply the inner turmoil of an intelligent Negro" (anonymous review 249) and for its "ruthless analysis of an emotionally unstable Negro" (Tracy 110). That the novel was simultaneously perceived as a reliable universal guide to the black man's psyche and as a work clearly derivative of *Native Son* offered critics little or no cognitive dissonance. "Since Himes is a realist," writes Carl Milton Hughes, segueing neatly from a discussion of Wright into one of Himes and thus emphasizing the perceived similarities between the two, "he finds the situation and its outlook for Negroes ... hopeless" (210).

Yet Hughes makes clear that Himes's novels are not on a par with Wright's. "American literature was enriched with the publication of Wright's *Native Son*," Hughes writes, citing reviews by Van Wyck Brooks and Alfred Kazin that labeled Wright's work a "masterly novel" by an "apostle of race" (Brooks 550; Kazin, *On Native Grounds* 372, qtd. in Hughes 250). However, Hughes concludes, Wright's successors, including Himes, suffer from "the limitations imposed by a narrow range of subject matter.... Varied as it is and inclusive of American interests, Negro writing concentrates on one weakness of American society [racism] rather than its virtues," an approach that is "hardly conducive to producing a great literature" (250–51). Bob Jones's fate, while obviously less tragic than that of his predecessor Bigger Thomas, ultimately was classed as a variant of it: (over)determined by events originating in racist societal conditions beyond the control of the African American individual, the future of the black man in America was bleak. At the same time, Himes was identified as a lesser light in the constellation of authors surrounding Wright, a promising student in the school of protest fiction. This diagnosis came as no surprise to Himes. A recipient from the beginning of Wright's intellectual and financial support, Himes had quite early recognized the difficulties he would face while writing in Wright's long shadow. In a 1945 letter, Himes thanked Wright for his detailed description of the collegiality among writers now inevitably classed as his followers: "It is really warming to a new novelist to learn that the petty jealousies, snipings, bickerings, animosities that have plagued Negro writers are being put aside in this new school which it has fallen your responsibility to head."

Hughes's reservations notwithstanding, contemporary reviews of *If He Hollers Let Him Go*, including one by Wright, were generally favorable. However, the novel was also regularly misinterpreted. Critics focused on the biographical similarities between Himes and his character, stressing that Himes (who held, by his own reckoning, twenty-three different jobs in the first three years of World War II, "all in essential industries" [*Quality* 74]) had experienced the wartime workplace racism that destroys Bob Jones's life firsthand and could testify that its depiction was "authentic." Even the novel's lack of a conclusive ending (the final paragraph consists of the single sentence "Two hours later I was in the Army" [*If He Hollers* 203]) could be read as a reflection of Himes's divided consciousness, his lack of solutions to the "Negro problem" he describes and to his rage. *If He Hollers Let Him Go*, opined Earl Conrad in a review in the *Chicago Defender*, "is at war with itself, as is Jones, as is Himes, as is the American Negro" (11). This conflation of Himes's life and his work underscores not only reviewers' investment in and narrowly defined criteria for determining the novel's authenticity as protest fiction but also the apparently willfully myopic readings this conflation entailed. As Himes biographers

Michel Fabre and Edward Margolies note, "critics dwelled on its sociological implications, often ignoring its wit and sardonic humor" (56) as well as its complexity.

Himes's response to early critics' laments appeared in "Second Guesses for First Novelists," a special feature in the *Saturday Review of Literature*. In *The Quality of Hurt*, Himes notes that "to those who had complained that I offered no solution for the problem my book presented, I wrote that I belonged to a nation which ... had learned to split the atom as a weapon more powerful than could be conceived by the average intelligence, and to ask me, an incidental black writer with a limited education and no status whatsoever, to solve its internal race problem was preposterous. Let the white people solve it their own goddamn selves" (77).

Today, *If He Hollers Let Him Go* is still cast primarily as a novel of "social rage" (as historian Eileen Boris classifies it [77]), but critics have also opened it up to some innovative readings. Examining the intersection between working-class literature and African American criticism, Bill V. Mullen has dubbed it a "labor classic" ("Breaking" 159 n. 3), while Christopher Breu situates it in the "hard-boiled" tradition and notes its transgressive depiction of racialized masculinity (769).[3] An attentive reading of *If He Hollers Let Him Go*, however, reveals not only such allegiances but also the novel's keen interest in foregrounding issues of presumed authenticity and in questioning the presentation of narratives of racial identity, especially those consistent with the conventions of the Wrightian protest novel. The two are, in fact, closely linked throughout the novel, as Himes's protagonist attempts, without success, to gain control of the narrative of his life by turning his experiences into absurdist jokes, reworking tragedy as comedic parody.

In so doing, Himes was following up on a possibility he had theorized in fiction written nearly a decade earlier. In one of his early short stories, "A Nigger" (1937), for example, the main character, Joe, is a young black man who is interrupted during an interlude with his black girlfriend, Fay, by an unexpected male visitor. As Joe hides in a closet, he listens helplessly to Fay trying to seduce the man, who is her elderly white lover. In his misery, he tells himself that the only way to persevere is by reframing the events: "If I can only get it funny.... It is funny! Funny as hell!" (*Collected Stories* 32). In this example, the joke functions, as most theorists of humor among marginalized groups have argued, to render oppression bearable.⁴ Yet it is also obviously a strategy to control the presentation of the narrative by shifting the terms of its interpretation. If he can place his humiliation in ironizing brackets, Joe's words imply, he can also question the racial identity that has been thrust on him, reclaiming the "nigger" of the title.

Jones, too, attempts to "get it funny," thereby offering a cutting evaluation of the racial authenticity of others around him. He brutally dissects the hypocritical behavior of Alice, his sophisticated, light-skinned, secretly bisexual girlfriend; the politically liberal social workers with whom she works; and her "smug and complacent" upper-middle-class parents, who "like to think [they] have contributed [to the advancement of African Americans] by setting an example, by showing our young men just what they can accomplish if they try" (*If He Hollers* 51). At the same time, he distances himself from the clichéd folk mannerisms and modes of expression of his fellow workers, who are less educated than he is and hail from the rural South. Angered by the truckling of one of the men on his crew when a white supervisor appears, Jones contains his temper by reminding himself that "He was just a simple-minded, Uncle Tom-ish nigger.... [H]e couldn't help it" (23). Emphasizing his alienation from his coworkers and his disdain for the educated middle class milieu into which he intends to marry, Jones insists on his own liminality in an urban setting in which he purports to feel at home only among "hustlers and pimps, gamblers and stooges ... my folks" (43). Yet he marks his distance from this group as well; the denizens of the "slick, niggerish block" to which he refers remain anonymous, known only as "weed-heads," "a raggedy chum," and "solid cats in pancho conks" (43). In short, Jones struggles to find a narrative of black identity into which he can fit his experience, gradually accepting that the reverse will occur, as his actions and perceptions mold themselves to the immutable requirements of the protest genre.

Recognizing that the absurdist role-playing demanded by racism dictates white behavior as well as black, Jones does not restrict his analysis to his fellow African Americans. He also notes the performative nature of racial identity among the whites he encounters, employing a series of metaphors to describe this phenomenon. He observes wryly that "the white folks had sure brought their white to work with them that morning" (*If He Hollers* 15) and wonders later "how it was you could take two white guys from the same place—one would carry his whiteness like a loaded stick, ready to bop everybody in the head with it; and the other would just simply be white as if he didn't have anything to do with it" (41), neatly encapsulating his view of whiteness as a series of behaviors rather than an essential quality. Although Himes implies that whites in a society defined by white race hegemony have the option of "bringing their white with them" or ignoring it, in practice, Jones's experiences demonstrate that racial difference is an insuperable divide between individuals, dictating even benign interactions, including those with the potential to use humor to overcome difference. Driving down the street with a pair of young white men and joking with them about women, Jones finds himself suddenly tongue-tied by the appearance of an old black woman "falling along in that knee-buckling, leaning-forward housemaid's lope, and frowning so hard her face was all knotted up." "If we had all been colored we'd have laughed like hell because she really was a comical sister," Jones notes ruefully. "But with the white boys present, I couldn't say anything" (42). Racial discomfort can naturally shade into danger for all concerned. Sitting in a bar with a predominantly African American clientele watching a white "Arkansas slick chick" whose companions are white soldiers flirt with two black men in an attempt to start a fight, Jones realizes that "all she's got to do now ... is to start performing. She could get everybody in the joint into trouble.... [I]f there was any kind of a rumpus with the white chick in it, there wouldn't be any way at all to stop a riot" (76–77).

Recognizing that interracial interaction follows a script does nothing to alleviate the inevitability of its performance, however hard Jones struggles to break out of character. His encounters with Madge, the white woman who is ultimately his downfall, follow an inescapable pattern. When he first comes face to face with her, they stand "for an instant, our eyes locked, before either of us moved; then she deliberately put on a frightened, wide-eyed look and backed away from me as if she was scared stiff, as if she was a naked virgin and I was King Kong" (*If He Hollers* 19). Though he knows that her "wide-eyed phoney look" is just part of a "scared-to-death act" (19), Jones finds he cannot control his participation in the raced (and racist) narrative Madge has set in motion: "It sent a blinding fury through my brain.... Lust shook me like an electric shock" (19). Meeting her for a second time at work when he approaches her to tell her that she has been temporarily assigned to his crew, Jones knows before a word is exchanged between them what will happen. "I knew the instant I recognized her that she was going to perform then—we would both perform."

> As soon as she saw me she went into her frightened act and began shrinking away. I started off with giving her a sneer so she'd know I knew it was phoney. She knew it anyway; but she kept putting it on me.... A wild, excited look came into her eyes and her mouth went tight lipped and brutal; she looked as if she was priming herself to scream." (27)

The limited scripts available for racial identity and interracial interaction are revealed to Jones in a series of dreams through which he, like Cassandra, foretells a future he can neither change nor explain to others. The compactly structured plot unfolds over a period of four days, each of which begins with a nightmare reflecting (accurately if sometimes sketchily) the coming day's events. The dreams are confused and disjointed, but each represents a struggle for control of the narrative of Jones's blackness, and in nearly all, the locus of that struggle lies in possession of the laugh. In his first set of dreams, Jones imagines that he is a witness to an investigation into the murder of a white man in which the police claim to be looking for a "big tall man with strong arms, big hands, and a crippled leg." They call in for questioning "all the colored fellows"; the first is "medium-sized, well-built [and] fast-walking" and is made to run up the stairs to view the body of the dead man:

> "Oh!" I said to the lieutenant. "You gonna keep 'em running upstairs until you find out what one's crippled." I fell out and rolled all over the floor laughing.
> Then I turned over and dreamed on my back. (*If He Hollers* 1–2)

Only in this first dream, however, does Jones manage to turn his circumstances into a joke. In subsequent dreams, he finds himself compelled to listen to the laughter of others, a situation that underscores his impotence in each scenario. He dreams that he is forced to ask two white men for a job, only to hear their excuse that he does not have the right tools and their mocking laughter (*If He Hollers* 2). He then envisages himself "lying in the middle of Main Street downtown in front of the Federal Building [while] two poor peckerwoods" beat him with lengths of rubber hose and the police stand "nudging each other and laughing" (69). He also sees a white boy stabbing a black boy "to death with a quarter-inch blade and laughing like it was funny as hell" (150). In one of his more symbolically laden dreams, Jones imagines Alice, whose self-image as a black woman is constantly undermined by her contact with liberal white colleagues in whose company she is encouraged to pass for white, being killed by smiling white women affecting sympathy for her:

> I saw what at first looked like a little rag doll, but when I turned it over I saw it was Alice.... [H]er body had shrunk until it was no more than a foot long and she was dead.... [T]here were millions of white women ... looking at me, giving me the most sympathetic smiles I ever saw. I woke up overcome with a feeling of absolute impotence. (101)

The dreams frame and surround the events in each of Jones's days, providing templates for the action, goading Jones toward the novel's resolution. "I woke up and I couldn't move, could hardly breathe.... Somewhere in the back of my mind a tiny insistent voice kept whispering, *Bob, there was never a nigger who could beat it*" (150). In his final dream, Jones, who has entertained parallel fantasies of killing a white man and raping a white woman throughout most of the novel, tells a giant laughing Marine that he has done both, then waits for the man to kill him in response. Jones awakens when he falls out of his bunk in a jail cell, just as he is summoned to his trial (199).

The dream sequences recall Himes's earlier, often more experimental, short fiction and are obvious precursors to the more directly antirealist strategies he embraced in later novels. In stories published in *The Crisis* and *Negro Story*, such as "All He Needs Is Feet" (1945) and "Make with the Shape" (1945), Himes produced narratives consonant with the "plotless realism" that Mullen argues allowed "novice working-class black and white writers ... to transform racist and sexist acts around the country into fictional polemics meant to charge readers' political awareness" ("Popular

Fronts" 8). Himes also experimented with nonlinearity and surrealism. "Heaven's Changed" (1943), for example, is told from the point of view of a dead man, while "He Seen It in the Stars" (1944) depicts a shipyard worker, "Accidental" Brown, who has an elaborate dream about being transported to Nazi Germany, where he predicts the future of the war for Hitler.

In *If He Hollers*, however, it is not just Jones's dreams that mirror, predict, and emplot the events in his life. Watching "Arky Jill," the "slick chick" at the black bar, he has a flash of recognition that what he is seeing is a premonition of his future: "All of a sudden, I thought of Madge; the two of 'em were just alike" (76). The complicity of whites in creating situations conducive to interracial violence even as they lament its occurrence, the paradox Himes found "funny (in a strange way)," emerges as well in Jones's conversation with a white leaderman, Don, after telling him the story of the altercation with Madge: "'Some stinker,' he said. 'What she needs is a good going over by someone.' I knew he wanted to say by some colored fellow but just couldn't bring himself to say it" (118). Don then offers Jones Madge's address, suggesting that perhaps he "can cure her" of her prejudice (119). Jones knows he should cut off the conversation, which he suddenly realizes is absurd: "I started shaking my head and laughing. He looked put out, slightly offended.... But he got it all out with the white man's eternal persistence" (119). Jones finds that he will not be allowed to make a joke of the idea of raping Madge, his last-ditch effort to avoid the narrative path along which Don is eager to help him. "We'd gone too far," he says, "to back out" (120).

Despite both conscious and unconscious warnings that contact with Madge will destroy him, once Jones has articulated to himself what he is expected to do ("What I ought to do is rape her.... That's what she wanted" [*If He Hollers* 126]), he cannot stop himself from going to her hotel room even as he calmly assesses the likely consequences. "All of a sudden," he announces, "I knew I was getting ready to go back and see Madge. Getting my gauge up to be a damn fool about a white woman, to blow my simple top, maybe get into serious trouble.... It was crazy; I knew it was crazy" (142). From the moment Madge opens her door to Jones, the novel begins its ineluctable descent into the specific tragedy associated in the novel of protest with the presence of a black man and a white woman in an intimate space. Although Jones and Madge ultimately do not have sex, they go through a ghastly rehearsal that parodies the racist fantasy of the murderous black rapist and his white victim:

> "The preacher said niggers were full of sin," she said. "That's what makes you black. Take off your clothes."
> I laid there and called her everything but a child of God, talking in a slow, slightly slurred voice. When I reached for her, she jumped back and wriggled free. "You know what you got to do first," she teased. Then I grabbed her and we locked together in a test of strength in the middle of the floor; I had her by the wrists, trying to break her down.
> "Take it, you can have it," she hissed.... [S]he looked me in the eyes, hers buck-wild.
> "All right, rape me then, nigger!" Her voice was excited, thick, with threads in her throat. (147)

Although Jones leaves Madge's apartment without harming her, his doom is nevertheless sealed as inexorably as Bigger Thomas's. Jones reconciles briefly with Alice, fantasizing for a moment about a future in which he will participate in *Native Son*'s courtroom scene not in the role of Bigger Thomas but as his lawyer:

> I could see myself at forty, dignified, grey at the temples, pleading the defense of a Negro youth.... "Gentlemen of the jury, I say to you it is as unjust to condemn this youth for a disease that society has imposed upon him...."
> ... Maybe by that time people would have gotten over the notion, I thought. Maybe they wouldn't be so prone to believe that every Negro man was the same, maybe they would have realized how crazy the whole business was. (*If He Hollers* 172)

Bob fails in his attempts to recast his part in the story he has now realized is the only one he will be able to tell. He apologizes to his supervisor, who agrees to rehire Jones, but as he is returning to his crew, he stumbles across Madge, napping in a storage room. Madge locks them in and makes a clumsy effort to seduce Jones; when he rejects her advances, she cries out that she is being raped:

Without moving, she said in a low flat voice, "I'm gonna get you lynched, you nigger bastard."

Out of the corner of my eye I could see the door swinging inward; people were surging into the room from the companionway. I saw a hundred million white faces, distorted with rage. (*If He Hollers* 181)

The narrative is inescapable, the mandates of the genre too strong. Allowed to question the utility of the trajectory of the protest novel, Jones is nevertheless confined to its conclusions, unable to conjure up an alternative narrative for himself. Although a humorous assessment of the absurdity of his circumstances has previously offered a glimmer of hope that he might control them, he finds that the joke has deserted him by the story's end. Pursued in his final dream by a drunken Marine who "laughed louder and louder" until he "panted and wiped the tears out of his eyes" as he contemplated the fact that he "ain't never got to kill a nigger" (*If He Hollers* 199), Jones finds his final joke in the kangaroo court that sentences him to a term in the army in lieu of prison as a punishment for his "attack" on Madge. "Suppose I give you a break, boy," the judge offers,

> "If I let you join the armed forces—any branch you want—will you give me your word you'll stay away from white women and keep out of trouble?"
>
> I wanted to just break out and laugh and laugh like the Marine in my dream, just laugh and keep on laughing. 'Cause all I'd ever wanted was just a little thing—just to be a man. But I kept a straight face. (203)

Himes himself "kept a straight face" in his subsequent fiction, producing a series of novels that could only with great difficulty be considered remotely parodic or experimental. *Lonely Crusade* (1947) is a sprawling novel about the treatment of African Americans by a villainous Communist Party; *Cast the First Stone* (1952) is set among white prisoners and loosely based on the author's prison experiences; and *The Third Generation* (1954) is a semiautobiographical treatment of Himes's parents and siblings. Just over ten years after the publication of *If He Hollers*, Himes, by this time an expatriate who believed with some justification that he had found a more appreciative and sophisticated audience in Europe, again took on the theme of the absurd humor of interracial sex and violence in the United States. *The End of a Primitive* (1956)⁵ was an ambitious novel he described in an interview with John A. Williams as his "favorite book" (67). Himes considered *The End of a Primitive* to be the book that best represented the lived experience of African Americans in the United States at the time, despite (or perhaps because of) the fact that he wrote it in Mallorca "filled with tranquilizer pills" (Williams 37). Contrasting it to *The Third Generation* (his most "dishonest book"), Himes told John A. Williams that *The End of a Primitive* was written "out of a completely free state of mind from beginning to end, where I saw all the nuances of every word I put down" (67). Himes also identified *The End of a Primitive* as "the transition between the protest fiction and" his later fiction, a series of detective novels set in Harlem (Fabre 88).

As its title suggests, the novel confronts head-on the idea that the African American is the final repository of the primitive in technologized postwar society. At the same time, however, it interrogates, in ways that illuminate Himes's conflicted acceptance of the protest formula in *If He Hollers Let Him Go*, the process by which black writers of protest fiction are complicit in this narrativizing of blacks as primitives through an insistence on the importance of race as an organizing principle for writing by African Americans, a strategy that could only result in Wright's "blueprint." In *The End of a Primitive*, Himes openly rips off and riffs off the prototype that provides the narrative for the black protest novel, rewriting the central event of narratives from *Othello* to *Native Son* to *If He Hollers Let Him Go*: the "rape" and/or murder of a white woman by a hapless black protagonist invariably doomed to suffer white vengeance. In so doing, he also suggests still more clearly than in *If He Hollers Let Him Go* the notion that the dominance of specific narratives of African Americanness spills over into the lived experience of the creators and readers of stories as well as the characters who inhabit them. Moreover, in *The End of a Primitive*, Himes deliberately elides the distinction between autobiography and fiction by building in stories and events that are easily recognizable as having been lifted directly from his early writing career, suggesting most clearly that the novel provides a corrective lens through which to read interpretations of his previous work, especially *If He Hollers Let Him Go*.

Himes's parodic revisions and subversion of the African American protest novel must be read as a searing critique of a postwar theoretical-critical apparatus, endorsed by African American writers in the interest of strategic essentialism, that allows Hughes to state with certainty that "*since* Himes is a realist," he must find "the outlook for Negroes ... hopeless." *The End of a Primitive* is the story of the encounter with "civilization" of the latest in a series of primitivized Othellos, Jesse Robinson, a black novelist who kills his white female lover in an alcohol-induced blackout. Although the story is ultimately tragic, like *If He Hollers Let Him Go* it relies on humor for its effect. *The End of a Primitive* brings to its apex Himes's obsessive fascination with the power of the joke not only to exclude outsiders but also to subvert, to tolerate, to rationalize, and to comprehend. For the most part, as we have seen, Himes's humor partakes of the gallows genus, wringing bitter amusement from situations that can hardly be less hilarious.

But in another sense, the brand of humor Himes exploits in *The End of a Primitive* participates not merely in the tradition of African American black humor but also in the postwar project of "black humor," usually identified with "American Surrealist" Nathanael West and with Kurt Vonnegut, Joseph Heller, and Thomas Pynchon. Himes's work operates at the crossroads of these two modes of understanding the black joke. His "black joking" constitutes a disruption, both ideologically and narratologically, and thus resists the established narrative of the protest novel and of the novel form generally. He obviously belongs among those writers identified by Bruce Janoff, in an early attempt to codify the tenets of "black humor," as having a perspective existing "in a terrain of terrifying candor concerning the most extreme situations" (37). But Himes also must be recognized in *The End of a Primitive* as a writer of parody as well as a deeply subversive satirist in the sense that his work is, as Steven Weisenburger writes of Ishmael Reed, "a revolt against ... the fictions of power" (162). In *The End of a Primitive*, Himes makes clear what *If He Hollers Let Him Go* struggles to articulate: the protest novel form is, like any narrative, a structure dedicated to the support of other structures, some if not all of which work to select, restrict, and maintain access to avenues of knowledge and power.

African American humor has always provided outlets for the articulation of sentiments that otherwise had to be suppressed and has thus traditionally functioned as a progressive and even liberating force. As Lawrence Levine suggests in *Black Culture and Black Consciousness: Afro-American Folk Thought from Slavery to Freedom* (1978), African American humor is "closely related to the humor of absurdity . . . which reveal[s] the gap between appearance and actuality and perform[s] what Anton Zijderveld has called 'the unmasking function'" (312)—here of the absurdity of American racism. Writing of the "creative resourcefulness involved in reversing an accepted joke and turning it to one's own advantage," Mel Watkins cites Ellison's remark that African Americans "couldn't escape, so we developed a style of humor which recognized the basic artificiality, the irrationality, of the actual arrangement" (33). Such a kind of humor allows the black jokester to make use of a situation in which, as Henri Bergson suggested nearly a century ago, a black face is ipso facto comedic: "Why does one laugh at a Negro? . . . [A] black face, in our imagination, is one daubed over with ink or soot. . . . And we see that the notion of disguise has passed on something of its comic quality to instances in which there actually is no disguise" (86). The notion of the disguise or of the mask is central to an understanding of the potential for subversion inherent in blackface humor, which historians have in recent years come to recognize and redeem as a vehicle for satire.[6]

A humor based on the ironized playing of societally designated roles necessarily foregrounds the parodic and performative aspects of identity construction, but beginning with *The End of a Primitive*, Himes allowed his black jokes a still more aggressive punch line, using a specific brand of parodic impulse that refuses to relinquish the most two-dimensional of stereotypes, to question realistic form altogether, as well as the limits and conventions of narrative. In his Harlem detective fiction, for example, the unremitting barrage of blaxploitative language (combined with an exquisitely detailed catalog of grotesquerie and violence) both establishes the characters as brutal caricatures and creates a knowing metacommentary on "realist" African American fiction, an effect that is only heightened by the quasi-bowdlerizing behind such terms as the awkward yet omnipresent "mother-raper." For example, Himes offered exaggerated treatment of the use of "vernacular" language in a description of T-Bone, a short-lived character in Himes's last (and easily most brutal) detective novel, *Plan B*:

T-Bone was clad only in a pair of greasy black pants. . . . His long, narrow face was hinged on a mouth with lips the size of automobile tires. . . . He had his bare black feet propped up on a kitchen table with the white soles toward the television screen. He was white-mouthed from hunger but was laughing like an idiot at two blackfaced white minstrels on the television screen who earned a fortune by blacking their faces and acting just as foolish as T-Bone had done for free all his life.

In between laughing, he was trying to get his old lady, Tang, to go down to Central Park and trick with some white man so they could eat.

"Go on, baby, you can be back in an hour with 'nuff bread so we can scoff."

"I'se tired as you are," she said with an evil glance. "Go sell yo' own ass to whitey, you luvs him so much." (4)

Abandoning the terms and conditions of "realistic" representation that "whitey . . . luvs . . . so much" allows Himes to foreground the issues that concern him—specifically, the sense in which African American identity, no matter how inherent and "authentic" it might be romanticized as being, exists only in and through representation and is thus inescapable except insofar as its grip can be loosened through parodic revision.

In *The End of a Primitive*, the narrativized quality of experience and identity construction as well as the obvious revisiting of *If He Hollers Let Him Go* are emphasized by the narrator's obsession with writing his life. Robinson, a not-very-well-disguised Himes stand-in, is the author of twelve published novels pigeonholed both by reviewers and by his editor as "typical protest" fiction, a genre understood here to preclude any interpretations that are not entirely sanctimonious. The opening of *The End of a Primitive* finds Jesse, recently separated from his wife, living in a room in a Harlem apartment with two older men, one of whom makes constant advances toward him, and a pair of spoiled and superannuated Pomeranians. Throughout, Himes leans fairly hard on the idea of Jesse as hypersexualized ur-primitive, giving him a steady diet of Scotch and raw eggs, which the alcoholic Jesse believes will enhance his virility. His status as nonmodern is also emphasized by the contrast between his living arrangements and those of his erstwhile white lover, Kriss; Jesse's communal apartment is crammed with old-fashioned furniture and outmoded junk, while Kriss's Gramercy Park flat is decorated in coolly modern pastels and sleek furniture of 1950s' functionalist design.

Like Bob Jones, Jesse tells himself jokes, generally centering on his playing the role of one modern primitive or another, in dire circumstances; in jail for recklessly allowing a white woman to hit his car with hers, he feels "laughter ... welling up from the depths of his despair. 'You should have stayed in that tree, son,' he thought" (*End* 93). Here, the black joke performs the function Levine identifies, springing from "the desire to place the situation in which we find ourselves into perspective; to exert some degree of control over our circumstances" (300). Also like his predecessor, Jesse observes, as he examines his haggard, hungover reflection in a mirror, that white hegemony is "'funny, really. Funny as hell if you just get the handle to the joke.... No point in being mad, son. Better get your black ass glad.'... He raised the glass to his reflection. 'Smile'" (123).

Yet Jesse's jokes have no place in the white establishment's understanding of his actions or of his writing; comedy is the province of the white writer, whose novels are not valuable primarily for what they communicate about "experiences inside the restricted and isolated Negro world" (Hughes 267) and who can afford the luxury of humorous and thus "inauthentic" representation. At the same time, however, the protest genre confines and limits Jesse. He recalls "an editor who'd rejected his second novel," asking why "you fellows ... don't try writing about people, just people?":

> "What I really ought to have told the son of a bitch," he thought, "is why don't you read the Old Testament? Or even Rabelais for that matter. That's how I should have started the damn book.... The nigger woke, sat up, scratched at the lice, stood up, farted, pissed, crapped, gargled, harked, spat, sat down, ate a dishpan of stewed chitterlings, drank a gallon of lightning, hated the white folks for an hour, went out and stole some chickens, raped a white woman, got lynched by a mob, scratched his kinky head and said boss, Ah's tahd uh gittin' lynched.... [A]nd the Boss said Go on home and sleep nigger, that's all you niggers is good for. So he went back to his shanty, stealing a watermelon along the way, ate the watermelon rind and all, lay down on his pallet, blinked, yawned and went to

sleep hating the white folks." "We can't print this crap," the editor would have said. (*End* 55)

Indeed, Jesse later has the opportunity to invoke Rabelais in his defense when his latest editor puts the institutional kibosh on his new work because it sounds too much like "fictional autobiography." The lack of differentiation between the events Jesse hallucinates and those that "really" take place in the narrative emphasizes the fundamental inescapability of stories, the interdependence of fiction and "life"; furthermore, the misidentification of Jesse's novel as autobiography suggests that the narrative framework into which his identity will be made to fit depends largely on the reader's expectations. Jesse's editor, felicitously named Pope, demonstrates not just the faith in the enlightened, universal, and rational that his name implies but also a fundamental inability to recognize the black jokes in Jesse's novel:

"Funny!" Pope stared at him incredulously.
"That part where the parents wear evening clothes to the older son's funeral," Jesse said, watching Pope's expression and thinking, "What could be more funny than some niggers in evening clothes? I bet you laugh like hell at Amos and Andy on television."
"That made me cry," Pope accused solemnly. (*End* 117)

Here Himes, as Robert O'Meally has written of Ellison, "brilliantly exploits the tension over black/white humor" (12) by calling attention to the dynamics of the joke self-reflexively, providing both joke and white reader and by making it incumbent on the actual white reader to participate in a perhaps incomprehensible discourse in which he or she wants desperately not to find anything funny. The black joke here destabilizes the reader/text relationship by rupturing the seamlessness of the narrative with a metatextual prod. In addition, the black joke serves a weapon not merely against the stereotyping impulse of minstrelsy but also against the subtler oppression of white liberal guilt that demands a "success story," replacing one tale of blackface with another. "Why don't you write a black success novel?" Pope asks Jesse. "I don't have that much imagination," Jesse responds. "How about yourself?" Pope insists further, unable to stop conflating Jesse's autobiography and his fiction. "You're certainly a success story" (*End* 117). The unspoken joke, of course, is that Jesse's life is evidently not a success story, as the preceding conversation makes clear.

Pope's dismissal of Jesse begins his spiral downward into the long joke of the book—that his life and his art really will be forced willy-nilly into the preestablished parameters of the protest genre. Wandering in a drink-induced blackout, Jesse decides to embark on a compulsive binge weekend in the company of Kriss Cummings, his alcoholic, sex- and narcotics-addicted white ex-lover. Kriss is driven by different demons than is Jesse but is similarly obsessed by the narrative of her life, which she reviews often and ever more lugubriously. (The target of her constant refrain, "You ruined me, you son of a bitch," is generally unclear.) Despite her insistence that she is "tired of listening to ... blacks whining" (*End* 62), Kriss is a self-proclaimed "Negrophile," and most of her friends and lovers are black. Invited to her Gramercy Park apartment for what he assumes is a weekend of nonstop sex, Jesse finds Kriss desperately unhappy and dangerously filled with rage; the book proceeds inexorably toward its conclusion, in which Jesse emerges from another booze-induced stupor to discover that he has "unknowingly" stabbed to death the woman he initially believes is sleeping peacefully in the next room. The conclusion is heavily foreshadowed (before killing Kriss, Jesse sinks a knife into both his own manuscript and uncooked dinner rolls that resemble "mutilated mammoth white testicles" [*End* 157]); only the most resistant reader could doubt its inevitability, which is the point Himes is making.

In addition to being an obvious reworking of the crucial scene in *Native Son*, in which Bigger Thomas accidentally kills the daughter of his white employer as she lies drunk in bed, the final pages of *The End of a Primitive* also reference the death of Desdemona at the hand of Othello. As Jacquelyn McLendon points out ("'Round'" 133), Jesse's attempts to rouse Kriss from what he assumes to be a deep sleep, presumably for sex, suggestively recapitulate Othello's much-analyzed words before killing Desdemona: "I will kill thee / And love thee after." Jesse himself remarks at the outset of his encounter with Kriss that "I'm going to have you whether you like it or not" (*End* 68); his last words before discovering that she is not ignoring him but is dead echo this initial vow: "You know, Kriss baby, you can be a very unpleasant bitch ... and whether you like it or not" (197).

From the moment in which Jesse exclaims that the "bitch wants to die" (*End* 181), the novel unfolds as horrific and ineluctable parody, highlighted by Jesse's metatextual musings on the process of writing the black joke as he "amus[es] himself with this parody on a fine novel written by a fellow black author":

—Ah likes chiddlins, do you like chiddlins?
—Ah likes chiddlins.
—Chiddlins is good.
—Ah likes de big gut, do you likes de big gut?
—Ah likes de big gut.
—De big gut is good. (90)

The point of the novel is its grotesque inevitability stemming from a kind of narrative certitude, a sense that only a limited number of stories can be realized and that all "reality" must succumb to the Procrustean bed of fiction. Walking aimlessly through Times Square, Jesse muses that it is a "good thing you like movies, son.... Otherwise you'd believe all that crap about your country you experience every day" (*End* 42). The feeling of being trapped in or at least in the audience of the wrong film never leaves him; much later, during a heated argument with Walter, a friend of his and Kriss's and the editor of a successful black picture magazine, Jesse observes with amusement that "it was as if he were watching, with impersonal interest, some vaguely valid but not very novel exhibition of idiocy, like a Hollywood treatment of a Negro theme" (184). The final moments of the novel are heavily mediated by this pre-scripting of events; Jesse learns of his crime the following morning while watching a television news report delivered by a talking chimpanzee. (Chimpanzees are cast throughout the novel as fellow primitives. Jesse considers writing a novel about chimps, only to dismiss the idea because "some white woman" would no doubt object that she had once been "leered at" in a zoo [86]). The chimpanzee's commentary takes in not merely current events but also imminent ones: "Defense will allege that he was completely blotto all during this time ... will dismiss the insanity plea ... and Robinson will be electrocuted in Sing Sing prison, December 9th" (193). Temporal differentiation collapses here, but this development is not unexpected given that the narrative plays fast and loose with the conventions of linearity from the outset. Jesse's blackouts structure a narrative filled with lacunae, the details of which are never supplied. Here, however, the joke shifts, taking aim at the conventions of the realistic novel form itself; Jesse is abruptly interpolated into a surreal three-way conversation with the chimp and the newscaster Gloucester that ends when Jesse reminds the chimp of a joke about Generalissimo Franco.

Returning to the bedroom, Jesse discovers Kriss's dead body between the sheets, and "when the full realization of what he had done penetrated his intelligence, his mind turned inward and became sealed within a sardonic, self-lacerating humor" (*End* 199). He assesses his situation in a fiercely condensed summary that both acknowledges and seems to mock the existentialist overtones of the final chapters of *Native Son*: "End product of the impact of Americanization on one Jesse Robinson—black man. Your answer, son. . . . BLACK MAN KILLS WHITE WOMAN. . . . Proof beyond all doubt. Jesse Robinson joins the human race" (199). His words recall the encounter with Walter, in which Jesse, in a flash of inebriated insight, outlines the ironic conditions under which black men are allowed to "join the human race," suggesting that only by performing the identity they are assigned, especially vis-à-vis white women, can African Americans hope to be recognized as people. Kriss's machinations arouse Walter's sexual interest and his fury, leading him to try to attack Jesse with a knife. Walter's (black) wife restrains him,[7] and Jesse muses that "the bitch has got us niggers killing off each other. . . . [N]ow I really do believe the sonofabitch has joined the human race . . . right attitude . . . good nigger . . . footsteps of tradition . . . no wonder they let the nigger join" (184).

As Jesse congratulates himself on his "successful" entry into humanity, the language degenerates into a sick commercial, the discourse of the media completely suffusing the narrative: The nonhuman status of black men is the "best thing [white Americans] ever had for all their social ills. . . . Be Happy—Go Nappy. . . . Feel Low? Lynch Negro!. . . . Can't Fuck? Shoot a Buck!" (199). Picking up the telephone to turn himself in to the police, Jesse, determined to have the last laugh (and underlining the vicious circle his life has become by echoing his earlier remarks), comments that it is a "damn good thing [he] read[s] detective stories; wouldn't know what to do otherwise" (*End* 201).

This insistence on the articulation of African American identity as both prenarrativized and performative lends plausibility to the claim that Himes must be considered a postmodern satirist whose satire is directed less at the societal conditions surrounding the novel's production and more at the form of the novel itself. Though his satire might be construed to have a "real" external target, whether that target is black/white relations or Cold War–era domestic policy (the other major subject of the chimpanzee's commentaries), it is impossible to say that a traditional definition of satire can begin to encompass such a self-contained narrative, particularly if that definition chooses to suggest that satirists write "in order to benefit society as a whole" (Gilbert Highet qtd. in Weisenburger 19). Himes's narrative worries less about inspiring righteous anger against the political and social oppression that supposedly inspires the protest novel than about wreaking havoc on the oppressive structure of the protest novel itself.

Thus, in *The End of a Primitive*, Himes's parodic reworking of the central event of the "classic" protest novel (the alleged rape and murder of a white woman followed by the inexorable punishment of the black protagonist) allows the narrative to regain a measure of control over events whose absurdist momentum would otherwise spiral out of control. By eliding the fictions of Jesse Robinson's novels and of his life, Himes creates a multilayered commentary on the strictures that result from the conceptualizing of African American writing as "protest"; by giving Jesse the role of parodically reworking his self as fiction, Himes allows for a space outside the pre-scripted identity construction so closely linked to the novel form itself. Himes's metatextual and postmodern version of Ellison's "change the joke and slip the yoke" strategy combines with what Weisenburger calls the "violence" and "suspicion of all structures, including those of perceiving, representing and transforming" (5), of the black humorist degenerative satire to create a form that is paradoxically hyperreal in its refusal to surrender stereotype and obsessively formal in its challenge to traditional narrative and mimesis. Thus, extending a long tradition of African American humor as resistance to white hegemony while reflecting suspiciously on the ways in which meaning can be made, Himes's primitive refuses to let pass unremarked the fact that he joins the "civilized culture" of Wright's blueprint only under protest.

CHAPTER THREE

Frank Yerby and the "Costume Drama" of Southern Historiography

While only a careful rereading of Chester Himes's *If He Hollers Let Him Go* reveals its critique of the strictures of the protest novel form for black postwar writers, the briefest glance at *The Foxes of Harrow*, Frank Yerby's 1946 debut novel, seems sufficient to judge its author's lack of commitment to Wright's blueprint. The cover, featuring illustrations of handsome white people in period costume and trumpeting the "fire and blood and whitehot passion" of the story of Stephen Fox, an Irish immigrant turned antebellum plantation owner, suggests the irrelevance of further discussion of the novel's position vis-à-vis literature, let alone literature specifically of racial protest. An almost immediate best seller, the book was read by teenage girls in their suburban bedrooms as well as servicemen in their lonely barracks, many of them unaware, despite hints on the dust jacket, that Yerby was African American. The fact of Yerby's blackness was little more than an interesting biographical aside for the many reviewers anxious to recommend the novel to the "general reader"; as an anonymous reviewer for *College English* observed, following a gushing synopsis of the "spectacular life" of *The Foxes of Harrow*'s protagonist, "The author is a Negro, but this is not a race-problem book."[1]

The persistent misconception that Yerby's publishers made a concerted effort to conceal his race speaks to the cultural and critical anxieties about race. Although knowledge about his race may well have eluded white writers, the brief author's biography on the dust jacket of the first book club edition of *The Foxes of Harrow* includes the information that Yerby both attended and taught at historically black colleges in his native state of

Georgia and mentions that he, like Himes, worked in the "Ethnics Division" of the Federal Writers' Project. Furthermore, a photograph of Yerby appeared on the back cover of his third novel, *The Golden Hawk*, in 1948; readers who subsequently remained unaware of his race must have been willfully obtuse or at best thoroughly incurious.

The "prince of pulpsters," as Robert Bone memorably dismissed Yerby (167), seemed to have produced a major and controversial anomaly for the 1940s—a novel by a black writer apparently not only deliberately unengaged with social realism and race but also entirely disinclined to court critical approval of any kind. Though the book met with some enthusiastic reviews that characterized it as the future of "raceless fiction" (Woodson 353; Locke, "Reason" 20; Gloster, "Significance" 13), Yerby's use of the conventions and tropes of historical romance fiction (what the author referred to as the "costume novel") made it difficult for academics and serious critics to argue that it was anything but the lightest literary fare. Scattered praise for the novel was overwhelmed by a general critical attitude of dismissal. Accordingly, historian Carter G. Woodson calls *The Foxes of Harrow* "one of the truly historical novels of our time" (353), and English professor Hugh Gloster weighs Yerby's "lack of restraint" with his "assets as a writer," including his knowledge of his subject, his balanced treatment of controversial subjects, his "faculty with words" and his "power to maintain interest" in a narrative ("Significance" 13). Gloster provides the most perceptive reading of Yerby's potential influence on the genre, describing the author's "chief contribution" as "shak[ing] himself free of the shackles of race and [using] the treasure-trove of American experience—rather than restrictively Negro experience—as his literary province" (13). Similarly, Alain Locke not only calls the novel "superior to most novels of this genre" but claims it gave Yerby "the right to a vast audience and a deeper influence when and if he should choose to write more seriously realistic fiction" ("Reason" 20).

Yet such reviews were exceptions, overwhelmed by a general tone of condescension. Even the reviewer for *Time* (a publication arguably not as invested as academic journals in maintaining its reputation as an arbiter of high culture) calls *The Foxes of Harrow* "drugstore fiction" ("Scarlet" 113), while critic Blyden Jackson bluntly asserts that "the book has no great positive values" and reminds readers that "fiction which serves only as entertainment is, at its best, trivial and at its worst, dangerous" (652). *The Foxes of Harrow* and its numerous successors, including its sequel, *The Vixens*, have continued to be regarded in much the same way, and although Yerby receives a mention in nearly every encyclopedia of African American writers, his work is rarely anthologized and almost never taught. This general dismissal marks a failure of the field of African American literary studies to fully recognize and encompass the complexity of its intellectual and artistic history. As Gene Jarrett, one of the few scholars who has written recently on Yerby, summarizes, "The long-standing stigma applied to his novels as lowbrow pulp fiction, hack writing and therefore representative of a subliterary genre is problematic and complicit in his absence from the African American canon" (*Deans* 145). The stigma to which Jarrett refers is linked not only to Yerby's choice of genre but also to his record-breaking sales. Jack B. Moore's blunt assessment of the state of Yerby scholarship in 1975 retains most if not all of its validity today: "How did Yerby become such a bad writer?—he must be bad, we feel, because he is a very popular writer" (747).

Moore here articulates an academic anxiety about subjecting popular culture to serious intellectual investigation that has, in the wake of several decades of just such intellectual endeavor, largely lost its force. However, despite contemporary recognition that popular fiction has often been unfairly penalized for its commercial success, recent efforts at critical reconsideration have nevertheless remained focused on Yerby's status as a "good" or "bad" writer, tending to include corollary value judgments even when raising more complicated questions. Indeed, rather than questioning the necessity or validity of these judgments, critics have for the most part been content to note that although Yerby's books are not very good, they are significant for extraliterary reasons, such as the history of their critical reception. As Jarrett concedes, Yerby deserves more attention. After noting that Yerby insisted that he was inspired not by contemporary ephemera but by canonical literature of the eighteenth and nineteenth centuries, Jarrett observes that "in all honesty, Yerby's talents as a writer do not come close to those demonstrated by these [canonical] novels. Yet his artistic exploration and attempted replication of 'how they were read then' and 'are being read now' are intellectual causes that should at least earn him a look in current scholarship on African American literary history" (*Deans* 165).

In addition to Yerby's reputation as a writer of potboilers, his insistence that he was largely uninterested in race as a theme in his fiction has worked against his recovery into the African American canon. Nevertheless, the apparent disparity between Yerby's earliest work, consisting of poetry and prize-winning short stories with explicitly racial themes, and the "racelessness" of his first published novels, which has been noted by virtually all of his critics from 1946 to the present, has led to a scholarly investment in locating a hidden continuity, thematic if not stylistic, that links the Yerby of the early 1940s with his postwar incarnation. For Darwin Turner, one of Yerby's first serious readers, that continuity manifests itself in the desire to "debunk" the history that characterizes Yerby's historical fiction, an impulse Turner sees as yielding a variety of valuable historical critiques related to but not actually including a critique of racial inequality. (Eugene Stovall, author of a recent fictionalized account of Yerby's life, concurs with this assessment.) For James L. Hill, Yerby's focus on the figure of the "anti-heroic hero" links his earlier realistic fiction with his later popular romances. Moore reads Yerby as revealing the unconscious "guilt of the victim" in novels that became more focused on race as Yerby's fame increased.

I do not (entirely) refute this view. However, it is important not to understate the significance of the difference between the Yerby who in 1944 published "Health Card," a terse story of the effects of racism on a young black soldier and his wife, and the Frank Yerby who two years later produced *The Foxes of Harrow*, dubbed by the *New York Times* an "obese" story of southern plantation life (Match 118). We probably should not take seriously Yerby's later contention that he "tossed off" his early novels "thinking all the time ... how correct is Mencken's dictate that nobody ever went broke underestimating the tastes of the American public" (Graham 70) or his possibly facetious remark in "How and Why I Write the Costume Novel" (1959) that he "made rather a serious study of the elements that go to make up a novel of wide appeal ... immediately prior to writing *The Foxes of Harrow*, in order to eliminate as far as possible its chances of failing" (145).

Still, Yerby's attitude toward his popularity is extremely difficult to gauge. While he boasted publicly that he understood (and exploited) the tastes of the American reading public, he also confided privately to an editor, "I believe the connection between a book and its sales should be a fortuitous accident; and that if you try to do it on purpose, you're dead." Whatever his attitude, a close reading of the novel reveals a clear link between its generic choices and its broader political project, a connection that has never been properly recognized. Yerby's shift from the protest genre to the southern historical romance needs to be understood not only as commercially canny but also as a shrewd attempt to exploit the form to further an embedded political agenda. Having essayed the poem and the short story with some critical success, Yerby had attempted in 1943 to interest a publishing house in a novel featuring a well-educated, middle-class African American protagonist, tellingly titled *This Is My Own*, only to see it rejected as not "wholly credible" by Edward Aswell, Richard Wright's editor at Harper, even after Yerby made substantial revisions to his manuscript.[2] Frustrated and determined to find a readership, Yerby turned from his black Ph.D. to a white plantation owner, looking, as the author later put it, to reach not the "semi-liberal" reader of social or racial realism but rather the "bigots" he believed made up the bulk of the American reading public: "I was trying to get to the nigger-haters," he confessed in an interview with James L. Hill (211).

Yerby's use of the costume novel formula in both *The Foxes of Harrow* and *The Vixens*, however cynically undertaken, met with spectacular success despite the fact that the latter novel convinced those critics still on the fence that his work was entirely unredeemable on either political or aesthetic grounds. However, the original manuscript (titled "Ignoble Victory") of Yerby's much-maligned second novel shows that previous assumptions about its author's total desertion of political conviction or literary value in the wake of his best seller are at best limited. The original *Vixens*, never before examined by scholars, reveals that Yerby was engaged in an ambitious attempt to manipulate and deconstruct rather than simply to profit from the genre that had made him famous and to intervene in the ongoing historiographic debate over the Reconstruction period. Together, *The Foxes of Harrow* and "Ignoble Victory" present a response to the Dunning School and its adherents of the 1930s and 1940s and offer a calculated reworking of the subgenre of the historical novel that Alfred Kazin dubbed "the Confederate romance" (*On Native* 511).[3] Other critics have gestured to the fact that *The Foxes of Harrow* is in obvious conversation with its best-known generic predecessor, Margaret Mitchell's *Gone with the Wind*, but have never explored the connection with any degree of thoroughness. Critics have generally been satisfied merely to note that Yerby's novels explore roughly the same narrative terrain as Mitchell's work, sometimes offering a reductionist reading of Yerby that suggests that he merely "borrowed characters and subject matter from . . . the best-seller sensation of the previous decade" (Turner, "Introductory Remarks" 141). In her exploration of the making of the film version of *The Foxes of Harrow*, Phyllis Klotman comes closest to discussing the two novels in tandem, noting that the films offer a "dramatic contrast" to each other while still belonging to the same genre of historical fiction, though in Yerby's case, the film substantially alters the novel. However, Klotman's palpable distaste for *Gone with the Wind* (emblematized perhaps by her insistent references to "Scarlet" O'Hara) causes her to overlook tantalizing issues of filmic intertextuality (such as screenwriter Wanda Tuchock's introduction into Yerby's narrative of tropes, images, and plot devices drawn directly from David O. Selznick's film); Klotman also frequently misrepresents the novel itself, as when she argues that Rhett Butler is "prejudiced against [Scarlett O'Hara's] aristocratic (read: female) snobbery" (212), a nonsensical conclusion given that Butler, by far the more "aristocratic" of the two characters, is also coded throughout the novel as being the more feminine as well.

While *Foxes* has been misunderstood, *The Vixens* has always been ignored, consigned to the oblivion traditionally enjoyed by less original and less successful sequels to popular first books. Yet the two novels demand concomitant consideration. An evaluation of *The Vixens* in its original manuscript form sheds light on both its predecessor and its unfortunately thwarted contribution to a barely nascent and bitterly contested attempt to revise the then-dominant historical view of the South in the decade following the end of the Civil War.

Yerby was not entirely alone in his interest in rewriting Reconstruction-era history, but he was unique in realizing that literary representations of the period had been inextricably linked to the form of the historical romance (not only through *Gone with the Wind* and its literary and cinematic antecedents but also through the army of imitators who followed Mitchell's example). As a result, the only way to effect a significant intervention in the popular realm was to use the same form in response.

To understand the relevance of genre here, one need only consider the example of Howard Fast's 1944 novel *Freedom Road*, which tells the story of an ex-slave who becomes literate after the war and is elected to Congress. Fast's work constituted the first real attempt in fiction to write about Reconstruction from a black perspective. Though the novel sold fairly well, its sales never approached those of Yerby's novels (or, for that matter, the sales of Kathleen Winsor's 1944 *Forever Amber*, a *Gone with the Wind* rip-off set in seventeenth-century England). Fast's novel did not begin to develop the appreciation it deserved until the 1970s, when it was made into a television movie starring Muhammad Ali; in 1995, the novel was reprinted with a foreword by W. E. B. Du Bois and a critical introduction by Eric Foner.

Yerby's two-pronged attack simultaneously challenged the conventions of the historical romance and the assumptions of popular historiography, laying bare the power of fiction to reshape historical fact in the minds of the general public. At the same time, Yerby's work insisted that readers consider textual pleasure's role in making extratextual meaning. By asking his readers to reevaluate their emotional investment in the hero, heroine, and trajectory of the romance narrative, Yerby also asked them to reconsider the biases and misapprehensions on which their enjoyment of that narrative, which might influence their acceptance of its historical accuracy, was based.

The published version of *The Foxes of Harrow*'s sequel bore little resemblance to the text Yerby clearly initially envisaged as continuing and extending its predecessor. Yerby detested *The Vixens*, calling it his worst novel and averring that he was unable to read it after it was published because "my stomach revolts" ("How" 147). To the book's legions of readers, Yerby later offered "my humblest apologies. It should have been banned, or burned" ("How" 147). Yet he repeatedly insisted that the novel in its original form represented his best work: "Ignoble Victory" "was a true literary piece of art.... It was a great novel"; however, Yerby and his editor, George Joel, had "fucked it up between us" (J. L. Hill, "Interview" 238). Given the second novel's far heavier focus on overt sexuality and relatively spartan investment in character development, critics have always assumed that *The Vixens* was hastily penned when Yerby realized that he had stumbled on a winning formula with *The Foxes of Harrow*, which was released as a film in the same year that *The Vixens* appeared. In fact, Yerby had almost certainly completed "Ignoble Victory" before *The Foxes of Harrow* began to sell; the promotional materials accompanying *The Foxes of Harrow*'s first book club edition (also released in 1946) note that "Mr. Yerby is at work on a new book, tentatively titled 'Ignoble Victory,'" while the manuscript itself demonstrates that it was written before its predecessor had undergone its final prepublication alterations. In any case, the novel's final incarnation bears little resemblance to its manuscript, and the excised portions of the original demonstrate Yerby's full project. Reexamination of the manuscript clarifies that Yerby's historical romance needs to be considered not as diametrically opposed to the goals of the protest novel but rather as extending them in ways that, though undercut by the published version of *The Vixens*, are clearly at play even in *The Foxes of Harrow*.

The Foxes of Harrow was subjected to multiple revisions that included the insertion of a different ending shortly before publication. In the novel, Stephen Fox's son, Etienne, returns from the war to find that his wife, Ceclie, believing him dead, has been unfaithful. He threatens to kill her but breaks down when she confronts him, reminding him of their sexual passion, and they reconcile. In the manuscript, however, Ceclie leaves Etienne and their children in a near-perfect, strongly pro-feminist inversion of the end of *Gone with the Wind*, returning to her previous life in Texas. "Ignoble Victory," continues the story of Etienne and his children after the original version of these events, making it clear that the two narratives were written at roughly the same time.

In both *The Foxes of Harrow* and "Ignoble Victory," Yerby moves African American characters and their intellectual and cultural contributions to American exceptionalism and southern identity from the margins in which they then languished in both popular and historiographical representation to a central narrative position. Accordingly, *The Foxes of Harrow* should not be read as the "assimilationist" product of a disillusioned black writer resigned to the notion that racial protest and popularity must be mutually exclusive. It is a biracial book by a biracial writer, not "raceless" but rather profoundly interracial. Furthermore, although Turner argued in 1968 that Yerby has been found "unacceptable" as a black intellectual because of his success ("The charm of the symbol" writes Turner, "is its aura of failure" [569]), popularity is crucial to his racial project. It is not, as Gloster argues in "The Significance of Frank Yerby," just significant that Yerby sold a lot of books and thus demonstrated that black writers could move "beyond" race in the commercial realm. Instead, the fact that Yerby sold a lot of books on the theme of the ways miscegenation is central to American identity—on, in other words, the blackness at the heart of whiteness—serves as an implicit argument not only that black culture and white American life have always been inextricably, undeniably imbricated but that Americans on some level recognized this fact in the 1940s and responded to its validity. In other words, Yerby might be arguing that African American literature need not take as its raison d'être the explication of the esoteric realities of black life. Instead, *The Foxes of Harrow* suggests that it merely expresses the obvious—that blackness and whiteness are inseparable in American culture—with the overwhelming acceptance of ordinary readers.

For all that *The Foxes of Harrow* was and is evaluated as a "raceless" narrative, even a cursory read reveals not only that it is full of black characters but that miscegenation, literal and figurative, structures the story and informs every aspect of it. The main character, twenty-five-year-old Stephen Fox, comes to the United States in 1825 from "old Europe" (Ireland), seeking to found a dynasty outside New Orleans. A talented gambler, Fox wins the land on which he will build his plantation, Harrow, from a brutal German planter, Hugo Waguespack,[4] in a poker game. Once the land is tilled and Harrow is established, Fox seeks a wife, wooing and winning the daughter of local Creole aristocracy, Odalie Arceneaux. He determines early on that she is the only woman in Louisiana suitable to be the mistress of Harrow, little dreaming that she will turn out to be at first frigid and subsequently (once her ardor has been awakened) unable to bear Fox the many sons he desires to carry on his name and to found his dynasty.

Any 1946 reader of the first hundred pages of the novel would have been struck by the points of convergence between its characters and those of *Gone with the Wind*. Scrappy Irishman Gerald O'Hara, Scarlett's father, also emigrates under questionable circumstances (Fox is accused of theft, O'Hara of murder and theft); gambles and wins a plantation, which he names after a battle fought on May 26, 1798, in the Irish Rebellion (the defeat at Tara Hill and the Battle of the Harrow, respectively); builds the land up through hard work; and despite social inferiority finds a wife with enviable French ancestry among the southern aristocracy. A bit of close reading and elementary math also reveals that Stephen Fox and Gerald O'Hara are near-perfect contemporaries; both, it seems, were born in the first year of the nineteenth century, and both die immediately after the end of the Civil War, as Reconstruction begins. These parallels matter. Though Yerby later criticized *The Foxes of Harrow* as containing "every romantic cliché in the world," it seems clear that while he borrowed certain clichés from *Gone with the Wind* (and by extension, the conventions of its predecessors in the Confederate romance genre), he also dispensed with others, adapting the genre to suit his variety of racial realism.

Specifically and most importantly, Yerby refuses the conventionalized narrative partitioning of race that characterizes *Gone with the Wind* and its many predecessors in the genre. Even the casual reader of *Gone with the Wind* today notices a glaring absence of mixed-race characters, a lacuna exploited by Alice Randall in her caustic recent parody *The Wind Done Gone*, which envisages an alternate Tara from the perspective of Scarlett's mulatto half-sister, Cynara. *The Foxes of Harrow* overturns this convention in its opening pages, introducing light-skinned blacks as a central feature not only of plantation life but also of social life in sophisticated New Orleans, where they are not slaves but rather free blacks who may be tradesmen (like the tailor Lagoaster, who clothes Fox and every other "man of refinement" in the area) or the paid mistresses of well-off white men. Fox initially expresses distaste for the miscegenation his Creole friends take for granted but later takes a quadroon mistress and fathers her child. By the novel's end, Fox has reconsidered his earlier stances on nearly everything related to race, accepting with relative equanimity the fact that his legitimate (white) son is a violent bully, an undereducated bigot, a rapist, and a drunk while his former slave, a character based in part on fugitive slave Anthony Burns, is an intelligent and ambitious young man destined for political greatness in the Reconstruction-era South. Like O'Hara, however, Fox has nowhere to go once the war has ended, and so although he survives the war, he dies a short time later, his outstanding vitality (of which the book makes much, implying that Fox's strength derives from his Irish peasant ancestry) sapped by the physical, intellectual, and moral strain of the war.[5] Also like O'Hara, Fox's dreams of founding a dynasty come to naught. Though Scarlett is devoted to "saving" Tara after the war, the novel ends with the strong suggestion that neither of her two surviving children will be capable of managing the plantation after she is gone. For their part, Fox's two sons are temperamentally unsuited to run Harrow and/or illegitimate.[6]

Stephen Fox's birth and death dates, then, follow closely the contours of the antebellum nineteenth century. His historical positioning suggests that for Yerby, the figure stands as an embodiment of that era, a sort of bridge between the Age of Reason and the Industrial Age. As such, he is Yerby's repudiation of the notion that prosperity in the antebellum South derived from what southern revisionist historians in the 1920s and 1930s preferred to think of as the South's dedication to an agrarian ideal inherited via the cavalier ancestry of its ruling class. Though Fox can be read as the perfect emissary of all that is Western European (he is Irish but spends his youth in London, Paris, and Vienna, so that he is perfectly trilingual when he reaches the United States), he is also emphatically American in ways that make him incapable of completely assimilating into the culture and politics of the antebellum South. He pauses to pontificate at various junctures throughout the novel, espousing basic Jeffersonian democratic credos justifying his faith in American exceptionalism and explicating his increasing unwillingness to support the class and racial divisions of the South: "We must not destroy the brightest hope of human freedom of all the ages," he tells his friend, Andre, justifying opposition to secession. "I've seen a goodly part of this land of ours . . . and there is something about it that is different. . . . 'Tis a big land . . . for big men to carve out and build and conceive the shape of human destiny" (*Foxes* 175–76). He later lectures Etienne, "The thing we would destroy is infinitely precious to me. I don't believe any longer in aristocracy. . . . Ye can't have a land like America unless the people—all the people—have a hand in its shaping" (375). Yerby argued that Stephen Fox's development from a European into an American should be seen as mirroring the author's development from solipsism to a love of all humanity that made his support of racism philosophically and morally impossible: "It would have been easier, of course," Yerby wrote in a letter to an editor at Dial, "to equip him from the first with a set of readymade ideals, concepts and motivations, but such a character, to my mind, would have been almost completely lacking in validity. All of the implications of this development [however] are present in the first part of the book." Finally, Fox also exhibits a resolutely Ben Franklin–esque pragmatic attitude toward work and a progressive view of technology. Seeing, for example, that New Orleans is flooded with waste after every rain, Fox wonders aloud why a little engineering could not be employed to ameliorate the situation; he subsequently imports machines from the North, against his neighbors' advice, to revolutionize the cane industry.

His initial attitudes toward racial issues make Fox an amalgamation of what were, in the first half of the nineteenth century, relatively progressive views for the South as well as a character of complex and often contradictory impulses. Though he alleges at first to find black people unattractive, he also sees the institution of slavery as regrettable. Yet he buys a crew of slaves, among them an aged black woman named Caleen who initially appears to be an analogue to the O'Hara family's Mammy but who ultimately proves to be Harrow's saving grace. Gifted with shrewd perceptions that she passes off as the gift of prophecy, Caleen saves Harrow from destruction by accurately forecasting a major storm that other plantation owners do not see coming and that destroys all of their crops. When Fox emerges as the only planter with a product that season, his fortune is made. Though he refuses to believe that Caleen is capable of second sight and goes through the motions of forbidding her to practice her voodoo ("If ye continue with this witchcraft, I'll send ye up to the calaboose and order thirty lashes" [*Foxes* 120]), he recognizes the value of her professed devotion to his household and her folk knowledge and accepts without much introspection or contestation her argument that there are "some things . . . no good for whites to know" (120). Fox's repression of the centrality of Caleen's role in his success mimics his adopted society's broader repression of the contributions of blacks to the antebellum South's economy and culture more generally.

Fox's lack of curiosity about the mysterious means Caleen employs to achieve her remarkable effects has its complement in Caleen's campaign to veil her secrets. While asserting that whites need not be privy to her knowledge, Caleen intensifies her inscrutability by hinting that the things she perceives are legible to her fellow blacks if not to whites, implying the existence of a vast communication network among the slaves. The reader knows of Caleen's desire, revealed only to her grandson, Inch, to see the slaves revolt, making her words sound like a coded threat against the aristocratic class represented by Odalie. In showing Caleen's interactions with

Inch and other blacks, Yerby offers a significant revision of the black characters in typical southern historical fiction, who exist entirely through the perspective of whites and thus occupy a separate (and unknowable) narratological space. As she attempts to convince Odalie that a *mamaloi* will be able to help her win back her husband's attention, Caleen lectures,

> White man wise, all right; he wise one way; but Negre wise too, he wise another way—a old, old way. White man can't understand that way. I sing a song, me, out in the kitchen house. Maîtresse hear me sing it a hundred time, but tonight I sing it different, just one sound different; hold one word a little too long, maybe. Cook, her hear me sing it. She hear that one word held a little too long. She go outside to empty water and she sing it too, her. And she hold that one word too long. Negre passing by hear it, him. He go through all the fields singing it the same way, till finally it go from mouth to mouth and the Negres in the fields next to ours done got it too, them. Then tonight, Negres from every plantation in fifty miles meet me tonight in the black bayous when the moon is dark. Ain't no white man can do that, maîtresse. Ain't no white *docteur*, no white priest can tell maîtresse what to do. Got to fight magic with magic: *gris-gris* with better *gris-gris*. We get maître back—you watch. (*Foxes* 217)

Though Caleen positions herself here as the bearer of "a old, old" wisdom, she is nevertheless also incontestably modern in ways that link her to Stephen Fox's insistently "progressive" mentality and undermine the conflation of authentic blackness and an allochronic folk identity that offered the lone accepted format for black southern fiction prior to 1940. While Caleen burns representative figures and deploys mysterious potions in her stereotypical performance of voodoo ritual, she also employs commonsensical health care solutions to save the lives of everyone at Harrow, dismissing the Foxes' adviser as a "great fool of a *docteur*" (*Foxes* 171). She midwifes the birth of Fox's only legitimate son, Etienne, encouraging Odalie through a difficult labor after the doctor informs Fox that his wife cannot be saved. Caleen stops a doctor from bleeding the infant Etienne when he is dying of yellow fever, instead lowering his temperature and getting him to take fluids. She uses psychological incentives to help Fox recover from a gunshot wound made more serious by his profound depression. And she persuades Odalie to discover her own sexuality by arousing her with pornography (a live sex show hosted by a voodoo priestess). Although Caleen lives to see her medical knowledge incorporated into the methods of "more than one progressive young doctor" during an outbreak of yellow fever, her contributions to Harrow go largely unacknowledged until her death. Yet if her influence is a secret, it is an open one. Without Caleen, there would be no Stephen Fox, no Harrow. Again, if Stephen Fox is a figure for the antebellum nineteenth century, it is no stretch to read Caleen as what Toni Morrison calls the "Africanist presence" beneath mainstream white American literature and culture (2). *The Foxes of Harrow* suggests that for Yerby, as for Paul Gilroy, modernity (here, specifically American modernity) is inherently a hybrid construct.

If Caleen is the black heart of the white (very white, as the description of the architecture indicates) Harrow, Desiree, Fox's mixed-race mistress, occupies the center of the web of miscegenation surrounding the plantation. The product of generations of interracial relationships, Desiree is a beautiful, intelligent, and sensitive woman who has been trained from birth for the one occupation for which she is deemed suitable—high-end prostitution—by her mother. Her "black" son by Stephen Fox is a replica of his father, down to his "white skin and red hair and freckles that dusted his forehead" (*Foxes* 403). Her brother, Aupre, who can also pass for white, expatriates to France, where he becomes a celebrated playwright by presenting the story of *The Foxes of Harrow* to a white Parisian audience. Aupre's metafictional positioning in the novel invites parallels both to Dumas and to Yerby. But Etienne Fox befriends Aupre abroad, unaware that he is black; when Etienne discovers Aupre's heritage, Etienne orders his slaves to beat Aupre to death.

Etienne, who emerges in *The Vixens* as the leader of the Knights of the White Camellia, a prototype of the Ku Klux Klan, is the key to understanding what *The Foxes of Harrow* teaches us about biraciality and American culture, bizarrely embodying both the "tragic mulatto" figure and the white supremacist. Etienne is the product of the union of two white people, Stephen and Odalie, yet is described from birth as "strangely swarthy" and "dark as a mulatto" (*Foxes* 158). (Stephen's best friend also names his son Stephen, so that Etienne's best friend is Stephen LeBlanc, literally "Stephen the White.") The darkest white man on the plantation,

Etienne is also the most virulently racist, as free with his diatribes as with his fists. His insistence on the separation between black and white and on blacks' subservience comes back to haunt him by the novel's end. When his former valet, Inch, orders Fox's release from the prisoner of war camp in which he is being held, Fox and Etienne are called to Inch's office for a meeting. Shocked to learn that Inch is now in a position of authority over him, Etienne is appalled to discover that Inch has married Desiree and adopted her son by Stephen, Cyrus, who is a perfect physical replica of his father. Stephen Fox vacillates between finding the situation wryly amusing and deeply disturbing; he has long since realized that the effort to enforce racial supremacy by maintaining an imaginary divide between hopelessly miscegenated peoples is bleakly comedic at best, yet he realizes that that struggle's viciousness can only intensify. When Inch encourages Cyrus (who, in a final twist on Yerby's reworking of *Gone with the Wind*, has emerged from the war as insane as Gerald O'Hara) to reveal his knowledge of the infidelity of Etienne's wife, Etienne offers violence, forcing Inch to remind him that the political situation has changed and that whites now can be lynched for threatening blacks.

Though Etienne's inexplicable darkness (especially alongside Cyrus's almost equally implausible fairness) allows him to embody the notion, elsewhere so prominent, that blackness and whiteness are inextricably mixed, Etienne stubbornly insists that black and white must not and cannot overlap. This separatism, however, is undermined so rigorously and consistently throughout *The Foxes of Harrow* that Etienne emerges as a pathetic figure, railing against the irrefutable reality of American interraciality when everyone, including Yerby's readers, knows better. Yerby's great contribution to the postwar debate over racial authenticity and literature is marked by this restoration of the integral role played by blackness in the progress narrative that is Stephen Fox's long journey from European to American, from superstition to reason, from racial prejudice to the recognition of human equality, all wrapped in the generic confines of the southern historical romance. In an American culture in which blackness and whiteness do not merely coexist but commingle, the notion that progressive racial realism has generic limits that demand the dichotomizing of fiction into black and white proved for Yerby problematic at best, untenable and destructive at worst. Indeed, Yerby's novel argues, everyone knows about the multiraciality of American culture, and it need only be acknowledged; only in denying the fact of our miscegenation do we, like the hapless Etienne, make our mistake.

While *The Foxes of Harrow* offers a rereading of one of the central conventions of the Confederate romance (the allegedly unbreachable racial divide characteristic of the first half of *Gone with the Wind*), "Ignoble Victory" tackles the greater challenge of revising the troubling historiography of the latter half of Mitchell's novel. As several scholars note, *Gone with the Wind* presents its history of Reconstruction in wholly "unreconstructed" form, just as it proffers a version of the Civil War itself that has drawn fire for its numerous inaccuracies, belying Mitchell's claims that her history was "as water proof and air tight as ten years of study and a lifetime of listening to participants would make it" (qtd. in Chadwick 211).[7]

As historian John Hope Franklin thoroughly chronicles, dissenting views to the reactionary notion of Reconstruction as at best a failure and at worst a nightmare visited on an innocent South by a vindictive North had already begun to be published by black historians as early as 1910, when W. E. B. Du Bois published "Reconstruction and Its Benefits." Du Bois went on to produce his eight-hundred-page defense of African American participation in the postwar period, *Black Reconstruction in America*, in 1935.[8] Despite such dissenting views, however, Mitchell's novel solidified the work of historian William Archibald Dunning and his acolytes (and the popular representations of their academic monographs, including the fiction of Thomas Dixon, Joel Chandler Harris, and Thomas Nelson Page) into received wisdom for millions of readers newly converted to belief in the plantation myth. Bruce Chadwick notes in his history of American Civil War films, *The Reel Civil War* (2001), that given the international coverage of the Scopes trial, the South was by the 1930s a target of worldwide ridicule, with southerners defined "as stubborn, unthinking, Bible-thumping dolts, stuck forever in the past, living in small towns up in the hills and firing potshots at wandering tax collectors" (213). However, Chadwick further argues, the region underwent a tremendous makeover in the public mind in the wake of the success of *Gone with the Wind*, whose sentimentality-cloaked but ideologically bound depictions of the "tragic era" influenced a generation of readers to identify with the South's noble victimhood. As Helen Taylor ably documents, millions read the novel in the year of its publication and millions more were inspired to buy it in the next few years when Margaret Mitchell won the Pulitzer Prize and when Selznick's film version became a media event. For every reader of Du Bois's *Black Reconstruction*, there were thousands who read *Gone with the Wind*. The readerships of popular and academic history may be largely though not entirely mutually exclusive; however, what is striking here is the remarkable convergence of the two genres just at the juncture when African American scholars were beginning to make strides toward overturning white apologist historiography.

Gone with the Wind's version of the 1865–73 period emphasizes the rapaciousness and cruelty of northern "occupiers," referring, sometimes obscurely and sometimes in great detail, to the machinations of the Republican state government and its Scalawag and Carpetbagger minions and the genteel suffering of the defeated southern aristocracy. Newly freed slaves have virtually no role in their own destiny in *Gone with the Wind*, where blacks exist as pawns to be manipulated by unscrupulous whites, as would-be rapists, or as both in a society in which the Ku Klux Klan is a regrettable necessity.[9] "The negroes were on top," thinks Scarlett O'Hara,

> and behind them were the Yankee bayonets. The South was too beautiful a place to be let go without a fight, too loved to be trampled by Yankees who hated Southerners enough to enjoy grinding them into the dirt, too dear a homeland to be turned over to ignorant negroes drunk with whisky and freedom. (639–40)

The implied and overt racism of *Gone with the Wind*'s reactionary historiography, which echoes the conclusions of Claude Bowers's *The Tragic Era* (1929) and anticipates E. Merton Coulter's influential *The South during Reconstruction* (1947), finds its near perfect obverse in the manuscript of "Ignoble Victory." Yerby was fascinated by the work of historians, especially its lacunae and biases, and his study of the Reconstruction period left him outraged. "I can tell when a historian is lying," he told James L. Hill.

> And historians lie; they lie like dogs. Let's take, for instance, the Reconstruction period.... [T]hey have written history about the thieving and robbing of the Reconstruction. The Reconstruction built

schools for the first time in the South's history. The Reconstruction passed the first humane, decent and enlightening laws in the history of the South. The Reconstruction period was a magnificent social phenomenon. It was killed by barbarians and savages, which basically the Southerners were. (230)

Yerby's reference to southerners as "savages" evokes W. J. Cash's notion of the "savage ideal," set forth in his 1941 response to the Southern Agrarians, *The Mind of the South*. Cash's work explodes many of the same southern political and historical mythologies that Yerby's work attacks, among them the notion of an insuperable divide between the lineage of the cavalier and the cracker populations. This concept bolstered the Agrarians' view of the South as an idyllic community dedicated to an "antique conservatism" but irretrievably altered by Reconstruction, which John Crowe Ransom describes as a "period of persecution" that inaugurated industrialism, a new "foreign invasion of Southern soil, which is capable of doing more devastation than was wrought when Sherman marched to the sea" (17, 23). Cash's book, which emphasizes repeatedly that the "mind of the South" is neither especially aristocratic nor inherently conservative, clearly situates itself as an intervention in an academic debate over the identity of the New South that carried with it an implicit call to resurrect the antipathies of the immediate post–Civil War period (and, by extension, concomitant institutions such as the Klan) some seventy years later. "It will be in order," Ransom continues, "to proclaim to Southerners that the carpet-baggers are again in their midst" (23). The revisionism of Ransom and his contemporaries is seductive, Cash admits, especially when paired with what he describes as an intellectual leadership, "emanating from the University of North Carolina Press," that is "wholly unarticulated with the body of the South" (418). In the final pages of his study, Cash turns specifically to the phenomenon of *Gone with the Wind*, noting that it is not that the South lacks intellectuals willing to debunk its myths but that writers such as Thomas Wolfe and William Faulkner have an "incredibly small" readership that often approaches their work with "squeamish distaste and shock," while "Margaret Mitchell's sentimental novel, *Gone with the Wind*, which had curiously begun by a little offending many Southerners, ended by becoming a sort of new confession of the Southern faith" (419–20). For Cash, this short circuit between the South's readers and its intellectual critics is the major problem facing the region at the beginning of the 1940s: "The tragedy of the South as it stood in 1940 centrally resided" in this lack of connection (421).

Though Yerby's texts converge at several points with Cash's work, Yerby extends and revises substantially Cash's treatment of the issue of race and, in the case of "Ignoble Victory," of Reconstruction. Cash is arguably the first white southern historian to acknowledge, albeit somewhat imprecisely, the centrality of the African American experience and influence on southern culture. According to Cash, the "Negro entered into white man as profoundly as white man entered into Negro—subtly influencing every gesture, every word, every emotion and idea, every attitude" (49–50). Yet Cash generally leaves the nature of these interactions unspecified. Rejecting the argument that only southerners could really understand African Americans, Cash refers instead to what Darlene Clark Hine later labels "the culture of dissemblance" (37), arguing that behind a smiling face "a veil was drawn which no white man might certainly know he had penetrated" (Cash 317).

Cash seems to bemoan the replacement of a sophisticated attempt to grapple with "the race problem" with the careless bigotry encouraged by narratives such as *Gone with the Wind*. However, he replicates many of the errors he seeks to correct in that he does not explore the actual contributions of African Americans to the southern history about which he writes, let alone to their own history. Consequently, blacks are visible in Cash's narrative exclusively through their effects on whites and are seen only through their eyes. Cash's narrative of the period of Reconstruction, which argues that it engendered a political and economic "frontier" that provided a continuation of the geographical frontier against which the South had historically defined its identity, differs from Mitchell's only in its replacement of the literal figure of the black would-be rapist with a metaphorical one; Cash leaves unchallenged the notion that blacks were helpless victims of Yankee greed and trickery: "In his manipulation of the unfortunate black man, [the Yankee] was of course generating a terrible new hatred for him," argues Cash. "Ignorant and ductile, the Negro was in fact a mere passive instrument, no more to be blamed than a cudgel in the hand of a bully" (114). Nowhere does "the Negro" emerge as an actor in his own destiny; rather, Cash concludes, the post–Civil War African American southerner was "the obviously appointed scapegoat" and nothing more.

Given his impatience with nearly every other article of faith to which he saw his fellow southerners clinging, and given his heated excoriation of apologists for slavery and Jim Crow, the fact that Cash uncritically accepts the basic premises of the Dunning School is difficult to fathom. Only in his insistence that the southern focus on the black rapist was a disastrous literalization of the South's gendered and raced psyche rather than a reaction to an actual threat by real people does Cash make a substantial break with his racist forebears.[10]

"Ignoble Victory" seeks to contest precisely this sort of characterization of Reconstruction-era African Americans as "ignorant and ductile" and entirely lacking in agency, which Cash recognized but failed to fully reject. "Ignoble Victory" offers a fictional correlative to the revisionist historical work of Du Bois and various less well known black historians who had by this time written similarly ignored regional studies of nineteenth-century black political figures (see, e.g., Rankin). Yerby most likely read and relied on Du Bois's work in particular: Yerby's project not only recapitulates Du Bois's in ideological terms but also repeats Du Bois's minor inaccuracies in the biographies of black Louisianan activists. For example, both Du Bois and Yerby assert that Oscar J. Dunn, the first black lieutenant governor of Louisiana, was an ex-slave and that the Roudanez brothers, who founded the *New Orleans Tribune*, the first black daily newspaper in the United States, were Santo Domingan refugees.

Yerby recognized the power of bringing together the conventions of sentimental fiction with the unvarnished facts of historical research. In his manuscript, he amalgamates the two approaches to historical writing that historian and novelist Henrietta Buckmaster dubs "a woman without a head, a man without a heart" (173).[11] At the same time, Yerby's proposed novel signals its break with tradition generically, simultaneously rewriting both the "history" and the "romance" in the historical romance. "Ignoble Victory" offers an unexpected narrative of Reconstruction, couching its critique of the racial politics of *Gone with the Wind* in the story of Land Moreau, a southern journalist who fights for the Union and returns to Louisiana as Reconstruction begins; Hope Varrick, a Yankee schoolteacher who devotes her life to improving literacy among ex-slaves; Tennessee Rhodes, a nineteen-year-old backwoods soldier who has implausibly fought on both sides and survived imprisonment in both the infamous

Andersonville prison and Camp Douglas; the surviving members of the Fox family, specifically Etienne and his children; and, most important, Cyrus Inchcliff, known in *The Foxes of Harrow* as Inch, and Isaac Robinson, the leader of an all-black settlement based on socialist principles that stands at the manuscript's end as the truly democratic, antiracist answer to the assumptions underpinning the now-destroyed Harrow.

As this list suggests, "Ignoble Victory" deviates almost immediately from the plot of the standard romance by replacing the stock figures of the romantic hero and heroine with a variety of characters among whom the story's sexual tension is distributed. In stark contrast to the rules Yerby later prescribed in "How and Why I Write the Costume Novel" (and followed in the process of reshaping "Ignoble Victory" into *The Vixens*), "Ignoble Victory" offers, in lieu of a single identifiable hero, a short, balding, fortyish journalist, Moreau, whose regular abuse of alcohol and underage prostitutes is presented in unromantic detail, and his friend Rhodes, strikingly handsome but completely lacking in strength of character. Moreau is drawn throughout the novel to Varrick, a Bostonian whose sexual appeal is initially overshadowed by her thick-lensed eyeglasses, though he later beds Gail Fox, the former mistress both of a Yankee soldier and of Hugh Duncan, a southerner who has made a fortune through unscrupulous business practices and now bankrolls the Knights of the White Camellia, a loose affiliation of white supremacist terrorist groups. Rhodes marries Hugh Duncan's cousin, Sabrina, a southern belle from a "good" family with whom he intends, like Stephen Fox, to found a dynasty; she, however, is insane at the time of their marriage and ends a suicide, whereupon Rhodes also embarks on a relationship with Gail Fox, who is unironically described by her father, Etienne, as "a true flower of the South." In the manuscript's closest approximation of a stable, middle-class marriage, Desiree, the erstwhile sexual partner of both Gail's father and grandfather, remains happily married to Inch, who has adopted Desiree and Stephen Fox's son, Cyrus.

If Yerby undermines the traditional romance novel's format by refusing to focus on any particular couple for too many pages, he also rejects the standards of the Confederate romance more specifically by making all of his female characters unconventional by its lights. The lone woman who might be classified as a "lady" is Desiree, now in her forties and described as "regal" ("Ignoble" 85) and possessed of the superior manners and circumspect behavior so central to the myth of the genteel plantation mistress. The white Gail Fox, by contrast, is beautiful but amoral and sexually indiscriminate, as seductive as Scarlett O'Hara but far less restrained by contemporary codes for women's behavior. Yerby renders Gail an object of almost universal sexual appeal, even as a child (Land Moreau first becomes aware of his sexual interest in her when she is only ten) and even under circumstances strongly suggesting incest.[12] Sabrina Duncan, the aristocratic scion of a formerly wealthy family, is a typically spirited southern belle at the narrative's outset but goes mad when her father is shot in front of her during the violent suppression of a political demonstration by blacks in New Orleans; the ordeal strips her of her genteel exterior and turns her into a shrieking racist. The other major female character, Hope Varrick, is a northerner, an intellectual, a feminist, and a political idealist. In valorizing the figure of the Yankee schoolteacher, Yerby works perhaps most strongly against the tropes characteristic of the Confederate romance and even of *The Mind of the South*. In one of the frequent narratorial disquisitions on post–Civil War southern society in *Gone with the Wind*, the reader discovers that "it was hard to know who was more cordially hated by the settled citizenry, the impractical Yankee schoolmarms or the Scallawags" (866). At the same time, Cash's description of the "Yankee schoolma'am who ... moved down upon the unfortunate South in the train of the army of occupation to 'educate' the black man" as "generally horsefaced, bespectacled, and spare of frame ... no proper intellectual, but at best a comic character, at worst a dangerous fool" (137) is perhaps his harshest indictment in a chapter devoted to demonizing the Reconstruction effort as a whole. Again, Yerby's manuscript curiously echoes Cash, describing Varrick as hidden behind "enormous black-rimmed spectacles" and possessed of a body repeatedly described as "too thin" and even gaunt. Yet unlike Cash's and Mitchell's teachers, Hope Varrick is neither impractical nor a fool; an idealist, she bravely lives as the lone white in the otherwise all-black Lincoln community, where she escapes an attack by murderous Klansmen and works with Isaac Robinson, whose respect and trust she has gained, to rescue both Robinson's sons and the badly wounded Land Moreau.

Yerby's manuscript lacks neither adventure nor sexual intrigue. However, "Ignoble Victory" makes a still more radical break with the conventional historical romance by pointedly subordinating these elements to the narrative's primary focus, which is political in nature. "When it was over," Yerby writes in the prologue, "it was not really over, and that was the trouble" (1). Like the prologue to *The Foxes of Harrow*, the introduction to "Ignoble Victory" sets up the historical context for the rest of the narrative from a vantage point sometime after its events occur, indicating that its scope will encompass the events of Reconstruction—roughly the period covered by the second half of *Gone with the Wind*. However, Mitchell does not describe the era of Reconstruction in its entirety; rather, Rhett Butler walks out on Scarlett sometime in the early 1870s, apparently just after the election of Ulysses S. Grant and the passage of the Fifteenth Amendment. "Ignoble Victory," by contrast, shows not only the beginning of the Reconstruction era but also its end following the Compromise of 1877, in which congressional Democrats agreed not to contest the decision of a majority Republican electoral commission to declare Rutherford B. Hayes the winner of the 1876 presidential election in exchange for the return of home rule in the South. The resulting withdrawal of Federal troops from the South set the stage for a resurgence of violence against blacks and the introduction of Jim Crow laws. Whereas *Gone with the Wind* left readers with the impression that Reconstruction was simply a failed policy that had somehow faded away in the unnarrativized years following the conclusion of the novel's action, "Ignoble Victory" explains that Reconstruction's policies were reversed not because of the incompetence of gullible blacks but because of the greed and corruption of wealthy white politicians, carefully delineating the process by which Samuel Tilden won the popular vote but was forced to cede the presidency: "We're witnessing something new in history," comments Land Moreau, "we're witnessing the process of having a national election stolen from the rightful winner" ("Ignoble" 325). "Ignoble Victory" ends with the flight from Louisiana of Isaac Robinson's followers, who have recognized that with the return of legislative power to the southern states, they have no legal defenses against white terrorism. The effect is to privilege the historical narrative over the imperative to provide closure to the "romantic" plot, further complicating and undermining the genre of the costume novel. While Yerby ultimately discarded this strategy (*The Vixens* truncates the historical narrative, structuring the novel instead around a story of thwarted but ultimately reunited lovers), "Ignoble Victory" shows clearly that Yerby originally intended to privilege his novel's historiographic imperative. If the narrative of *The Foxes of Harrow* "was not really over" with the end of the Civil War, so the action of "Ignoble Victory" cannot properly end until Reconstruction does.

Not only does Yerby tether his novel's chronology to that of Reconstruction, but his description of the period offers a sharp and recognizable contrast to the historiography central to the Confederate romance. While Yerby laments the "ravished earth" of the South, in his formulation, both northerners and southerners enrich themselves during Reconstruction, while white men are pawns in the game of Reconstruction: "Their creatures were the Carpetbagger and the Scalawag, the White Leaguer and the Ku Kluxer. And if the one was a thief, the other was a murderer." Yerby pays lip service to the notion of the noble Confederate soldier and reassures his reader that while "no man who had seen Bob Lee kneeling in prayer before his boys could stomach such dishonor . . . there were enough ex-slave drivers, Negro stealers, traders in human flesh for it, enough mudsill scum to do the job" ("Ignoble" 3; *Vixens* 9). Yet the narrative itself undermines this reassuring class division, introducing a tidewater Virginian (shorthand for a representative of the cavalier myth) as the archvillain, Hugh Duncan, and shows Etienne Fox, described repeatedly as recognizably a "gentleman," as Duncan's right-hand man. It is also no coincidence that Yerby gives the name *Wilkes*, with all of its intertextual resonances, to the most repellant of the Ku Kluxers, Etienne Fox's colleague and a prewar overseer, slave trader, and "nigger stealer." Yerby's canny borrowing from Mitchell neatly elides the false distinction between slave owner and slave provider designed to obscure shared moral culpability beneath an unbreachable social divide.[13] Furthermore, the prologue to "Ignoble Victory" continues to explicate the continuity between those whites who "could not stomach such dishonor" (3) and those who could, holding up to critique a society "too enraptured by the mystical brotherhood of whiteness to comprehend democracy" (3) and ending with a powerful catalog of Reconstruction-era violence against blacks in Louisiana: "So there was Bossier Parish and St. Landry and St. Bernard and Mechanics Institute in New Orleans and Colfax and Coushatta and Clay's Stature. There was the sky reddened with the flame of the burning schoolhouses of the black children, and the earth splattered with their blood and brains.... It was against this flameshot smoke that black Inch dreamed his foredoomed dream" ("Ignoble" 3).

The introduction of Inch at the end of the prologue (in a line cut from the published version) signals Yerby's final and most important revision of the Confederate romance and his challenge to contemporary Reconstruction historiography. Inch's "dream" of equal rights for African Americans and Isaac Robinson's intention to (re)found a black utopia outside the South bookend the manuscript, and throughout the text, Yerby allows African American characters the opportunity to expand on these ideas in concrete terms. Unlike its many predecessors in the genre, which show black characters exclusively through their dealings with and relevance to white characters, "Ignoble Victory" puts the focus on active black characters who debate their role in the struggle for equal rights and ultimately for their lives in the face of harassment and persecution. In its original form, the novel is structured neither by a love story nor by a series of events functioning as a de facto apologia for the plantation myth; rather, it is centered on African Americans' postwar work in Louisiana to build their future and secure their freedom and their response to the many acts of violence perpetrated by whites who sought to thwart those efforts. The manuscript's title page, a map of Louisiana charting the sites and dates of various massacres between 1866 and 1877 and apparently drawn freehand by Yerby, indicates graphically his intended focus.[14]

The narrative emphasizes the horror of these events and their tragic effects but also foregrounds black agency and perspective. In a series of scenes cut from the published version of the novel, Inch explains not only the realities of black life during Reconstruction but also the intricacies of Louisiana politics, with which he is intimately familiar. (In *The Vixens*, these explanations are given in abbreviated form and primarily by a third-person narrator.) A member of the state legislature, Inch accuses some of his "colored brethren" of corruption, accurately predicting their future assessment by racist historians eager to make of them "beautiful scapegoats": "Didn't they know that every little error they made would be seized upon, magnified, exaggerated out of all proportion to its magnitude, blown up into a gratitudinous [sic] insult to Southern white manhood, which could only be wiped out in blood?" ("Ignoble" 175). Inch recognizes that "some good has been done" (181), but he articulates the clearest understanding of the forces opposing lasting change in the South, tempering the idealism of white characters such as Land Moreau and Hope Varrick when he resigns from his Senate seat, averring that the "hour of opportunity has passed for" African Americans in Reconstruction politics:

> The only thing we can do now is salvage what remains.... For many curious reasons the South has lived outside the main current of American thought. They don't know what freedom means. They can conceive of life, liberty, and the pursuit of happiness as rights belonging only to the privileged orders. Now the re-enslavement begins. And not only of us, but of the landless, moneyless, hopeless whites as well. (211)

Inch's speeches, which often couple pragmatic appraisal with the ability to abstract larger historical meaning from the immediate political situation, mark his position in the narrative as analogous to that of Stephen Fox in *The Foxes of Harrow*. Unlike Fox, however, Inch's observations reflect not the white patriarchal wisdom that leads Fox to his often Panglossian view of antebellum American society but black intellectual honesty that ends in bitter disbelief. "Holy Mother of God," Inch thinks, "how did it ever happen that the accidental coloring of a person's skin could come to be of such importance?" ("Ignoble" 214). After fleeing New Orleans for what he hopes will be the relative safety of Isaac Robinson's community of Lincoln, Inch is killed in the massacre in Colfax on Easter Sunday 1873. At Colfax, a white mob gunned down a group of blacks who took refuge in the courthouse in response to a campaign of intimidation launched by local white supremacists.[15]

The description of the massacre, which *The Vixens* retains in a shorter form, is shown from Inch's perspective. He recognizes early on the futility of the black men's resistance (they are outnumbered, their weapons are greatly inferior, and the brick courthouse they believe impregnable will become, as Inch observes, "a kiln" [276] once it is set on fire) and the perfidy of the whites, who shoot an old man through the head as he attempts to signal a truce by displaying a Bible. As Inch watches, Etienne Fox, who leads the mob, is strangled by Isaac's enraged brother, Nimrod, who dies moments later as the courthouse burns and the white vigilantes line the black men up in rows to shoot them more efficiently, a historically accurate detail whose foregrounding allows Yerby to link the systematic murder of blacks with the rational mass killings of the Holocaust. Inch dies a martyr, smiling cynically at the thought that writers later put "noble words" into the mouths of doomed men ("Ignoble" 278).[16]

Inch's metafictional musings draw attention to the narrativizing of history, foregrounding for the resistant reader the notion that *these* stories of Reconstruction, unlike the more familiar narratives of white southern suffering and the exploitation of blacks at the hands of northern carpetbaggers, had in 1947 not yet been written. Indeed, by the time Yerby began to research the Colfax massacre, it had become known as the Colfax "riot," with white men "defending" their community against a rampaging black mob, most of whose bones still lay unidentified in the mass grave into which the bodies of the dead had been thrown. The white leaders of the attack had, after a lengthy series of trials and appeals, been essentially acquitted, and a memorial honoring the three white men who were killed in the massacre was erected in 1921 in the Colfax cemetery, while a state historical marker placed in front of the rebuilt courthouse in 1951 notes that the "riot" marked "the end of carpetbag misrule of the south"; both still stand today. It is impossible to know exactly what sources Yerby consulted in rendering his account of the massacre, but his version rejects the prevailing historiography in favor of the account kept alive for decades after the event through oral histories maintained by the black participants' descendants. Yerby does not shy away, for example, from rendering the role of Christopher Columbus Nash, the white sheriff whose participation in the massacre was subsequently deemed "heroism," in damning detail. *The Vixens* shows Nash driving two black prisoners at the gunpoint to torch the courthouse rather than bribing them to do so, as he later testified. Such details as well as others that did not survive the editing process indicate that Yerby's research encompassed more sources than white-authored regional histories and courtroom testimony.

Although Inch is clearly the most important African American character in "Ignoble Victory," the manuscript also introduces a series of forgotten black historical figures as the narrative immerses itself in the complexity of Reconstruction-era regional politics. Among these secondary characters, those playing significant roles include Louisiana politician Pinckney

Benton Stewart Pinchback; Louis Charles and Jean Baptiste Roudanez and Paul Trevigne, the publishers and editor, respectively, of the *New Orleans Tribune*; Francis E. Dumas, the highest-ranking nonwhite officer in the Union Army; and the first black lieutenant governor of Louisiana, Oscar J. Dunn. These characters illustrate a wide range of attitudes and approaches to the political and social issues of Reconstruction and directly refute the Dunning School's image of blacks as an undifferentiated herd of ignorant freedmen easily manipulated by unscrupulous whites. Yerby's remarkable effort to overturn stereotype and redirect historiographic discourse is revealed by a close examination of a lengthy passage in an early chapter of "Ignoble Victory" excised before *The Vixens*'s publication. In it, Yerby imagines these historical figures attending a heated political meeting at Inch's elegant home to discuss the Louisiana special gubernatorial election of 1868. All present wish to nominate a black candidate in lieu of Henry C. Warmoth, the white Republican who ultimately wins the election. The discussion underscores the complexity and variety of class and regional alliances, shattering the accepted essentialist fiction of a homogenous African American population.

Most vocal in his opposition to Warmoth is Paul Trevigne, described as "a black man, and a genius": "Editor, teacher, linguist, firebrand of the blacks ... Trevigne sparkled, he scintillated, radiated force and brilliance" ("Ignoble" 49–50). Trevigne argues that blacks have already missed a key opportunity in failing to stage an armed revolt at the end of the war, and in making his impassioned case, he revisits the political history of Haiti, locating American blacks' racial obligations within a diasporic rather than an American context:

> "You could read a newspaper from one end of the island to the other by the light of the burning plantations! They broke Ogé on the wheel, every bone in his body broken with iron rods. They took Toussaint away to France and starvation. But the blacks smashed them! Still they had Dessalaines [sic] and Christophe! And they hurled the soldiers of Bonaparte back into the sea! They were the first to do that. There was a greatness there!" ... "Sacre Neg!" Trevigne roared. "Who on earth had a better chance than we [of revolting successfully]? Here was the land,

defenseless, ours for the taking! With scythes we could have done it! With cane knives! In a night there could have been not a manor house standing the length and breadth of the South! Why didn't we? Name of a name of God, why didn't we?"

"Perhaps because we aren't Santo Dominicans," Inch said evenly. (51)

Trevigne's account of the Haitian Revolution elides the myriad differences among the black historical figures he names, creating a powerful but inaccurate portrait in which Vincent Ogé, a wealthy mulatto who refused to ally himself with slaves even at the cost of his own revolution, is effectively equated with the heroic Toussaint L'Ouverture and his successors, the brutal military tactician Jean-Jacques Dessalines and the autocrat Henri Christophe. Again, however, "Ignoble Victory" problematizes simplistic historiography. Just as Yerby clearly draws on and draws attention to Du Bois's neglected *Black Reconstruction*, "Ignoble Victory" also implicitly evokes C. L. R. James's similarly ignored 1938 Marxist analysis of the Haitian Revolution, *The Black Jacobins*, in the other characters' responses to Trevigne's words. Inch's swift reply interrupts Trevigne's fantasy of a transnational insurrection based on racial "purity" (Trevigne, described as "so black that under the light [his skin] took on a bluish tinge," notes, "They found it necessary to remove a number of mulattoes in Haiti! Once you lost the blackness and the kink, you learned the artistry of the whip quickly, didn't you?" ["Ignoble" 51]). Instead, Inch insists that Trevigne ground his analysis of the situation at hand in the reality of his own thoroughly interracial time and place. Dunn offers a more explicit, class-based critique, evoking the central thesis of James's book, Toussaint's attempt to forge a link between "the masses" and their leaders:

> Do you imagine for one minute that you represent the Negro? Have you ever cut cane in the fields? Do you know what the freedman wants? Oh, you know what you want all right—power! But beyond that, what is your program? What good are you going to do? What good can you do? What are you—Jacobins? Girondists? Sans-Culottes? (53)

Highlighting the meeting participants' awareness of the relevance of the revolution in Haiti to their political project gestures toward a broader reconceptualization of the historiography of the 1940s that takes into account what we now recognize as the obscuring of the centrality of race in the limning of modernity and suggests an extension of the critique that Yerby began in *The Foxes of Harrow*. While Trevigne, Inch, and Dunn are all well aware of the significance of the historical events they are discussing, almost no one else in the nineteenth century and few 1947 readers would have possessed such awareness. Although, as scholar Grant Farred writes, "*The Black Jacobins* is a major document of postcolonialism, one that is simultaneously reflexive and anticipatory" (27) precisely because it situates slavery, for the first time, at the center of Enlightenment discourses of freedom, its reception at the time of its publication and for decades thereafter was at best cool.[17] Still more significant, however, is James's attempt to restore agency to blacks in the narrative of the abolition of slavery, a revisionist move closely related to Yerby's project in "Ignoble Victory."

Dunn's excoriation of his fellow activists' motives presages his attempt to promote his preferred candidate for the governorship, Isaac Robinson, who even more than Dunn personifies the narrative's valorizing of African American efforts to gain equal rights and its concomitant interest in the ordinary freedman. As Inch ponders the possibility that Trevigne might "easily become the head of a black republic in Louisiana" until "his head ached from thinking" ("Ignoble" 55–56), Dunn presents Robinson, "a huge black mountain of a man" in "ornsaburg [*sic*] trousers and a ragged shirt" (56). Robinson, a former slave who initially eschews politics, is an autodidact, a natural leader and a radical thinker who leads the autonomous and all-black Lincoln. Robinson's settlement functions on a kind of Fourieristic, self-sufficient, but anticapitalist model:

> Got a place up in Grant Parish. Ten families. Old land, no good, nobody's land, but we make it grow. Stuff to eat, no cotton. Pigs and chickens. That way we eat. That way we live. Ask nobody for nothing. Free. Everything belong to everybody. This man grow corn, put it in the storehouse. This one raise pigs—same thing. Then we divide, and everybody have enough." (57)

Robinson, like Inch, overturns the myth of the semiamnesiac ex-slave whose inherent fecklessness makes him incapable of drawing on past experience to plan for the future and leaves him open to exploitation; the movement for equality, Robinson declares, must draw on "men who know what it was. Who know what they want" (58). Robinson's role in "Ignoble Victory" is crucial; although Inch dies at Colfax, Robinson lives on to lead his people north from Louisiana, in the process becoming a figure not only for progressive political action but for the coming Great Migration.

Like Dumas, Pinchback, the Roudanez brothers, and Trevigne, Dunn, who emerges in "Ignoble Victory" (as in his historical representation) as an incorruptible political figure who dies under suspicious circumstances[18] after registering his objections to Warmoth's corrupt administration, is mentioned only in passing in *The Vixens*. Isaac Robinson's role is also reduced substantially; though Robinson still founds Lincoln, little description of it appears in the published novel, and *The Vixens* depicts Robinson as the white hero's "magnificent lead hand" (214), establishing his devotion to his former master early on and diminishing his achievements. Although little of the focus on African Americans remains in *The Vixens*, enough survives to hint at Yerby's project in full—a scathing rejection both of the conventions of the costume novel as he would later codify them and of the historiographic discourses surrounding the antebellum South, the abolition of slavery, and the Reconstruction era. Against the backdrop of 1930s popular and academic historical representation, Yerby's two novels must be seen together as a stunning achievement. The first, a cliché-ridden romance, introduces the reader both to a dashing hero who reworks Gerald O'Hara and to a sweeping narrative that casually injects the miscegenation back into Tara, in the process revealing the biracial interdependency of American exceptionalism and the absurdity of the ritual racial segregation of the conventionalized Confederate romance. In manuscript form, the second novel abandons readerly expectation as it performs the extraordinary trick of upending the conventions of the romance novel while simultaneously overturning racist historiographic representations of Reconstruction, eschewing the traditional hero to concentrate on the central role of African Americans in molding their destiny and offering the reader instead two extraordinary black leaders, Inch and

Isaac Robinson. *The Vixens*, transfigured by the grafting on of a steamy love story and stripped of much of its historiographic resonance, renders Yerby's initial project nearly unrecognizable. His remarks in interviews suggest that he lost his nerve, fearing that the combination of an unconventional romance plot and a strong emphasis on revisionist historiography might be too much for audiences in 1947. Especially in its description of the massacre at Colfax, the finished novel retains some of its original focus; Yerby's strategy of making his novel more salable by wrapping horrific historical fact in a mantle of softer-focus romantic fiction is arguably understandable and even defensible. Still, only by examining the manuscript of "Ignoble Victory" does Yerby's unique version of the postwar black novel truly emerge, a vision that protests racism not merely thematically but also generically and provides a valuable testament to the costume novel's ability to convey both historical fact and its own kind of protest fiction.

CHAPTER FOUR

William Gardner Smith and the Cosmopolitan War Novel

William Gardner Smith's aesthetic and philosophical approach to his first novel, *Last of the Conquerors*, was the obverse of Frank Yerby's. Yerby's decision to write popular historical costume novels set in the antebellum South followed his limited success with protest-oriented short stories and unsuccessful attempts to find a publisher for a social realist novel with a contemporary middle-class African American protagonist. Smith, however, was a decade younger than Yerby and never expected to write protest fiction at all. Although Smith's biographer notes that Smith read and "admired" *Native Son* as a young adolescent (Hodges 6), he, like many other young African American writers of the period, resisted what he perceived as an onerous obligation to follow Richard Wright's "blueprint" and struggled to reconcile his commitment to what he saw as universal themes with the raw materials for fiction with which his experiences had provided him. Recognizing that the "raceless" fiction writer might find a substantial audience among white postwar readers, the young Smith initially determined that he would follow the model of best sellers such as *The Foxes of Harrow* and Willard Motley's *Knock on Any Door* (which appeared to great acclaim in the spring of 1947 just as Smith was beginning to write *Last of the Conquerors*) and write novels in which blacks were secondary characters—if they appeared at all. As he wrote to Carolyn Wolfe of Farrar, Straus, and Giroux on April 8, 1949, "I did not originally intend to write novels directly about Negroes, for this would reach only a certain, limited audience. I planned, rather, to write stories about white people, bringing in the racial theme only indirectly." Smith viewed his approach not only as pragmatic but also as a logical consequence of his orientation toward canonical European and American writers. In his letter to Wolfe, Smith listed among the influences on his writing "Proust (for his poetic allusions) and Dostoievsky (for his intensity)" as well as Hawthorne, Melville, Hemingway, Maugham, and Faulkner. The roster did not include a single black writer.

Not only did Smith never expect to write directly about African American issues, he also never thought (despite the obvious debt to Hemingway that *Last of the Conquerors*'s deliberately tough style conveys) that he would write a war novel. However, as he explained drily to Wolfe, "my overseas experiences changed my mind." Smith's laconic explanation understates the reality: His experience in the military transformed both his view of race relations and his approach to writing. Drafted in December 1945 and discharged in early 1947, Smith entered an army newly demobilized but still overwhelmingly segregated. He experienced firsthand the tense relations between black and white servicemen when, on furlough following his completion of basic training, he was attacked and beaten by a mob of white sailors angered by the fair complexion of a girl he had escorted to a nightclub (Hodges 11). Although Smith, then barely twenty, had lived in a poor black neighborhood in South Philadelphia all his life, his previous experiences with individual whites had been largely neutral or even positive, as in the case of the white high school teachers who encouraged him to write, and he struggled to maintain his optimistic view of race relations even after the incident. "I felt then and there that I should hate every white person who had ever lived, but I just couldn't. I have too many white friends whom I know and respect and the feeling is reciprocated" (qtd. in Hodges 11).

Yet as a series of high-profile incidents involving black veterans targeted by hostile whites made headlines in the United States that year,[1] the newly inducted Smith also witnessed the reception of the Gillem Report, a series of recommendations produced in 1946 by a committee charged with investigating the misuse of black manpower in the military. Although the implied impetus behind the committee's convocation was the fact that, as historian Robert B. Edgerton notes, "opportunities for black servicemen were markedly worse in 1946 than they had been at the end of the war in 1945" (163), the Gillem Board reached conclusions that ultimately were used as a rationale for continuing rather than ending military segregation. The discrimination black soldiers experienced even after the armed forces were officially desegregated has been ably documented: African Americans fought and died in two world wars while eating, sleeping, and seeking recreation separate from whites. Nevertheless, as historian Heide Fehrenbach notes, by the time the United States entered World War II, there was "considerable public pressure by a growing number of African American activists and organizations to democratize the United States and dismantle its discriminatory policies and practices toward its own citizens of color" (19). The report, issued in April 1946, suggested that the military needed to "eliminate, at the earliest practicable moment, any special consideration based on race" (qtd. in MacGregor 154). Yet the report's rhetoric was unmatched by a commitment to change: by "earliest practicable moment," the board clearly did not mean, as did the Supreme Court eight years later in its *Brown v. Board of Education* ruling, that desegregation should be accomplished "with all deliberate speed." On the contrary, the report did not conclude that segregated units should be eliminated, though it made a few suggestions about how they might be more flexibly assigned. It did, however, determine that blacks were overrepresented in the military as a percentage of the general population, a decision that effectively instituted a quota for African Americans that would restrict their numbers to approximately 10 percent of military personnel through selective enlistment and reenlistment. When these strategies proved insufficient, the army instituted policies that facilitated the early discharge of African American soldiers. The forced expulsion of blacks from the military under a series of pretexts (which Smith describes in detail in *Last of the Conquerors*) offered a vivid object lesson in the contradictory postwar U.S. approach to eradicating institutional racism.

Indeed, predictions that *Last of the Conquerors*'s treatment of the theme of interracial sex would prove both titillating to northern audiences and a hindrance to southern sales influenced the marketing strategy Farrar, Straus, and Giroux pursued. (The first edition of the novel, for example, hints at the interracial theme while deemphasizing it with cover art that obscures the race of the soldier it depicts). Nevertheless, letters from potential reviewers to Smith's editors also emphasize both the timeliness and the controversial nature of the novel's critique of the armed forces' policies on integration. Not only was public opinion strongly swayed by the resistance of Generals Omar Bradley and Dwight D. Eisenhower to President Harry S. Truman's directive integrating the military, but perceptions of the inadequacy of black soldiers lingered even among those who might have been expected to know better. Writing to Roger Straus and John Farrar on August 1, 1948, novelist James Michener, for example, strongly objected to Smith's portrait of the plight of the African American soldier: "But—and here is the confidential part—I think you as the publishers ought to know that the case *for* the Negro soldier is not so good as Smith presents it. In fairness to the Army, one should know all the facts.... If the files of the Pacific wars were thrown open one would find a pretty wretched story of Negro performance.... Negro troops could not be trusted in jungle warfare."

Thus, as a journalist whose tenure at the *Pittsburgh Courier* in the final years of the war had sharpened his appraisal of its impact on African Americans, Smith entered the occupation army in a unique position to observe the social and political ferment that characterized the years between the end of the war and the integration of the military that began with Truman's executive order in 1948. At the same time, Smith found himself in the divided city of Berlin, simultaneously a devastated symbol of the former might of the Nazi government and a cosmopolitan European cultural center. Out of the fusion of these two circumstances, *Last of the Conquerors*, the first novel about World War II written from the perspective of an African American, emerges as a unique contribution to the genre of the African American war novel. A text that is truly neither about war nor about race, *Last of the Conquerors* instead proffers an exploration of the power of a cosmopolitan approach to rebuilding a war-torn world and suggests that African Americans, as members of a diasporic community, can and must be in the cosmopolitan vanguard. Such is their duty as potential world citizens; their alienation in a racist American society gives them both a unique perspective and the liminality necessary to serve as global cultural liaisons. This notion had considerable currency among black intellectuals during and immediately after World War II, especially in the context of broader political movements among colonized peoples worldwide. As journalist Roi Ottley wrote in 1943, "Black men in this country—a group larger than some nations involved in the war—are feeling a great resurgence of racial kinship to other colored peoples of the world" (*New World*, foreword). Yet African Americans were also in a position to mediate between and among not only the colonized but also the colonizers, especially as postwar occupiers of European nations. *Last of the Conquerors* explores precisely this paradoxical situation and the unique and liberatory opportunities it holds for black soldiers.

Last of the Conquerors's generic innovations may have been one reason for the lack of attention it has received. For reasons of content and timing, the novel rarely appears in discussions of World War II fiction. Because the novel never deals with combat, it is often left out of retrospective overviews of war fiction of the period; it also had the bad luck to appear just a few months after Norman Mailer's best-selling *The Naked and the Dead*, which greatly overshadowed Smith's work. Yet even within the genre of African American postwar fiction, Smith's novel has been largely ignored. Alex Lubin's evaluations of Smith as a writer "not regarded as one of postwar America's most distinguished" (125) and of *Last of the Conquerors* as "a rather predictable novel" (127) are typical of critics' responses. As in the critical response to Yerby's work, these value judgments often obscure the importance of the ideological interventions these works performed. Recent work in twentieth-century German military and social history has done far more to rehabilitate Smith's novel than has African American literary studies; historians Fehrenbach, Petra Goedde, and Maria Höhn are particularly notable in this respect.

Last of the Conquerors is in every way a different kind of war novel. Indeed, if we consider the war novel as by definition a story of combat or a study of the psychological effects of combat on soldiers, it would not qualify. The war novel genre has historically been dominated by white male writers; however, even within the restricted subgenre of the African American war novel, *Last of the Conquerors* is unique. Unlike its predecessors, Smith's novel treats neither the foreign battlefield nor the experience of the African American veteran upon his return to the United States.[2] More familiar were works by African American novelists that specifically treated black soldiers' battlefield experiences, such as F. Frank Gillmore's 1915 *The Problem: A Military Novel*, about black soldiers' heroism in Cuba and the Philippines, and Victor Daly's 1932 *Not Only War*, about a pair of southern soldiers—one black, one white—who fight and die together in France in World War I. Nor does *Last of the Conquerors* describe the experiences of veterans, as did the better-known *Home to Harlem* (1928) by Claude McKay and *The Fire in the Flint* (1924) by Walter White. Rather, *Last of the Conquerors* is a novel of occupation that begins with protagonist Hayes Dawkins's first view of postwar Germany and ends, less than a year later, with his acknowledgment to another soldier that he is "shipping for home" later that day. A new recruit with no combat record, Dawkins also renders his personal and familial history with a notable opacity; furthermore, an insistent presentism characterizes his attitude toward the army, his fellow soldiers, and the white German woman, Ilse, with whom he establishes a romantic relationship.

Last of the Conquerors is indeed a novel of conflict; however, the war described is not that of one nation (a putative democracy) against another (a fascist dictatorship) or even that of an individual fighting for recognition of his rights in a society that denies them. Instead, the war Smith delineates here involves violence wreaked on the impulse toward hybridity, relativism, and shared humanity by an insistence on an exclusionary concept of identity and ideological orientation, an imperative that finds its clearest manifestation in a nation's armed forces. War is both the enemy of cosmopolitanism and the result of its absence, as the classic peace activist parody of the U.S. Army's motto makes clear: *Join the army. Travel to exciting, exotic places. Learn exciting skills. Meet exciting, exotic people. And kill them.*

For Smith, however, the aftermath of war also paradoxically creates an opportunity to bring individuals together in circumstances that force unforeseen and potentially transformative interactions; out of a society fractured and devastated by war, he posits, may be born an impetus toward recognition of an essential shared humanity and of our obligations to our fellow human beings—the basic components of the cosmopolitan outlook. Using the city of Berlin, with its history of diversity and artistic and political innovation, as his organizing metaphor, Smith dexterously weaves together ideas of interraciality, biraciality, and cosmopolitan duty in a deliberately utopian vision in which African Americans lead the way toward a future that is not "raceless" but rather free of outmoded, reified notions of racial difference. His depiction of Berlin, which emphasizes the city's vitality and energy, stands in stark contrast to its common postwar image as, in the words of historian Richard Mayne, "a city of the dead" (30–31) in the wake of its annihilation by the Allies. Though Smith's African American protagonist, Dawkins, alludes briefly to bombed-out buildings and the corpses hidden beneath them, he emphasizes far more strongly the quotidian activities of Berlin's inhabitants. Smith's approach is unusual in its lack of interest either in Berlin's various subcultures, a preoccupation of prewar chroniclers of Berlin from Alfred Döblin to Christopher Isherwood, or in the dominant postwar image, beamed worldwide by newsreels and feature films alike, of the city as a ruin presided over by stoic *Trümmerfrauen* (rubble women).[3] The city thus emerges not as a battlefield or even as a postwar zone but as a multicultural urban space with a vexed relationship with both its recent Nazi past and the rest of Germany.[4] The effect is to establish Berlin, a historically polyglot and multicultural city whose wholesale physical destruction in 1945 and strategic geographic position had left its postwar fate largely unclear, as an alternate space in which issues of race can be contested and rendered irrelevant. Furthermore, in Smith's novel, the city becomes a site of practices and interactions that allow it to be a transformative arena within which notions of occupation, democracy, and identity can be reconfigured.

As Lubin notes, interracial intimacy plays a central role in developing the protagonist's sense of self in *Last of the Conquerors*. Like Fehrenbach, who writes that the novel illustrates that "time spent in Germany was instructive to many black GIs because it provided them with the ability—via a different cultural frame—to think beyond their social experience as black men in the United States" (39), Lubin says that "at the core of Private Hayes Dawkins's military experience is the inescapable feeling that interracial intimacy confers a sort of assimilation and freedom to black GIs" (127). Goedde notes as well that seeing other interracial couples while on his first date with Ilse spurs Dawkins's feeling that he has paradoxically found equality in "the land of hate" (Smith, qtd. in Goedde 110); Goedde writes that "Smith's fictional account captured the general mood of black soldiers in Germany after the war" (111). Such readings, while valid, are incomplete.

Dawkins meets Ilse early in the novel and quickly becomes deeply involved with her; their sexual and emotional relationship, with which Dawkins initially feels some discomfort, is treated frankly. Although the novel includes secondary plotlines involving desertion and the murder of a white commanding officer who forces his African American troops to testify against one another to procure illegal discharges, most of the novel's tension derives from the question of how Dawkins and Ilse's relationship can survive given the fact that Dawkins is first transferred away from Berlin and then forced to leave Germany before the end of his tour of duty. The novel certainly was interpreted at the time of its publication as a treatment of what the 1949 paperback edition coyly described as "an explosive theme." (The cover art for that edition, which shows a smiling blond and a smoking GI, gives no visual hint of Dawkins's race, a concession to the southern market, where Smith's publishers feared his work would be unpopular, even banned.) However, it is more importantly a novel about the development of a global cosmopolitan consciousness in the postwar period and the leading role African Americans, from W. E. B. Du Bois to Richard Wright, saw themselves as playing in that development. Critics from 1948 to the present have overwhelmingly identified *Last of the Conquerors* as, in the words of a contemporary reviewer, about a black soldier whose consciousness is awakened when he "discovers that [in] Berlin there is no color line" (Rolo 110). But for Smith, interracial relationships and their "miscegenated" offspring are predominantly a metaphor for cosmopolitan interaction rather than a representative figure for an array of specifically American civil rights that blacks had begun to demand more vociferously during the war.[5] While earlier war fiction by African Americans had, like the real wartime experience on which it was often based, led readers to the obvious conclusion that blacks were being unjustly denied their rights as citizens of the United States, Smith's novel suggests instead that African Americans' liminal position in American society makes them better situated than white Americans to become *Weltbürger* (citizens of the world).

Making Dawkins such a world citizen enables Smith to write his character into what Ross Posnock calls "the often overlooked tradition" of black cosmopolitanism ("Dream" 804). Posnock, like most critics who have examined black contributions to cosmopolitan discourse, identifies W. E. B. Du Bois as "the pivotal figure in this lineage, positing a deracialized 'kingdom of culture' as the end of black American striving" (804).[6] Though Du Bois's contributions to cosmopolitan thought are complex and even at times contradictory, there is little doubt that they were inspired by his experiences as a graduate student at the University of Berlin from 1892 to 1894, a history to which Smith obliquely alludes when Dawkins announces his desire to attend the same university. *Last of the Conquerors* echoes Du Bois's assessments both in *The Souls of Black Folk* and in his 1940 autobiography, *Dusk of Dawn: An Essay toward an Autobiography of a Race Concept*, of his time in Germany as revelatory in that it allowed him to feel for the first time since childhood that he was not "a problem" but a human being. Most scholars assume that in Berlin, Du Bois first developed the commitment to maintaining "a dialectic that preserves the interplay of the universal and the particular" (Posnock, *Color* 92) that would lie at the heart of his cosmopolitanism. Historian Kenneth D. Barkin also persuasively argues that Du Bois's exposure in Berlin to the discipline of political economy both allowed him to develop the methodology underlying his landmark sociological study, *The Philadelphia Negro*, and inspired in him a "conviction" that the approaches of academic economists in "Germany provided him with a strategy for changing race relations in the United States" (95). Barkin's work problematizes the dominant reading of Du Bois's time in Europe as a period in which he was strongly influenced by Hegel, theories of the *völkisch* tradition, and European racial "science." Instead, Barkin argues, Du Bois focused less on philosophy than on political economics, seeing in the work of Heinrich von Treitschke, generally regarded as a proto-Aryan nationalist, an admirable insistence on the universal application of law to all citizens in a liberal democracy. Treitschke illustrated his point with the negative example of lynching in the United States, which he believed demonstrated that the United States was not just hypocritical but "uncivilized." In the work of social-reform-oriented economists Adolf Wagner and Gustav Schmoller, Du Bois saw a prototype for U.S. progressive reform to benefit black workers.

Dawkins, a "Philadelphia Negro," takes his instruction not in the lecture hall but at the level of the street, yet he ultimately reaches conclusions similar to those of Du Bois, learning to prize his cultural heritage as a liberatory force not merely for himself but for all "world citizens." As Paul Gilroy writes, "For Du Bois, their culture is what allows African Americans to be a world-historic people, to sit at that table and offer the world a conception of freedom which is richer, more complex, more compelling, and more dynamic than any conception of freedom which has been articulated previously" (Shelby 118–19). While there is no direct evidence of an early influence of Du Bois's work on Smith's, it is difficult to imagine that Smith would not have read Du Bois's work in the 1940s, especially given Smith's keen interest in Marxism. For example, on April 8, 1949, he told Carolyn Wolfe that he saw "no 'solution' to the race problem independent of a solution to the general world problems of cut-throat competition, economic uncertainty, etc. . . . Believe that the next era belongs to Socialism, which will be imperfect but at least a step higher." Moreover, Smith was friendly with Shirley Graham Du Bois from the late 1940s onward; he left Paris to join her in Ghana in 1964, just after W. E. B. Du Bois's death, at her request.

Posnock writes that the movement toward black cosmopolitanism that grew out of the systematic social and legal exclusion of African Americans from structures of power in the United States replicates the "historical affinity between the cosmopolitan and the egalitarian, which helped diminish the prestige of descent or blood relations" ("Dream" 804). Yet for Posnock, as for Gilroy in a British context, the institutional racism (and the raciology underpinning it) that spurs the desire for cosmopolitan understanding among minorities also prevents its realization in the context of one's own cultural environment. Only the dislocation of the foreign encounter can dislodge racist presuppositions. This is not necessarily to argue that race bias does not obtain outside one's own culture, nor is it to insist that the potential for cosmopolitan discourse can only be found in (newly) "enlightened" European contexts.[7] It is, however, to suggest that the newness of the foreign encounter can open up a space in which what Tania Friedel dubs cosmopolitanism's "valuable discourse [that] mediates between the universal and the particular" (48) can present itself. If, as Martha Nussbaum suggests, we can usefully envisage our identities as a "series of concentric circles" that collectively constitute an "interlocking commonality" (9), any encounter beyond the parochial limits of our experience can be liberating. Recognition of such limits is an unavoidable first step in moving beyond them, yet they can be virtually invisible in familiar surroundings. Thus, for Smith, a foreign, urban environment such as that of Berlin is necessary if these experiential boundaries are to be seen and overcome.

Berlin, therefore, gives Smith an ideal setting for investigating the cosmopolitan response to blackness, a setting that American cities, with their ossified racial dynamics, cannot provide. Smith does not naïvely suggest that the German people in general are somehow, despite their fascist history, inherently more color-blind than their American contemporaries; nor does he implicitly argue, as Fehrenbach does, that the defeated German citizenry learned from their American occupiers that they could retool the racist ideologies they had historically embraced within a new framework of democratic values. Smith also avoids the tendency of other African American expatriates, such as Wright, to make sweeping generalizations about the foreign populations among whom they resided. Wright famously declared that there was more freedom in a city block in Paris than in the whole United States; similarly, Ottley wrote in 1952 that "Negroes uniformly declare the German people freer of color prejudice than the French.... [T]he Germans have no color allergy" (*No Green* 156). Smith, however, carefully underscores the naïve idealization of his characters' encounters with racial and cultural Others. "Most of us would have preferred being assigned to France," Dawkins wryly remarks as he enters Germany, alluding to Paris's historical position as a center of black expatriate activity and his fellow soldiers' assurances that French women would welcome black GIs with open arms. Yet he quickly finds that the acceptance he encounters in Berlin surpasses all of his expectations and begins his process (under the circumstances ironic) of idealizing the color blindness of Berliners. Steadfastly differentiating between Nazi Germany and its capital, Smith limns a space in his mythical Berlin in which difference, simultaneously literalized and metaphorized as difference of skin color, is not an excuse for bloodshed but rather an impetus for conversation. Communication across linguistic and cultural boundaries is shown throughout the novel as a goodwill gesture in and of itself: Dawkins begins to learn German immediately upon his arrival and uses his language skills both to accelerate his acculturation and to win the trust of the Germans he meets; by contrast, the few Germans he meets who refuse to accept him demonstrate their hostility with silence. Yet Smith, like Kwame Anthony Appiah, goes further, using discussion as a figure for cross-cultural engagement and a representative act of tolerance. As Appiah writes, "conversation" is a metaphor for engagement with the experience and the ideas of others. [These] encounters, properly conducted, are valuable in themselves. Conversation doesn't have to lead to a consensus about anything, especially not values; it's enough that it helps people get used to one another. (85)

This conversation demonstrates not only that, as Appiah succinctly writes, "cultural purity is an oxymoron" (113) but that homogeneity of thought is also not desirable outside the confines of an entity, such as the army, whose primary purpose is to destroy an enemy entity designated as irretrievably Other. Thus, Berlin becomes a space that provides for the articulation of the civilian cosmopolitanism the novel argues is the true heart of democracy and the only way to avoid not only fascism (the apotheosis of anticosmopolitanism) but also future wars. Armed conflict, after all, can reasonably be understood as the polar opposite of what Kant called "hospitality" or "the right of a foreigner not to be treated with hostility because he has arrived on the shore of another" (328–29), which he argued was the concept most crucial to an understanding of "cosmopolitan right" (329). Although this portrait of Berlin as a center of diversity and worldly politesse has its basis in historical fact (as German playwright Carl Zuckmayer said, "Once you had Berlin, you had the world" [qtd. in Ronald Taylor 233]), it is also recognizable as a constructed figure for an urban ideal that is understood as such and need not be hampered by a strict reliance on a realistic representation of postwar Germany.

Because Smith intends to use Berlin as a figurative as well as literal space, *Last of the Conquerors* immediately establishes the geographical and cultural complexity of the postwar environment its characters must navigate, setting up a spatial analog to the novel's action that must be regarded at least partly in symbolic terms. Hayes Dawkins and a group of other newly drafted soldiers arrive in Bremerhaven, Germany, an American-administered port city on the North Sea in the British zone. All are transported together to a central location in Hesse, in the American zone, from which the men are divided up and deployed to various locations throughout Germany. Dawkins and the two men he has befriended, Charles Henry, a black reporter for the *Pittsburgh Courier* who is immediately dubbed the Professor, and a reenlisted combat soldier named Randy, also black, are shipped together to Berlin, itself divided into four zones but located in the Russian zone. The other black soldiers are sent to Bremburg, a fictitious base elsewhere in the American zone, presumably in the vicinity of Frankfurt. Dawkins does not pause to wonder why he has not been sent to Bremburg; only later, after he has established himself in Berlin and begun a serious relationship with Ilse, does he discover that the army, anxious to begin implementing the Gillem Report's recommendations, has begun segregating all black GIs on the same bases and then permitting their white commanding officers to discharge them prematurely. Once Dawkins is reassigned to Bremburg, a camp he quickly learns has been dubbed "nigger hell" (*Last* 111) by the other soldiers, he finds himself at the mercy of Captain Johnny Polke, a white southerner whose racist views are widely known. "He sure hates to see one of the boys with a white girl," Dawkins is told by Corporal "Steve" Stevenson, the company clerk who is his supervisor at Bremburg. "He'd a rather seen the Germans win the war" (122). Polke's capricious application of courts-martial results in Stevenson's violent attack on him and his right-hand man, Sergeant Brink. Dawkins's involvement in the attack, though largely involuntary, ultimately results in his discharge, forcing him to leave not only the army but Ilse and any hope of a return to Berlin.

Mapping Dawkins's journey through occupied Germany provides a visual correlative for the novel's narrative movement. Dawkins moves south from Bremerhaven to the American zone, then north again to Berlin, and finally back south when he is dispatched to Bremburg. The American zone of postwar Germany effectively encompasses Bavaria and Hesse, which, as James K. Pollock notes, is the southern portion of Germany popularly identified with Hitler, and Smith ensures that his readers make the link between the foreign white supremacist from Munich and the domestic version from Jackson, Mississippi. Fully understanding Smith's novel, however, requires an acknowledgment that portraits of support for Hitler by region or *Bundesland* (state) are often unfairly simplified. For example, the assumption that socially conservative Bavaria, where Hitler's political career began and which even today tends to lean right, was the mainstay of Nazi support before World War II is widespread despite the fact that it is not borne out by electoral records. According to Pollock, writing in 1944, the electoral map corresponding to the Reichstag and presidential elections of 1930–33 shows that Hitler's support was not confined to any particular region but rather that urban populations generally voted against National Socialism while rural populations favored it. Pollock also notes that turnout in urban areas was unusually high in these years, suggesting a strong distaste for Hitler that brought voters to the polls.

When, in Weilberg, the camp to which the men are sent before they are reassigned to Berlin, Randy argues that the Germans are "damn krauts" who are the natural enemies of any American, white or black, another African American soldier responds, "I know what Hitler said. I also know what [Mississippi governor Theodore] Bilbo says" (*Last* 14). By superimposing the culture, practices, and mentality of the American South onto southern Germany, Smith effectively aligns the American-administered zone, where Allied efforts at denazification and democratization were most concentrated, with the racism that the American government hypocritically embraces at home and abroad. Even the women in the area surrounding Weilberg have, it is implied, been influenced by the policies of the segregated camp; when the Professor, who speaks some German, attempts to approach them on behalf of Dawkins and Randy, he is invariably rebuffed: "The girls always shook their heads violently and walked rapidly away. 'This is a hell-fired country,' Randy said. 'I should have gone back to France. They don't shake their heads there'" (11).

Yet Smith's mapping of intolerance is more complicated than this broad sketch suggests. Though the location of Bremburg, like Weilberg, in southern Germany suggests that it is meant to be read as analogous to "nigger hells" in the southern United States, the camp is in a rural part of Germany depicted as profoundly unlike the metropolitan area Dawkins has just left. Again and again, Dawkins unfavorably contrasts the village of Wildsdorf, where Ilse lives after following him from Berlin to Bremburg, with the city of Berlin. The people are provincial ("Most Germans . . . had never been to the big city," Dawkins observes [*Last* 139]), and the landscape is flat and unvarying beneath a "heavy, low, smothering, spirit-suffocating sky" (112). Even the company's trucks, Dawkins notes with disdain, are "dull and unwashed, nothing like the clean, washed, always freshly-painted ones of the Berlin company" (117). Two Texans, Polke and Brink view Dawkins's service in Berlin as pernicious and, more to the point, suspiciously unmilitary. "I don't know what you were used to in Berlin," Captain Polke tells Dawkins. "But you're not in Berlin any more.... I might as well tell you right now that we like the American Army around here and we aim to keep it just that—an Army! ... We don't stand for a lot of foolishness around these parts" (116). Sergeant Brink is blunter still, informing Dawkins of the incompatibility of success in the military and liberal education: "You look like maybe you was a college boy. Educated, see.... [Y]ou think you're hell. Well, you ain't. Not in this company you ain't.... Big city boys. Hep cats. Know all the goddamn answers. I never did like your kind of guys, see" (120).

Polke and Brink's hatred of the "big city" and specifically Berlin has its echo in the capital's assessment by Hitler. Although Hitler intended, once his Third Reich had conquered all of Europe, to rechristen Berlin *Germania* and turn it into his *Welthauptstadt* (capital of the world), he planned first to raze it. Albert Speer's blueprint for Germania would have leveled most of the extant city, rebuilding it around a central three-mile-long parade route through the city's premier urban park, the Tiergarten, leading to a giant, domed *Volkshalle* (people's hall). Eschewing the glass and metal prized by the Bauhaus movement, Speer and Hitler envisaged enormous marble and stone structures designed to communicate the Third Reich's grandeur and power, thereby offering the added advantage of producing more impressive ruins in the next millennium. The weight of the proposed buildings would have necessitated extensive treatment of the marshy land on which Berlin is built, altering even the natural landscape itself.[8] (Apart from Tempelhof Airport and the Olympic Stadium, little of this plan was realized.) For Hitler, "the proposition that an evolving and changing 'modern' society needed ambiguous architecture ... was demonstrably false" (Balfour 115); demolishing whole blocks of private houses to make way for Speer's grandiose public monuments was a logical analog to and precondition for the forcible reconditioning of human behavior. For Hitler, Berlin's architecture and populace mirrored each other; both were unsystematic, representing everything he viewed as obstructing his goal of purifying Germany and the Aryan race. As historians Anthony Read and David Fisher note,

> Hitler's attitude to Berlin before he came to power was reflected in his newspaper, the *Völkischer Beobachter* ("People's Observer"),

which was published, of course, in Munich. A virulent diatribe in July 1928 denounced the capital as "a melting pot of everything that is evil—prostitutes, drinking houses, cinemas, Marxism, Jews, strippers, Negroes dancing, and all the vile offshoots of so-called "modern art." (23)

Politically and socially liberal and cosmopolitan, most of Berlin also never embraced Hitler. "While the rest of Germany was making the Nazis the largest party in the Reichstag in 1932, almost three out of four Berliners voted against them," Read and Fisher observe. "Even in March 1933, with brownshirt squads on the streets and their political opponents outlawed and locked up, the Nazis could only raise less than a third of the Berlin votes" (17). Possibly because they had been disproportionately affected by Germany's unemployment and rampant inflation during and after World War I, Berliners were in general also singularly lacking in enthusiasm for Hitler's military ambitions, a fact that did nothing to endear them to the Führer.[9]

Berlin's cosmopolitanism, which Hitler read as decadence, was unique in Germany both before and after World War II. The typical Berliner, like the typical New Yorker, was from somewhere else, often outside the country. Waves of immigrants had created a multilingual and ethnically and religiously diverse populace before the French Revolution; the economic boom and massive industrialization of the late nineteenth century had both dramatically increased the city's population and given "Rotes Berlin" its well-deserved reputation as a hotbed of left-wing thought. In the 1920s, under the Weimar Republic, the city became the recognized European leader in modernist art and architecture as well a center for sexual liberalism[10] that attracted still farther-flung expatriates with a combination of cultural sophistication and an extremely attractive exchange rate. The University of Berlin was one of the first German universities to admit women and had the highest percentage of female students in the country in the years before World War I.

The city's diverse population, investment in artistic innovation and experimentalism, and reputation for moral relativism, then, made it an obvious target for reinvention according to the brutalist kitsch style Hitler preferred in his buildings and in his view of appropriate public and private interpersonal interaction. His disdain for Berliners perhaps also helps to explain his refusal to allow an evacuation of the city's residents, almost all of whom were elderly, women, or children, as bombs fell on the city and the Red Army approached in 1945. Despite the horrors of its recent history, however, in *Last of the Conquerors,* Berlin continues to evince its prewar laissez-faire and to strike a responsive chord in Dawkins and his fellow soldiers. As the Professor observes on their first night in the new camp, "It's all according to yourself. If you don't believe something is a sin, I don't think it's a sin for you to do it" (33).

The atmosphere that Hayes Dawkins notes upon his arrival in Berlin establishes the city as well as the camp as urban—and urbane—spaces. The camp is described as clean, spacious, and modern, while the mess hall "looked like a first-class restaurant" (*Last* 13). Though the camp is segregated, the young white captain does not demean the men—unlike Polke, Captain Doyle is a northern urbanite who hails Dawkins as a fellow city dweller: "I'm from Chicago," he says after learning that Dawkins comes from Philadelphia. "Philly is a good town" (18). Doyle also recognizes and appreciates Dawkins's civilian talents as a photographer: "Good. That's really fine" (18). "The captain is a great guy," Homo, another soldier, tells Dawkins. "He's just one of the boys" (14). The offices are staffed mostly by young German women whose sophistication and command of English result in a steady stream of sexually charged banter: "Oh, I guess you want to meet our two lovely assistants, who do nothing but gossip all day long," says Sergeant Murdock, the company clerk, introducing Dawkins to two secretaries. "This is Margit . . . who laughs at everything and is a lot of fun but doesn't work worth a damn. . . . This one, over here, is Ann, a conceited wench, pursued by every soldier in the company" (20). Ilse, who works in the dispatch office, is quiet and largely unresponsive to the overtures of Dawkins's fellow soldiers. ("What are two beautiful women doing working on a lovely day like this?" Randy asked. . . . "You should join the Army . . . and you could eat without working. Also every night you could sleep with many soldiers" [33]). However, despite her apparent reticence, Ilse asks Dawkins for their first date, establishing the pattern that will later characterize their relationship. She also initiates their first sexual contact and lays many of the ground rules for their relationship, telling Dawkins, "You can say anything to me" (76).

Ilse announces from the beginning that she will teach Dawkins the German language and elements of German culture, such as popular dances with which he is unfamiliar, rather than attempt to Americanize herself to suit his expectations. Although she pampers him (cooking and washing his clothing, even bathing him), she also insists that he become familiar not only with her family and friends but with German culture and history. Gerri Bates reads Ilse as "good, girlish" and an "ideal domestic" (1–2), while Robert Bone sees her as "more a product of adolescent fantasy than a real woman" (177). However, such a reading ignores Ilse's strength, determination, candor, and pragmatism. She pursues Dawkins to Bremburg when he is reassigned, traveling illegally through the Russian zone despite having been raped by Russian soldiers during the liberation of Berlin in 1945. Once she learns that Dawkins is being discharged, she says that she knows he will not return and implies that she will have to exchange sex with the town's mayor for a pass back to Berlin. In short, Ilse is hardly a shrinking violet or a domestic fantasy. Furthermore, textual evidence suggests that her unconventionality is neither new nor a reaction to her situation in postwar Germany; Ilse tells Dawkins that when she was nineteen, she married a man she did not love, divorcing him two years later at the height of the war in direct defiance of the prevalent Nazi discourse of "Kinder, Kirche, and Küche" (children, kitchen, and church). Her choice reflects an independence that Goedde argues was highly unusual: "War casualties forced more women into the position of main provider for their families. . . . Young women faced not only increased responsibilities for their families but also the possibility of remaining single for the rest of their lives[, resulting in] a panic that took hold of young women who faced fierce competition in their search for the right partner" (106).

Most significantly, the other soldiers assure Dawkins that the army's more restrictive policies vis-à-vis fraternization, in force in other parts of Europe, will not affect his ability to take part in all of the city's intercultural opportunities. "Of course we have a club," says Murdock,

> "or we can go to a movie, or to an opera, or visit a German friend. It's really forbidden to enter a German's house at night, but everyone does it. A lot of things can be done. You'll discover them all, by and by."
> "Do you like Berlin?"
> "It's a great city," Murdock said. (*Last* 21)

Although Doyle apparently lacks hostility toward African Americans, he does, while drunk, make anti-Semitic remarks that appall Dawkins and his fellow soldiers (*Last* 91). (It is a marker of Smith's commitment to his model of a Berlin so tolerant it can only be intended symbolically that the novel's lone mention of Jews is made not by a German but by an American.) More than one critic points to Doyle's uncharacteristic comments as a false note in Smith's otherwise entirely believable characterizations of military personnel.[11] Such objections, however, miss the point of Smith's narrative, which implies that whites in the United States cannot evade their complicity in racism; regardless of their intentions, as Homo, whose cynical appraisals of the military's attitude toward blacks lead him to desert to the Russian sector, bitterly notes, "There ain't no swell white guys. Not Americans, there ain't" (59). Thus, Smith uses the notion of collective guilt to interpellate the unexamined discourse of Germany's postwar democratization by slyly applying it not to the Germans but to their occupiers.

Although the camp and its club are described in largely positive terms, from Dawkins's perspective, the real advantage to being stationed in Berlin is the relaxing of the military codes and regulations that might impede his blossoming cosmopolitanism, facilitated by his relationship with Ilse. Although the men are occasionally subject to bed checks and other monitoring, most of the soldiers have German girlfriends, Homo reports, adding the reassurance that the women of Berlin are especially faithful to their lovers. Indeed, according to Homo, interracial relationships in Berlin are far less problematic than they are in Paris despite the French capital's celebrated reputation as a haven for African Americans: "I seen race riots in Paris and Marseilles because a colored guy was out with a white girl," he remarks. "I seen white MPs beat a man half to death with a stick because of a French woman" (*Last* 58).

The captain (who has a long-standing relationship with a local woman who works in the dispatch office) takes a pragmatic approach to the situation that reflects accommodations in military policy generally after 1945. ("You are normal," he tells Dawkins, "and so I know things will occur between you and the women here. I have no objection to that as long as you are careful" [*Last* 17].) Fraternization between soldiers of any race and the desperate women of economically ravaged postwar Germany had initially been forbidden in an extension of the ban on contact between soldiers and civilians that had been considered a vital security measure while the fighting was ongoing. The wartime ban had not been a notable success; despite being inundated with unsubtle warnings about the dangers of sexual liaisons with disease-ridden "Veronikas,"[12] such as billboards showing a woman in a trench coat with "VD" on her chest, soldiers continued to seek out sexual encounters with local women. Furthermore, "enforcement of the fraternization ban became almost impossible once Germany had surrendered . . . and security was no longer the main concern" (74), writes Goedde. The presence of a long-term occupation force in a single place also changed the dynamics of the relationships between soldiers and locals. Where previous encounters between soldiers and women had been brief, the potential now existed for extended relationships; although these relationships were often based at least in part on the willingness of soldiers to serve as unofficial supply routes for scarce commodities, including food and other necessities, they also frequently became serious. By the fall of 1945, commanders were fielding petitions from GIs to marry their German girlfriends.

However, even after the army gave up its losing battle to keep the occupation forces chaste, relationships between black soldiers and German women were unofficially discouraged. According to historian Uta G. Poiger, "Such relationships once again raised fears about miscegenation, and after the fraternization ban was lifted, mixed-race couples found it much harder to receive marriage licenses from U.S. military commanders than their all-white counterparts" (35–36). Even when black soldiers and their German fiancées obtained permission to marry, U.S. antimiscegenation laws made it difficult for them to settle in the States. Also, Lubin writes, "the military used its ability to relocate soldiers without cause as a means to regulate interracial romances" (103). Black soldiers who had requested permission to marry white women might find themselves "punitively relocated" (Lubin 103) to bases located in the South, effectively terminating the legality of their engagements or marriages. German police generally accommodated the discriminatory policies of the armed forces, either as a result of their unwillingness to challenge U.S. supremacy or because those policies dovetailed with German prejudices. However, Fehrenbach points out that although the average German civilian was likely to have been influenced by racist Nazi propaganda before and during the war, after 1945 the attitudes of German civilians toward African Americans improved dramatically, offering a sharp contrast to the German view of white soldiers:

> The problems that confronted officials in occupied Germany did not derive for the most part from Germans' wholesale unwillingness to mingle with American troops. Quite the opposite.... [A]fter Germany's unconditional surrender, American officials reported an unanticipated "epidemic" of fraternization between African American troops and the native population.... Germans tended to consider them more affable, modest, courteous and compassionate than white soldiers and officers. (33)

Last of the Conquerors, too, shows the German response to the African American soldier as being predicated on the latter's desire not to impose a rigid program of democratization and Americanization on a vulnerable foreign population. In this sense, the novel offers a prescient response to Gilroy's complaint, perhaps as relevant to postwar Germany as to the twenty-first-century postcolonial world, that notions of cosmopolitanism may have been irretrievably "hijacked and diminished" by "the economic and military dominance of the United States" through "recast[ing] the ideal of imperial power as an ethical force which can promote good and stability" in a chaotic world ("Postcolonial" 59). Dawkins, like the other African American soldiers he meets, is too conflicted about the American democracy he is expected to promote to blindly embrace a jingoistic agenda in which Americans are benign occupiers spreading peace and capitalism; the title of the novel is intended ironically. Rather, Dawkins's relationship with Ilse is based on his interest in and willingness to learn about German cultural difference. Dawkins not only quickly learns the German language but also embraces German standards of propriety and even beauty, remarking that he can "no longer conjure up an image of the typical American girl" but that he knows vaguely that he prefers the "emphasis on naturalness" among German women, with their "abhorrence of too much lipstick, rouge or face powder" (*Last* 96).

For their part, Ilse and her fellow Berliners show interest less in the manufactured products of American culture they see imported into

Germany to meet the demands of an increasingly "Coca-colonized" market than in Dawkins's racially particular version of Americanness, alien as it may be. Stung by their characterization as "Hitler's children" (*Last* 27), most of the Germans Dawkins meets try to align themselves with the African American soldiers in their struggle against American racism and the racial hierarchy of the military, pointing out that "you fight for America, but it is not your country" (28). When she is picked up and held by the military police outside Bremburg, Ilse refuses to renounce her relationship with Dawkins, even after she is subjected to abusive language and threatened with rape. *Last of the Conquerors* idealizes the reaction to Dawkins's blackness among the Berliners he meets; he is told again and again what beautiful skin and hair he has, compliments he uncritically enjoys despite the fact that he "never understood fully about the hair" (51), and he never perceives or resents the comments as potentially exoticizing (or feminizing) gestures. His experience, he says, is typical: When he tells others in the camp how Ilse has described his curly hair as naturally beautiful, "the soldiers said it had been no joke, that they had heard that many times from Germans, sometimes from the men" (50).

Another reading is available of Dawkins's aestheticizing by Ilse and her fellow Germans. Critic Ashbel G. Brice argues in an informal and unpublished review of *Last of the Conquerors* that plotlines hinging on the tragic and thwarted love of a white man for a beautiful black woman were a staple of popular fiction of the late nineteenth century and that Smith's only innovation was gender reversal. While Brice's reading oversimplifies Smith's work, these observations draw attention to the continuity between descriptions of stereotypically "exotic" black characters in nineteenth- and early-twentieth-century fiction and those of Hayes Dawkins through the eyes of white Europeans. An obvious comparison might be made between Dawkins and Helga Crane, the black protagonist in Nella Larsen's *Quicksand* (1928) who finds that in Denmark she is exoticized (and sexualized) because of her unusual skin and hair color. Yet Helga, who is Larsen's rebuttal to the already well-established modernist trope of the exotic primitive, differs substantially from Dawkins. Helga, who learns no Danish and is largely content to be "exhibited" like "some new and strange species of pet dog" (Larsen 70), shows little curiosity about Denmark, while Axel Olsson, the Danish suitor Helga rejects, is not at all a cosmopolitan figure. Rather, despite his bohemian credentials (he is a successful but unconventional painter of portraits), he is the prototype of the white European racist, projecting onto her his fantasies of her racial difference as he tells her that she has "the warm impulsive nature of the women of Africa" and produces a portrait that she recognizes as "some disgusting, sensual creature with her features" (80). Unlike Dawkins and Ilse, Helga and Axel engage in far from a cosmopolitan conversation.

Dawkins's time in Berlin, then, is deliberately constructed as a sort of dreamlike idyll in which difference is remarked on only in passing and only in the context of the palimpsest of difference he sees in the most recent historical iteration of the city. Though Dawkins says repeatedly that he feels that he is in a "waking dream," the absence in Berlin of the barriers and obstacles that characterize his American civilian life is crucial to his discovery of a new, liberatory, fluidity of self. Unlike, for example, Wright, who in his 1957 description of his cosmopolitanism proclaimed himself a "rootless man" who does "not hanker after, and seem[s] not to need, as many emotional attachments, sustaining roots or idealistic allegiances as most people" ("White Man" xxix), Dawkins sees in the reassuring space of everyday Berlin a fertile ground in which his new identity can flower. Envisaging his future, Dawkins fantasizes about "a house in Wannsee" and an identity that is simultaneously German and "Negro," allowing "*Herr* Dawkins" to converse easily (using the informal pronoun *Du*) with his neighbors yet retain his pride in his difference as "everyone look[s] up at me in admiration, admiration, admiration . . . not disdain . . . because my skin is brown and healthy-looking and as a man's skin should be. With the barber saying, *Herr* Dawkins, you have wonderful hair" (*Last* 217). His experience of Berlin itself rather than his love for Ilse awakens Dawkins's belief in the power of cosmopolitan interaction to allow the recognition of racial difference while dissipating racism:

> Vacations. To Switzerland? Can you ski? No, but I'm willing to learn. Up in the beautiful Alps in the land of Swiss cheese and fresh milk. Fat, healthy (in mind as well as body) people. To Rome: Have you seen the Vatican? No, but I would like to go there. It is beautiful. The papal city is one of the wonders of the world. And the frescoes! To Vienna: Why, Herr Dawkins, how beautifully you waltz! Thank you. Where did

you learn? In Berlin. Yes? You waltz very well. To Budapest, and Marseilles, and Madrid, and Lisbon.... With no thought of prejudice. Forget race. No, don't forget. Be proud because of it.... I am a Negro. I am a black man. How beautiful the gold ring looks against your skin. (217)

Urban Berlin is implicitly contrasted not only with rural Bremburg but also with the urban United States, in which cities are shown to be made up of racially segregated spaces that are paradoxically far more cut off from one another than are the sectors of divided Berlin. In this sense, Berlin functions as the "visionary city" that Charles Scruggs argues is "a durable and ongoing tradition within black urban literature" (4). According to Scruggs,

> The city as a symbol of community, civilization, of home—this image lies beneath the city of brute fact in which blacks of the twentieth century have had to live. This kernel has never been lost. It is one of the aspirations expressed in an ongoing dialogue that the Afro-American community has with itself, a dialogue that sets a city of the imagination, the city that one wants, against the empirical reality of the city that one has. (4–5)

Though the "city of the imagination" of African American literary tradition is generally understood, by Scruggs and others, as a utopian space for blacks, Smith's ideal city cannot sacrifice cosmopolitan openness even for the benefits of communal closeness.

This insistence on the inherent cosmopolitanism of Berlin's populace as a whole is a feature only of Smith's early work. In *Return to Black America* (1970), published after he had lived as an expatriate for nearly two decades, Smith's definition of the cosmopolitan takes on a new, distinctly class-inflected valence: "The friends of black Americans were usually the cosmopolitans—the artists, writers, students, jazz enthusiasts, intellectuals. Their world was a gigantic and more subtle Greenwich Village. Beyond—hazy, distant, and somewhat mysterious—lay the 'real' Europe: the peasants, anonymous clerks and civil servants, the shopkeepers, the conservative middle class, the hard pressed workers and their employers.

It is among these that the black man began to perceive the fuzzy outlines of his old enemy, racism" (65).

In *Last of the Conquerors*, however, Berlin provides an enlightening contrast to American life. What little the reader learns about Dawkins's past life in Philadelphia appears in brief interior monologues written entirely in the second person and highlighted in italics that crop up in the text on the rare occasions when Dawkins contemplates the past. These carefully restricted passages echo formally the racially delimited Philadelphia ghetto they describe, which Dawkins says cannot be compared with Berlin:

> Not this city within a city. This could not equal Berlin. Berlin, with its bombed-out buildings and vegetable-growing parks and crowded houses and pyramids of rubble was still a marvelously beautiful suburban section compared to what I had known at home. (*Last* 66)

Berlin, by contrast, is shown as having ample public spaces whose openness is a spatial objective correlative for the human interaction that takes place within them. As spring fades into summer, Dawkins finds that

> now I knew Berlin almost as well as I knew Philadelphia.... I knew the city's wide, clean streets lined always by trees; the location of many of its once-beautiful parks and flower gardens... the absence of slums such as those in which the Negroes of New York and Philadelphia and Detroit and Chicago live. (49)

Free to be an intellectual as well as literal flâneur, Dawkins discovers that in Berlin, "high" art is also neither segregated nor rarefied. Attending operas with Ilse, Dawkins realizes that classical music, a form with which he has previously had no contact, is enjoyable once its exclusivity is demystified: "I liked it when I knew the story behind the opera and knew what the singing was all about" (*Last* 47–48). Access to cultural capital, so carefully policed in the United States through educational and social inequity, is unrestricted in Berlin. So too is achievement in the arts; Dawkins describes attending a concert "conducted by Dean Dixon, the Negro," sitting "proudly in the theater and applaud[ing] loudly when it was over" (48).¹³ In his final "waking dream" of Berlin, Dawkins lists "listening to operas and symphonies over the radio or in the theater" and dancing "the waltz and the tango and the rhumba and the samba and the polka" (216) as the final components of his ideal life with Ilse.

Finally, despite the fact that Berlin is officially divided into four politically and militarily distinct zones, Dawkins and his fellow black GIs mingle freely with British soldiers and Russians, with whom Dawkins says he and the other African American soldiers enjoy a special relationship unknown to white American soldiers. "We visited the British often because they liked 'you brown Americans.' . . . The Russian soldiers were friendly, too . . . to the American Negroes, offering us vodka and pounding us hard on the back when they greeted us in the street" (*Last* 48). The black soldiers find themselves in an intermediary cultural position by virtue of their racial difference; their marginalization in American culture offers them the liminality abroad necessary to go anywhere, communicate with anyone, and forge cosmopolitan links between dissimilar and even combative participants in the nascent Cold War. Far from being a problem, insuperable or otherwise, to be overcome, as the Gillem Report insisted, racial difference is shown to be the spark that can galvanize a million crucial conversations. Desirous of the equality they have historically been denied yet chary of exploiting the privilege of their dominant position as occupiers in a defeated country, African Americans are, Smith suggests, ideally suited to be global ambassadors of cosmopolitan goodwill.

Last of the Conquerors envisages the future of these ambassadors of goodwill in Sonny, a small boy Dawkins meets through Ilse. If interracial sexual contact serves in the novel as a metaphor for cosmopolitan conversation in a postwar world (intercourse as intercourse, so to speak), the figure of the biracial child must be interpreted as its corporeal manifestation, a visible marker of the encounter with the Other on which any cosmopolitan gesture rests. As Alexa Weik argues, drawing on the work of German philosopher Hans-Georg Gadamer, intercultural knowledge is not an achievable goal but rather a process, predicated on recognition of the Other through a "pre-judgment" (Gadamer's etymological gloss of *Vorurteil*, more commonly translated merely as "prejudice") that is subject to potentially endless revision through what Gadamer calls goodwill or openness to the Other. "Without goodwill," writes Weik, "there is no readiness to open up and revise previous pre-judgments into new pre-judgments. However, this disposition is how we function as understanding beings—by having our assumptions constantly challenged by other, new and differing information, without ever arriving at a fixed or final judgment" (469).

"The fixed or final judgment" of which Weik speaks is synonymous in *Last of the Conquerors* with the perception of fixity of racial or cultural identity and is coterminous with the bigotry that allows for the belief in a cultural or racial superiority that must be defended from adulteration. For Smith, then, the slide from individual incuriosity to fascism, from abdication of one's cosmopolitan responsibility to endorsement of armed conflict, is shorter and more slippery than one might expect. Biraciality, more even than interracial relationships, disrupts the will to ignorance that leads to "final judgments" by serving as a visual reminder of fluidity and hybridity; writing nearly twenty years after his experience in Berlin, Smith identifies the city's biracial children rather than its mixed-race couples as the signifier most closely associated with this disruption: "Walking down the street," he observes, newly expatriate black Americans were "pleasantly startled" by the unexpected juxtaposition of "so many gray-haired white women wheeling carriages containing brown babies—their grandchildren" (*Return* 63).

Sonny, the four-year-old adopted son of a couple Ilse has befriended, is one such "brown baby." As Ilse explains, "He is the son from an American soldier and a German girl.... He was a colored soldier and now he is home and the girl had no money to take care of him. So Frau Hoffman took the baby [and now] he thinks Frau Hoffman is his mother" (*Last* 78). Sonny is what was known in postwar Germany variously as a *farbiges Besatzungskind* (colored occupation child) or a *Mischlingskind* (mixed child), one of approximately three thousand biracial children among the approximately ninety-four thousand children presumed to have been conceived as a result of the occupation of Germany. These terms were used both formally and informally after 1945, though neither term is today considered appropriate. In general, however, such words were considered descriptive but not necessarily pejorative in the years immediately following the war, when children born to German women were classified according to their parentage based on other concerns, such as the likely circumstances of their conception. For this reason, the official term *Russenkinder* (Russian children) was far more politically fraught, since these children were assumed to be the products of the mass rape of women in Berlin by Russian soldiers during the city's "liberation"; after 1947, the term was dropped entirely, and such children, Fehrenbach writes, "from an official bureaucratic perspective . . . ceased to exist" (80). As Fehrenbach shows, the "colored occupation child" had a distinct niche in postwar German political and social discourse; as other children of "mixed" parentage (specifically the children of German couples in which one partner was Jewish and one was not and those whose fathers were Russian soldiers) were progressively reclassified as white, *Mischlingskinder* came to be identified exclusively with African American military personnel despite the fact that many black Germans had other backgrounds.[14] In a detailed historical explanation of the biracial occupation children, Fehrenbach argues that after about 1950, the illegitimate children of German women and black GIs were progressively recast as a major social problem, demonstrating that although the discourse surrounding their presence in Germany and their ability to assimilate into German society was "not monolithic," it was nevertheless often racist in ways that produced a "bureaucratic preoccupation with blackness" that "displaced, and ultimately erased . . . other racialized identities previously, obsessively, and sometimes lethally targeted by the German state" (78). Smith's depiction of the beloved Sonny thus may be read as reflecting a view of biracial children of occupation soldiers that was still relatively benign compared to the view of the *Russenkinder* or may be read as deliberately idealized. Either way, Sonny's acceptance in Berlin, realistic or not, is complete and unproblematic.

Sonny, who has effectively been abandoned by his birth parents, inhabits an identity hardly constrained by his parentage or his immediate circumstances. Sonny is welcomed not only by his adoptive family ("Trouble?" asks Frau Hoffman incredulously in response to Dawkins's question about the difficulty of raising a strange child. "Such a beautiful baby? Oh, no" [*Last* 79]) but also everywhere in his working-class neighborhood.[15] Avers Frau Hoffman, "He is liked by all of the little boys, and the girls think he is wonderful, even at so young an age. . . . Everyone near this house knows him, you know, and always they want him to come to their houses" (79).

Sonny inspires not just spiritual but also material generosity: "He is not small, you see. He has enough meat on the bones. It is because he goes to everyone's house and they give him to eat.... Always he is to somebody's house. Always. When I want him, I have to look for him" (79).

Furthermore, Sonny is connected not just to other *Mischlingskinder* but also to the black and biracial population of Berlin as a whole through his mysterious resemblance to Lela, a beautiful black dancer who is an absent presence throughout Dawkins's visit at the Hoffmans' house. "He looks like Lela," Frau Hoffman says, evincing surprise that Dawkins does not know Lela, who is another of Ilse's friends and is also involved in a relationship with a soldier: "I thought you knew her. I thought all of the soldiers knew Lela. Sonny looks like her" (*Last* 80). The insistence on Sonny's (improbable) resemblance to Lela functions narratively to link Berlin's cosmopolitan postwar future with its prewar past; Lela's parentage is unknown but is irrelevant, since she, like the rootless Sonny, is a citizen of the world: "She was born in Berlin," Ilse says, "and then went to so many countries to dance. She speaks so many languages, darling. You should hear her. She came back to Berlin maybe one year before the war" (80). Although Lela is unique in that her past performances have made her both rich and famous, she is only one of an extensive diasporic remnant spread across Berlin: When Dawkins says that he did not know that Berlin had "Negroes," Ilse replies,

> Most [are] French Africans who come here from France and marry German women. Then the children are German and stay here. When I was young I often saw a Negro man who was married to a German woman and lived not far from me. (80)

After being introduced to Sonny as "Uncle Hayes," Dawkins joins Ilse in taking the child to the camp for a visit. On their way back to the Hoffmans' house, Dawkins observes "an old German woman who glared at Ilse and then at me," a reaction Dawkins, staunch in his belief that Berliners do not practice racial discrimination, assumes stems from the woman's distaste for American servicemen and not from her bias against interracial couples: "The woman does not approve of soldiers, I noted" (*Last* 77). His optimistic view of the typical Berliner is subsequently borne out by the response he and Ilse receive when they return to the streetcar with Sonny, as his presence both legitimizes their relationship and "pleasantly startles" fellow passengers into a recognition of the pleasures of embracing hybridity:

> We rose and the three of us walked along the street toward the Strassenbahn Haltestelle [streetcar stop]. I felt good walking with the boy between Ilse and me. He held both our hands. We stood at the Haltestelle and people looked at the boy and smiled. When we boarded the Strassenbahn I picked Sonny up and walked into the car while Ilse paid the fares. Ilse took the one empty seat and I stood up, holding Sonny. Everyone on the Strassenbahn looked. I heard comments in German: "Is he not *sweet!*" . . . We rode back on the Strassenbahn and again the people stared and made exclamations. (81)

Sonny's identity is largely unknown, continually subject to assumption and revision; he is a walking illustration of a cosmopolitan encounter, evoking in spectators and interlocutors the requisite openness and goodwill to forestall the "fixed or final judgment" (Weik 469). As a *Mischlingskind*, he is beloved of all, for he belongs both everywhere and nowhere. Cast as the eponymous son of Berlin and linked closely to Lela, its native daughter, Sonny represents the chance for cosmopolitanism to emerge from and triumph over the wreckage and national rivalries and resentments caused by war and occupation.

Although Dawkins meets Sonny only once, the child occupies a crucial position in the narrative; in Sonny, Dawkins sees not only his potential future with Ilse but also a future in which race is only one of many axes of identity and as such does not limit but rather may encourage cosmopolitan interaction. The memory of Sonny haunts Dawkins until the novel's end; when he is told, after being sent to Bremburg, that he will never be allowed to return to Berlin, Dawkins laments not that he has lost Ilse but that he has been sent "away from Sonny" (*Last* 112). Later, when Dawkins determines to return to Berlin to live after his military service ends, he thinks "of Sonny, the little colored boy in Berlin. 'It is very cozy here,' I said softly, looking around the room. . . . 'How much would a house such as this cost?'" (177). Finally, near the novel's end, Dawkins thinks yet again of "little brown babies": "'Very many and all very fat,'" says Ilse's landlord, Pop, "'Little brown babies, yes?'" (235).

Yet Dawkins, who has envisaged not only "brown babies" but his own rebirth in Berlin as Herr Dawkins, must return to the United States and his old life. Like Chester Himes's Bob Jones, who is forced into the military in wartime rather than out after the war is over, Dawkins's dreams of escaping a life in which his identity is narrativized for him by racist discourses he cannot control are thwarted by the heavy hand of institutional power. After he witnesses Polke's cowardice and venality in his dealings with a vengeful soldier he has vindictively court-martialed on a trumped-up charge, Dawkins is abruptly discharged to preserve Polke's reputation, his silence bought with the promise that his discharge will be honorable, making him eligible for education under the GI Bill. Notified that he will ship out the next day, Dawkins goes to Ilse to say good-bye. *Last of the Conquerors* ends on an ambiguous note, as Dawkins promises Ilse that he will return to Germany but she for the first time acknowledges the artificiality of the "dream" they have been living together: "I know you will not be back," she tells Dawkins:

> You will go to Philadelphia, your home.... You will think that it was like a dream, that you were so far away in a country that speaks another language.... [M]aybe always you will say, far back in your head, "Someday I will go back to Germany." But you will never come back. Never. (236)

Dawkins reassures her that he "will be different," but as he walks away from the apartment he has shared with Ilse, her landlady warns him that he must not look back or, like Eurydice, he will never return from the United States. The implicit comparison of life in the United States with Hades recalls an earlier scene in which Sergeant Murdock, who finds Berlin "a great city," laments his early discharge, telling the other men, "I don't want to go back there. I don't want to go anyplace in the States.... I like this goddamn country, you know that? I like the hell out of it" (*Last* 56–57). The novel's final words make clear that not just Dawkins, Murdock, and their friends but in fact all of the black soldiers in Germany recognize the dilemma Dawkins faces:

> Along the dirt road toward the personnel building, a soldier shouts, "Hey Hayes, I hear you're shipping for home today."
> Hoarsely: "Yeah."
> "Tough." (237)

The novel leaves deliberately unclear the question of whether Dawkins will become an expatriate, as William Gardner Smith did a few years later, or will return to the segregation and racial prejudice of the United States. However, this lack of clarity, which compels the reader to weigh Dawkins's choice and render judgment, also serves as an implicit call to action. Like Dawkins, like Smith, the narrative suggests, we all must come to terms with our cosmopolitan responsibilities to ourselves as well as to others. If we do not do so openly and with goodwill, we can later expect to be forced to confront the difference we seek to avoid on the battlefield.

Thus Smith's rejection of the "raceless" theme in his cosmopolitan war novel must be read as resulting from his realization of raceless fiction's inherent limitations. The raceless novel's failure is its reliance on a misguided discourse of "universality" that denies the value of the particular except as it is illustrative of what purport to be themes applicable somehow to all. *Last of the Conquerors* makes its contribution in its understanding that a slavish devotion to the concept of the universal, while it may seem equitable and laudable, ultimately leads not to cosmopolitan openness and conversation but rather to the enforcement of homogeneity. For, as Ulrich Beck writes, "Universalism obliges us to respect others as equals in principle, yet for that very reason does not involve any requirement that would inspire curiosity or respect for what makes others different" (49). In a discussion with a young German ex-soldier who has spent time in an American prison camp, Dawkins is reminded that American policies toward African Americans might be reasonably compared to those of the Nazis; the solution, the young German suggests, is a "strong man ... who can make sure that everyone is treated the same" (*Last* 147). Dawkins's response contains the heart of his—and Smith's—cosmopolitan philosophy:

> People can either hate or like, for that is inside of them. No Hitler can change that. Hitler could make the people *say* that they have no hate,

but he could not change them inside. We want no one to make anyone like us ... or hate us. The friends we want are friends of the heart. To have no one smile at us is better than to have someone *forced* to smile. (147)

For Smith, the only answer to fascism is curiosity about and openness to the Other. In the words of historian Rayford Logan in his "primer" on black history, *The Negro in the Post-War World* (1945), "Interest in one's neighbors, five thousand or more miles away, can be one of the most valuable bases of a just and lasting peace for all mankind" (v). For Logan, as for his contemporaries, this curiosity begins with a "revolution in education" (v) at home driven at least in part by politically oriented and specifically African American educational initiatives. Yet the role of black academics and historically black institutions of higher learning in reshaping the contours of American race relations at midcentury was by no means obvious or unproblematic, as is shown by J. Saunders Redding's 1950 academic novel, *Stranger and Alone*.

CHAPTER FIVE

J. Saunders Redding and the African American Campus Novel

Like so many of his contemporaries, eminent African American literary historian and critic J. Saunders Redding is today largely unknown. Yet his long and complex career, in which he was excoriated for holding positions deemed too radical in the 1930s and insufficiently radical in the 1960s, as Henry Louis Gates Jr. observes, "reflects the irony and paradox of Afro-American thought" in the mid–twentieth century ("Introduction" xi). Redding, whose politics were sometimes inconsistent, has the distinction of having been roundly criticized as both too liberal and too conservative. He was dismissed from his first teaching position, at Morehouse University, because his support of W. E. B. Du Bois's demands for political and social equality was judged to be too radical; by the 1960s, however, Redding's refusal to embrace the essentialist and separatist discourses at the heart of the Black Arts and Black Power movements earned him the opprobrium of black nationalists.

Yet even as his iconoclastic views threatened repeatedly to marginalize him, Redding remained crucial to the postwar debate over race, politics, and literature. His work spans an extraordinary range of genres, both fiction and nonfiction, critical and autobiographical. He published groundbreaking studies of African American history, among them *They Came in Chains: Americans from Africa* (1950), *The Lonesome Road: The Story of the Negro's Part in America* (1950), and *The Negro* (1967); candid autobiographical works such as *No Day of Triumph* (1942) and *On Being Negro in America* (1951); a postcolonial study of India, *An American in India: A Personal Report of the Indian Dilemma and the Nature of Her*

Conflicts (1954); and *To Make a Poet Black* (1939), which many observers judge to be the first sophisticated critical appraisal of African American literature by a black scholar.[1] Redding came under fire in later decades for maintaining what was considered to be an outdated, ideologically conservative stance; Lawrence Jackson writes that Redding's work "tended to discomfit black readers. He did not cleanly pick a side in the aesthetic and political debates between modernists and social realists. He was too much a frustrated 'race' man to join easily the reconstituted liberals of the 1950s. To his dismay, Redding's prolific and compulsive writings about his racial identity earned him the title not of a thoughtful humanist, but of 'traducer' of his race" ("Irredeemable" 714). However, Redding's influence as a scholar-critic was at its apex in 1950 when he published his largely forgotten novel, *Stranger and Alone*.[2] Overshadowed by his nonfiction works, *Stranger and Alone* was dubbed "perhaps his most glaring mistake in judgment" (160) by his friend and coeditor Arthur P. Davis. Long unread, Redding's novel is nonetheless key to understanding not only the author's oeuvre but also the development of African American literature up to 1950, that midcentury marker so many critics, black and white, regard as pivotal. Furthermore, in Redding's struggle with the changing form of the African American novel, amply documented in nearly a decade's worth of manuscript revisions, today's readers can see the outlines of the issues of form and content, politics and style, genre and innovation that inflect our understanding even today of what the form can, should, and might do.

Redding's work, like that of the other authors discussed in this book, reflects a deep understanding of the interactions among generic form, political action, and the realities of African American life. Like Chester Himes's *If He Hollers Let Him Go* (which Redding disliked, misreading it as sloppy protest fiction and objecting to what he saw as its gratuitous use of slang), *Stranger and Alone* is an ideologically complex work, showing a keen awareness of the strictures of the protest genre and an effort to subvert them. Also like Himes, Redding depicts the contradictions unique to middle-class black life in the decades immediately preceding World War II with an ambivalence that contemporary reviewers generally interpreted as undifferentiated hostility. More significantly, just as William Gardner Smith's and Frank Yerby's revisions of the war novel and the historical romance, respectively, demand a reconsideration of the generic implications of the African American novel of the late 1940s and link the subversion of literary convention with extraliterary political action, so *Stranger and Alone* provides a commentary on its generic choices and simultaneously intervenes in a broader political discussion.

Stranger and Alone, which depicts the inner workings of two historically black southern colleges and reflects the research Redding had done nine years earlier for *No Day of Triumph* as well as his lengthy teaching career, tells the story of one man's rise from poverty to a position of power in the African American educational system in the South and his ultimate betrayal of his community. Though it has been categorized as a novel whose "theory is mimetic and [whose] verisimilitude is within the text" (Berry 6), *Stranger and Alone*'s relationship to formal conventions is far more complex than its surface "realism" allows. Resisting the urge either unhesitatingly to idealize or merely to ridicule the middle-class black educators who are its main characters, *Stranger and Alone* rejects not only the tenets of the protest fiction model but also the established templates for mid-twentieth-century academic fiction, which generally relied on satire to achieve a more or less humorous effect. In so doing, the novel offers what may paradoxically be seen both as a scathing critique of the practice and an implicit defense of the theory of African American education in the South at a historically resonant moment. Just four years later, the Supreme Court's historic *Brown v. Board of Education* decision, which put an end to segregated education, opened up a public debate whose repercussions were felt nationwide.

In describing Redding's novel as "academic fiction," I encompass both the college novel and the later "campus" novel. The college novel, a largely pre–World War II form that focused on the experience of college life as lived by undergraduate students, is distinct from the campus novel, a version that, like its British counterpart, owed its postwar rise to the expansion of opportunities for higher education among the members of the working class and the increasing professionalization of academic work. The former emphasized college life from the student's perspective, while the latter often focused on the petty politics, intellectual dishonesty, and general hypocrisy that supposedly characterized the contemporary university. While the college novel's general goal is the nostalgic reproduction of an idealized undergraduate experience, the campus novel usually at least implies a critique of the university system itself, albeit nearly always leavened with humor. Students in the campus novel play marginal parts; instead, the action centers on conflict and intrigue among the faculty and administration. Kingsley Amis's *Lucky Jim* (1954) is usually considered the classic postwar British campus novel; on the other side of the Atlantic, critics point to Mary McCarthy's *The Groves of Academe* (1952) as the defining text of the genre.

Other novelists had depicted life on historically black campuses, but the setting had typically served purely as a backdrop for a plot aimed at presenting a moralistic story consonant with the basic premises of social realism and protest fiction.[3] Unlike in these novels, the setting of *Stranger and Alone* is not incidental; instead, the colleges and their administration are central to the narrative. *Stranger and Alone* is thus the first black academic novel by an African American. Comprising the forms of both the college novel and the campus novel and applying both to the historically black college, *Stranger and Alone* anticipates not only *Invisible Man* (1952) but also later novels ranging from Alice Walker's *Meridian* to recent novels by popular black writers Omar Tyree and C. Kelly Robinson.

Stranger and Alone does not appear in *The American College Novel* (1981), John E. Kramer's otherwise exhaustive annotated bibliography of academic fiction written in the United States. In fact, the only work by an African American in the anthology is *Invisible Man*, despite the fact that Ellison may have borrowed characters and incidents from Redding. As John Vassilowitch Jr. shows, Ellison's Dr. Bledsoe closely resembles a composite figure based on an actual college president Redding describes in *No Day of Triumph* (1942) and his fictional Perkins Wimbush. Indeed, Redding's work seems to have provided several unacknowledged models for Ellison. For example, *Invisible Man* arguably also draws on the anecdote of accidental incest between a sharecropper and his daughter that Redding transcribes in *No Day of Triumph*. For that matter, Chester Himes may have based the character of Alice Harrison in *If He Hollers Let Him Go* on Redding's description of his alcoholic lesbian cousin, Rosalie Hatton, in *No Day of Triumph*. Like Himes's character, Hatton is the only daughter of a wealthy doctor and is so color-struck that she cannot function in black society.

Only two novels concerning historically black colleges preceded Redding's, with both published in the 1940s by white authors and featuring white characters interacting with heroic, self-sacrificing, or tormented African Americans. The college setting is largely irrelevant except as a narrative excuse to force interracial interaction. Worth Tuttle Hedden's *The Other Room* (1947) tells the tale of Nina Latham, a young white teacher who, after implausibly discovering that she has "accidentally" accepted a position at a black college, learns to accept and appreciate her black students and colleagues. The novel ends when Nina's African American lover, a history professor at the college, decides that he must break off their relationship because they can never marry because the pressures of race prejudice in the South would destroy their lives and his career. Bucklin Moon's *Without Magnolias*, which won the 1949 George Washington Carver Award for fiction by and about African Americans, describes the conflict between a white, apparently liberal newspaper editor and the black president of a local college over the retention of a politically radical sociology professor.[4] The president, admitting to himself at last "in a revelation that was so crystal clear as to be almost as dazzling as a blinding light" that he has been "bought . . . wholly . . . his mind, his loyalty, but most of all his personal integrity" (272), decides that the only honorable course of action is to resign his position in protest in a moral, if professionally Pyrrhic, victory. The novel's end suggests strongly that the president, Ezekiel Rogers, will not follow through on his plan; his cowardice is motivated by his fear of being forced to leave his snobbish wife, who he knows will never agree to abandon her social position in their small southern town. His decision echoes that of Cal Thornton, the white newspaper editor, who opposes forcing Rogers to fire the sociology professor but does so at the urging of his racist wife, whose family money supports his failing newspaper. The novel's misogynist choice to blame both men's moral failings on their narrow-minded spouses thus links the two men, despite their race, and marks the book as participating in what Barbara Ehrenreich points out is a trend in postwar fiction toward identifying women as exploitative figures whose social pretensions and consumerism provide the driving force behind men's enslavement in the world of the gray flannel suit (42–51). It is fitting then, that in one of the few reviews that did not praise Moon's work, Henry Cavendish of the

Chicago Tribune summed up its plot in his seven-word title: "Negroes All Good... White Folk All Bad."

Redding was aware of these precedents. As a prolific book reviewer from the 1940s to the mid-1960s,[5] he extensively read fiction by and about African Americans, and his papers suggest that as a career academic, he had a particular interest in fiction dealing with college campuses. One of his most vitriolic reviews, in fact, is of *Youth of Color* (1952), by Caroline Wasson Thomason, a former professor at the University of Wisconsin, about mixed-race students at Oberlin. *Youth of Color* is "fantastically infantile," writes Redding. "Such books... are not only crimes against art; they are crimes against nature herself" (review of *Youth* 4). His review characterized *Without Magnolias* as lacking "a vigorous sharpness of new insight," and he disliked its narrative because "nothing happens" (YYY), though he admitted that he expected the book to be widely read. Although he did not produce a review of Hedden's novel, he also knew of her work. Furthermore, *Stranger and Alone* was reviewed by both Hedden and Moon, and he considered their evaluations important enough to retain copies in his files until his death.[6]

As unsparing in his criticism as he was catholic in his literary selection, Redding discussed a wide range of fiction and nonfiction, writing in his weekly column that he considered himself a plainspoken alternative to the two types of reviewers then in existence, literary critics who produce "brilliantly written criticism of the kind almost no one understands" and "well-paid press agents" ("Second Look," May 18, 1946, 4). Proudly individualistic in his judgments, he did not shrink from panning even critical darlings. Fannie Cook's best seller, *Mrs. Palmer's Honey*, for example, which in 1946 had, like *Without Magnolias*, won the prestigious George Washington Carver prize, Redding unhesitatingly pronounced "tripe," adding "and tripe makes me sick" ("Second Look," May 18, 1946, 4). As he drily noted in a 1953 review of Carl Milton Hughes's *The Negro Novelist*, "as few people know (and they have missed nothing by not knowing) the field of the Negro novel between 1940 and 1950 was littered (I almost said "illiterate") with trash... which no one except the respective authors, their dearest kin and this plagued reviewer ever read."

Given his low opinion of the state of "Negro" letters, it is unsurprising that Redding would attempt to remodel the African American novel, producing work that seeks to reconceive the relations between form and content. Redding likely began thinking about writing a novel drawing on his experiences at historically black colleges as early as the 1930s, but his focus on producing scholarly works forced him to delay its completion. As a result, his numerous revisions to the manuscript under several titles clearly reflect his ongoing engagement with the shifting conventions of the African American novel of the 1940s. Though he intended from the beginning to include a character representing the black educational system in the South, Redding wrote and discarded literally hundreds of pages as he sought the appropriate generic form, auditioning narrative options ranging from a somewhat melodramatic love story about an African American political activist and his married lover to a modernist-inflected folk narrative about an interracial orphan in a rural community that included dialogue rendered in dialect.[7]

Only gradually did his work emerge as a campus novel, and then only with multiple caveats, chief among them his decision to strip his story of the tropes Hedden and Moon had used to mark their narratives as protest fiction aimed at convincing the reader of the unjustness of the educated African American's position in a racist society. By the late 1940s, Redding had realized that the protest fiction model was inadequate for his purposes; his goal in writing was not (or not merely) to demonstrate that white society discriminated against educated blacks but rather to show that discriminatory practices and discourses in fact made black education itself impossible. Novels such as Hedden's, in which black students and professors are shown as hardworking and devoted to intellectual endeavor, or Moon's, in which the hero is a brilliant political progressive, gave the impression that the problem lay not with the African American educational system per se but with the reception of educated blacks in the broader American society. Yet Redding's long-standing position led to a quite different conclusion. As he had written in 1943, "Insofar—and it is considerably far—as the Negro problem lies in the range of interpretations and meanings of concepts and postulates that surround it, education is at fault." Thus,

> It is re-education that is needed. Of necessity it would be a re-education of the whole people, North and South.... Under our present

system of education, it would have to be largely voluntarily undertaken, and this, as Pearl Buck says, would make it a "long and difficult process." Its design would be to change the behavior of the people, their emotions and convictions. ("Black Man's" 590–91)

Showing a well-rounded, sympathetic, intellectually gifted black character whose aspirations are thwarted by whites, therefore, would pair a narrative cliché with an inaccurate portrayal of the state of the African American educational system. Thus, Redding began to rewrite his novel, marginalizing the black activist who had originally been the narrator and jettisoning portions of the narrative that readers might use to humanize and justify the misanthropy of his new protagonist. Redding also removed passages devoted to explicating the political and philosophical views of the token "radicals" among the faculty members. For example, in the manuscript versions, Howden encounters and is influenced by thoughtful resistance to white hegemony, often pungently expressed, by characters such as Edward Pettijohn, a lecturer at Arcadia College whose political views result in his firing by President Wimbush. In the novel, Pettijohn is replaced by Spurgeon Kelly, a lecturer who objects much more vaguely both to "playing monkey for white folks" (*Stranger* 145) and to contributing a dollar to a staff social. Similarly, the activist figure, consistently named Curtis Flack in both the manuscripts and the novel, disappears almost completely after Redding's revisions, emerging only at the narrative's end to tell a detailed story to Shelton and his wife about having endured racist treatment at the hands of northern airport staff. The story is presented explicitly as a protest narrative designed for maximum effect; Flack has just given a speech at a meeting of local activists and is now telling personal anecdotes illustrating his points at his wife's urging. ("You ought to use that story in a speech," she suggests. "It's a wonderful commentary" [283].) Yet Flack's tale does not move Howden, through whose perspective the reader's response is also filtered; he responds that "the whole thing was exaggerated, that its meaning was forced, that too much was made of too little" (289). *Stranger and Alone* thus provides a commentary on the protest genre not unlike that offered by Bob Jones's dismissal of *Native Son* in *If He Hollers Let Him Go*—the protest narrative has lost its ability to surprise the reader and thus its efficacy.

Reducing the story to its barest essentials and its characters to their flattest delineations, Redding allows the novel's subject, the current state and future significance of black education, to emerge as the central "character." At the same time, by removing the generic markers of protest fiction from his text, Redding also engages the broader literary issue of the ideological work of genre itself. What does it mean for a black writer at midcentury both to reject the protest form and to make use of, even while substantially revising, another form never before associated with African American literature? From his affectless main character to his repurposed campus novel, Redding disrupts the reader's expectations, all the better to foreground his real subject: the impact of educational policy on postwar African Americans.

Stranger and Alone, set on the Louisiana campuses of the fictional all-black New Hope and Arcadia Colleges, tells the story of its black antihero, the awkwardly named Shelton Howden. The awkwardness is no accident. Multiple early versions of Redding's manuscript, under titles including "If There Be Any Praise" and "The Secret Life of Gaynor Howden," indicate that Redding apparently discarded the name *Gaynor Howden* only shortly before publishing the book. The change has two purposes. Howden and Wimbush are linked throughout the novel not only by their racial heritage (both have black mothers and white fathers) and their worldviews but by their nicknames (Howden is "Old Lady" to his only friend at New Hope, while Wimbush is widely known as the "Old Man" at Arcadia). The change from *Gaynor* to *Shelton* gives both men two surnames, a marker ironically often associated with the WASP culture Wimbush venerates. Also, however, the change strips Howden's name of its original euphony as well as its more obvious etymological irony (*Gaynor* is a Welsh name derived from the words meaning "white" and "soft"), which is consonant with Redding's broader project of making Howden's character a representative textual signifier rather than a well-wrought character aimed at evoking readerly sympathy.

The story is told as an inverted bildungsroman, an ironic novel of education. In lieu of the traditional movement in this genre from ignorance to knowledge and alienation to social integration, Redding presents Howden's academic education as stunting his personal and spiritual development and positioning him irrevocably in a liminal position between a white community he envies and fears and a black community he pities and despises. A work-study student at the private, coeducational New Hope College, Howden follows a career trajectory that ensures that he experiences the full range of educational opportunities available to African Americans from the 1920s to the middle of World War II. He completes his undergraduate education at a historically black college, acquires a master's degree in education at "the University in New York" (references to Morningside Heights clarify that it is Columbia), and ends up parlaying a faculty position at another historically black college, where he is hired as the assistant to his mentor, the unscrupulous college president Perkins Wimbush, into a second job as supervisor of "Niggra schools" (*Stranger* 215) for the state.

But this range of educational experience leads him neither to a greater understanding of the importance of race solidarity nor to a sufficiently broad understanding of events in the outside world to enable him to manipulate them. He strikes a Faustian bargain when he agrees, at Wimbush's prodding, to spy on other black educators to keep white local politicians apprised of incipient "radicalism." Yet his corruption gains him nothing. Though he congratulates himself on disdaining idealism in favor of "pragmatism" in the face of implacable realities, his reactionary interpretation of the "real world" ironically prevents him from recognizing the political and social changes that are about to overtake him. The novel ends in the autumn of 1943, as World War II rages and the civil rights movement gathers steam, yet Howden ponders a phrase he has heard in a local activist's speech, "the time on the clock of the world,"[8] without even the slightest insight. ("It doesn't mean anything," he ultimately decides. "It's just clever rhetoric" [*Stranger* 270]). His final perfidy is to infiltrate and then betray a group of political activists who are planning to protest the imposition of the poll tax on the county's black residents, an act that occasions in him no distress beyond the realization that "betrayal" ought not to be "this simple and easy" (307). He cynically believes that this move will further ingratiate him with influential whites. However, Howden's stagnant career prospects in the coming civil rights era are foreshadowed by his description in the novel's final paragraphs, as he enters the office of Judge Reed, the white congressman whose patronage he seeks, to give his evidence: The receptionist "let her eyes slide over Howden as if he were a familiar unused piece of office furniture" (308).

Shelton Howden is, in short, a remarkably unlikable protagonist—unkind, incurious, unwaveringly self-serving. Ralph Ellison's review of the novel compared Howden to a "collaborator with his own enemy," a term today perhaps less loaded than in 1950, when it could only have evoked Nazi sympathizers; reviewer W. T. Scott still more bluntly characterized *Stranger and Alone* as "Saunders Redding's novel of a heel." A comparison of the manuscripts with the published book shows clearly that this Shelton Howden emerged from a series of revisions that stripped all of Howden's interpersonal relationships of nuance and characterized him as impervious to human emotion. For example, Redding early on removed passages describing Shelton Howden's past as the unwanted child of a black mother abandoned by her white lover ("Secret Life" n.p.), opting in the end to allow only the briefest allusions to an orphanage (*Stranger* 66, 70, 108), filtered through Howden's consciousness and consequently tinged with a paranoiac self-pity that undermines their validity. Instead, the reader meets Howden as he embarks on his undergraduate career at New Hope resentful and envious of his fellow students, whom he finds overprivileged and carefree. He is determined to do well in school because of a vague ambition, never articulated with any specificity, to "show them" by becoming "a doctor or a lawyer or—something" (3, 11).

Howden's final "career," as an informer who works against grassroots social justice movements, is logical, even overdetermined by his inability to connect to other people. Howden's college roommate, Fred Thompson, attempts to befriend him, bestowing a familiar nickname ("Old Lady") on him and running interference between Howden and the other work-study students, who are characterized as vulgar and sometimes violent-tempered. Thompson suffers from tuberculosis, an illness that only becomes obvious to Howden when Thompson coughs up blood in the room he and Howden share. In one of the earliest versions of the manuscript, Howden worries about Thompson's illness, nursing him when he has an especially bad spell; when Thompson's death occurs during a semester break, Howden is saddened to learn the news through a notice sent by the school and discovers that "he missed Thompson very much" ("Secret Life" n.p.).

In the novel, however, Howden rejects Thompson's overtures from the beginning, callously sizing up Thompson's worth: Thompson "smiled warmly, but Howden felt an immediate sense of resentment and kept his eyes narrowed. He could tell that Thompson was no great shakes at New Hope College; he could tell that Thompson was a nobody" (*Stranger* 7). Thompson's death serves as the first definitive marker of Howden's implacable self-absorption: "Fred Thompson was ill, and his illness would have been noticeable to anyone but Howden" (35). Howden's main response to Thompson's plight is an "impatience" he can barely conceal; he leaves the room each time Thompson experiences another of a series of hemorrhages, finally deciding to request another room: "No one could make him stay with Thompson's sickness. There were plenty of vacant rooms" (38). On his deathbed, Thompson begins to speak of the inevitability of his death, talking of his absent father and his mother, who also died of tuberculosis. Howden reacts angrily, flinging "himself so violently from his chair that it tipped over" and deserting Thompson, who is clearly in extremis: "When [Howden] returned at dawn, Fred Thompson had drowned in his own blood" (39, 40). No further mention is made of Thompson, and two paragraphs later, the reader learns that Howden, who subsequently procures the single room he desires, "exulted in his loneliness" (40).

Similar changes to Redding's earlier manuscript denude Howden's other relationships at New Hope and beyond of warmth and reciprocity even as they strip his character of a colorful interior life that both enlivens the third-person narration and provides context and depth for Howden's actions. In both the manuscripts and the novel, Howden is befriended by the school's lone black faculty member, the near-white Professor Clarkson, who invites Howden to regular family dinners and holidays and encourages him to attend medical school. When an accident cripples Howden's right arm, ending his dreams of becoming a surgeon, Clarkson exerts his influence so that Howden can receive a fellowship that will enable him to pursue a master's degree in New York. A comparison of Howden's reaction to Professor Clarkson's revelation of Howden's acceptance in an earlier manuscript and in the final novel shows the stark contrast between the two Howdens, the original Gaynor and Shelton. In the manuscript, Howden smiles to hide his disappointment so that Professor Clarkson will not be hurt by his indifference; later, alone, Howden attempts to raise his own spirits: "He lay there staring up into the ceiling, telling himself that everything worked out for the best. . . . Then, without fully realizing what had happened or what had caused it, he felt something roll across the bridge of his nose and drop heavily onto the pillow" ("Secret Life" 135). After Redding's revisions, however, a far more indifferent Howden emerges: "He had not asked them for anything. He didn't owe them anything. And if they thought he owed them something, he had nothing to give" (*Stranger* 102). Once Howden completes his master's degree, he never again contacts the Clarksons.

Howden's tears in the manuscript version of this scene result not only from his injury and the fact that he will be unable to study medicine but also from the breakup of his relationship with Valrie Tillet, a character who also appears in *Stranger and Alone* but plays a very different role. In the novel, Howden meets Valrie, a fellow student, when she is his lab partner in a chemistry course. Valrie is intelligent, kind, and attractive, but Howden's interest in her, like his later interest in President Wimbush's daughter, Gerry, is motivated primarily by his fascination with their middle-class status, which he envies. Although he tells Valrie that he loves her, Howden's true feelings for her are mostly hostile, and the relationship ends when he attempts to rape her on their graduation day after verbally abusing and psychologically controlling her for weeks. Again, the novel emphasizes the untrustworthiness of Howden's recasting of past events, as he recalls that "all he had wanted to do was kiss her":

> His intentions were misunderstood. Valrie had always misunderstood him, he told himself.... From the very first day she had made him suffer—and she had no right. She had made him crawl and beg and suffer. It was her doing and her fault. Last night was her fault. She had put him at odds with his inclinations, with his very nature. She always had. (*Stranger* 80)

When Howden receives a letter from Valrie in which she tells him she hopes never to see him again, he is "not sure that he [feels] anything at all" (83).

In "The Secret Life of Gaynor Howden," by contrast, Howden, attempts to maintain a long-distance relationship with Valrie while working as a waiter on a railcar to earn money to send himself to medical school. Although theirs is largely an epistolary love affair, it is described as genuinely affectionate and serious, and its end shows Howden at his most imaginative and sympathetic. Valrie invites Howden to visit her in Philadelphia over the Christmas holiday, but he not only feels he cannot afford to do so but asks himself, "What did a young man do when he called on a girl in a city that was not her home?" (121). Daydreaming about Valrie, Howden decides to leave his job and in a fog of desire tries to jump from the moving train, sustaining the injury that destroys his medical career. As he lies in his hospital bed, he spins an elaborate fantasy in which Valrie is "the physician attending him." In it, he is no longer the victim of a foolish accident but the heroic subject of a romantic narrative:

> He had fallen ill of the dangerous and baffling disease upon which he had been doing medical research, and she had come two thousand miles to look after him. He was not in a big city hospital, which had a ward for Negroes in the basement, but in a straw-thatched hut, ingeniously set up partly as a laboratory and partly as Spartan living quarters, in some disease-ridden tropical country where he had gone to conquer one of the great scourges of mankind. By train, by plane, by crude canoe, she had come to be with him. Gravely, with tenderness and courage she worked over him. (129)

In the final version of this incident, Valrie plays no part. Instead, Howden falls from the train in a fit of rage against the uneducated men with whom he works on the railcar. As in the scenes with Valrie and Thompson, Howden's interactions with the rest of the crew change substantially from the manuscript to the final text. While the novel's Howden has "no curiosity" about the nameless men with whom he works, having "catalogued them within three days" (*Stranger* 88), in the early drafts, he admires their "careless expert haste" and describes each man in some detail: "The chief cook, Glassco, was a card. Peet, one of the waiters—a flat-eyed, axe-faced dandy—was straight out of the gallery of the more sinister characters of Octavius Roy Cohen. Sperling, 'the Spade,' was a regular humdinger" ("Secret Life" 112). The men, for their part, are "proud of him," showing "a certain diffident consideration and respect for him" ("Secret Life," 112). In their truncated form in the final novel, the episodes on the railcar are marked by mutual distrust, as Howden withdraws from contact with his fellow workers "as completely and as arrogantly . . . as a plane in flight"

(*Stranger* 90). The crew members, who refer to Howden as "Joe College," spend most of their time discussing news items in the black press, while Howden refuses to acknowledge the validity of their perspectives. By eliding all commonalities between the crew members, who are knowledgeable, literate, and engaged participants in current events, and Joe College, who refuses to learn anything from them, Redding limns the irony of Howden's condescension: higher education steeped in the verities of racism is no education at all.

As the disappearance from the final novel of such passages makes clear, Redding's most significant change to Howden's character in the quest to flatten it was to strip him of a desire for understanding or empathy. The decision to pair Howden with Nan, his race-conscious but timid wife, and his mistress, Gerry Wimbush, was one of Redding's last. In every earlier version of the manuscript, Howden's wife is Tressa, a foreign-born, smart, and outspoken "race woman" whose father is a prominent activist. Tressa's commitment to knowledge marks her as one of the success stories of the traditional progress narrative associated with black education: "There were arguments you couldn't use with Tressa," thinks Howden, "because she knew the answers" ("Secret Life" 6). She is also well aware of black history and culture to an extent Howden is not, as her possessions, inherited from her father, indicate:

> [Howden] remembered the cries of delighted recognition with which she had unpacked all the stuff that came from the storage place in Charleston. There were editions of Dunbar's works, including his fiction, which Howden had never known he wrote. There were books by a man named Chesnutt, of whom Howden had never heard; and by Sutton Griggs and Frederick Douglass and a half-dozen other ex-slaves; and all those books by that trouble-maker, Du Bois; and the various histories of the Negro's part in the various wars. ("Secret Life" 61–62)

Nan, by contrast, is a radical revision of this character, a timid local woman who prizes an inheritance of "gaudy china" as much as her "old illustrated books about 'Illustrious Negroes'" (*Stranger* 276). Even the late addition to the story of the embittered, neurotic, and promiscuous Gerry

Wimbush is carefully deployed to make Howden's character, like the narrative as a whole, more detailed but no deeper. Like Howden, Gerry's actions completely lack narrative motivation, and she is presented as being so insistent on maintaining her superficiality that she literally refuses to have a serious conversation. (She speaks in a brittle parody of Jazz Age slang, exaggeration, and repetitive empty endearments; in response to Howden's marriage proposal, she says, "Don't be neurotic tonight, honey baby" [173].) Howden's desire to marry Gerry, though he articulates it as being prompted by love, is both a way for him to align himself permanently with Wimbush and a mode of attaining the middle-class security he seeks, as he acknowledges:

> When Gerry talked, the world of her friends contracted to the size of a tent, and Howden liked the feeling of being in it. It was a world on a level of habits and attitudes and adjustments subtly different from the one in which, but for the Old Man, he would still be a poke. The social world, Gerry's world, complemented and afforded escape from the other. . . . It was a small world, but he was not really in it. . . . "Gerry," he said, turning impulsively toward her. . . . "Gerry, will you marry me?" (170)

Howden's relationships with Nan and Gerry ultimately mirror his earlier encounter with Valrie. After convincing Nan to engage in premarital sex, he taunts her for her provincial attitudes; in bed with Gerry after taking a phone call from his wife, he informs her that Nan is now pregnant, a revelation that makes him feel like Gerry's "master . . . somehow triumphant" (265).

The reader who may begin the novel seeking justification for or an explanation of Howden's attitudes ends it, as Redding scholar Pancho Savery notes, by despising him (x), at least in part because he seems to have failed to learn anything. Yet this response reflects the reader's assumptions about what the narrative structure of Howden's story should look like and frustration when those expectations are denied. Not only does the novel resolutely refuse to build to a climactic conclusion (the significance of Howden's final betrayal is undercut by its presentation), but Howden's character does not develop in any way. Rather, his moral, emotional, and intellectual outlook remain fundamentally the same from the beginning of the narrative to the end. As the inability of education to elevate Howden indicates, the novel's treatment of the world of black academe is a bleak one. Redding portrays Howden and Wimbush as thoroughly selfish opportunists who, unlike Moon's college president, are unable even to recognize their corruption. Despite having received their degrees from Ivy League institutions, both men disdain universities, their faculties and students, and even the pursuit of knowledge as an abstract good. As an undergraduate, Howden realizes that "the learning of such knowledge as books held" is to him a "useless, heartbreaking chore" (*Stranger* 22); years (and an advanced degree) later, Howden's preferred reading material is *Success* magazine, with its "section called 'Culture for the Successful Man,' which, month after month, showed the same distinguished-looking gentleman of early middle years absorbing or about to absorb some kind of culture" (271–72). Wimbush uses his considerable wit and rhetorical skill primarily to design smugly paternalistic public addresses aimed at increasing his power and to invent racist puns. (One of his many "jokes" is that black women who join the Women's Army Corps are "Waccoons" [256].) Unlike the protagonist of the bildungsroman who finds through education a stake in his or her own society, Wimbush and Howden remain entirely alienated from the impending political movement around them: "No one seemed to realize, the Old Man had said, that the only struggle worth anything was the personal struggle and that whatever fulfillment there was in life was a personal fulfillment" (249).

Redding makes his most daring choice, then, in refusing to honor one of the articles of faith not only of the members of his and previous generations but also of an African American literary tradition founded on slave narratives: the idea that education is inherently enlightening and liberating and thus is the basis for racial uplift. As Lindon Barrett observes, in academic criticism of the slave narrative, "no single issue holds the preeminence granted literacy" (418). Building on Valerie Smith's criticism of the privileging of literacy in such narratives as "pay[ing] homage to the structures of discourse that so often contributed to the writer's oppression" (qtd. in Barrett 418), Barrett sees the focus on literacy as at best unduly limited. Redding's literary contemporaries agreed that, as Robert Stepto succinctly writes in *From behind the Veil*, "The primary pre-generic myth for Afro-America is the quest for freedom and literacy" (xv).

While *Stranger and Alone* refuses to idealize higher education and its redemptive potential, it also refuses to go to the other extreme made available by midcentury trends in fiction about the nonblack college experience: the nullification of the value of higher education implicit in the traditional academic satire. Where Himes's fiction seeks to take the situational tragedy of the typical protest novel and, through satire, "get it funny," Redding's consciously eschews the humorous model that had by 1950 become recognizably dominant in academic fiction. Rather, Redding, whose lengthy academic career spanned a series of prestigious appointments beginning at Morehouse College and ending at Cornell University and who was just beginning an appointment at Brown University as he made final revisions to his manuscript in 1949, opted not to embrace the postwar trend toward the humorous academic satire, which included a number of novels written by academics (or their spouses). Given that this approach had already proven generally successful, it is necessary to ask why Redding disdained it. The answer can be found in the incompatibility of the exigencies and implications of the white campus novel genre with the realities of black educational life.

The growing popularity of such satires at midcentury has been usefully interpreted as reflecting, at least in part, educators' dissatisfaction with the increasing professionalization of the university and with growing public anti-intellectualism and antipathy toward the left-wing political views commonly ascribed to university faculty. In addition, as Leslie Fiedler implies in his 1964 essay, "The War against the Academy," the portraits of the absurdity and venality of university teachers and administrators that litter what Fiedler calls the "anti-College novel" of the late 1940s and 1950s bespeak and even propagate a cynical dismissal of the purpose of higher education, especially in the liberal arts.[9] The Anglo-American academic novel's long history of exhibiting what Robert F. Scott calls "a seemingly irresistible tendency to trivialize academic life" (83) reduces its ability to offer any kind of serious social critique. The genre of campus fiction may be seen as inherently conservative in that sense, tending as it does toward the insularity of the comedy of manners made up of a series of conventionalized figures engaging in rituals at once arcane and silly. In the words of literary historian John O. Lyons, "The thinness and pallidness" of academic life as a subject for fiction "are perhaps a convention; perhaps as much a convention as that which demands that the life outside the academy be vital and interesting.... The academic type in fiction has often been conventionalized and labeled [with] satire and ridicule so that the novelist and his readers can quickly get back to the real world of men or the forest where true education takes place.... Such conventions are formidable" (xvii). As Hester Pine summarizes the prevailing characterization of college faculty in her satiric campus novel, *Beer for the Kitten* (1939), "All people on college faculties can be divided into the following categories: social termites, academic guppies, intellectual poor-white trash, and literary stumble-bums" (136). According to David Lodge, "The ultimate secret of the campus novel's deep appeal" is that "academic conflicts are relatively harmless, safely insulated from the real world and its somber concerns—or capable of transforming those concerns into a form of stylized play.... That is why it belongs to the literature of escape, and why we never tire of it" (35).

Whereas the mid-twentieth-century academic novel and its many offspring in subsequent decades take as a given the notion that the college campus is a circumscribed environment whose hothouse ideas and politics wilt in the harsh light of the real world, *Stranger and Alone* takes the position that, for blacks, higher education *is* the real world. Demonstrating both the relevance of education to "real life" and the centrality of "academic" debate to political discourse, *Stranger and Alone* presents the reader with a generic revision that is simultaneously a political intervention, presciently revealing the ease with which the typical narrative of the postwar campus novel would make itself complicit in marginalizing the intellectual work of university communities. At the same time, Redding's novel explores the complexities of the position of historically black colleges in the decades preceding the civil rights movement: these campuses were hardly ivory towers. Historically black institutions found themselves prey to a host of problems largely irrelevant to the small liberal arts colleges and state universities that provide the settings for most campus fiction; many of these problems derived from practical issues of funding and accreditation as well as more abstract questions about their utility and purpose. Consequently, these institutions were in no position to shelter their faculties and students. White intellectuals commonly perceived these schools as spaces in which African Americans could find respite from the burden of life in a racist society, if only for the period of their study; Redding debunks such myths.[10]

Contemptuous though Redding might have been of some of his colleagues in black higher education, to produce a narrative arguing for the complete irrelevance of the black college at this moment in history would have been an unhelpful assault rather than the constructive criticism he sought to offer. Specifically, Redding demonstrates that, far from being sheltered from the viciousness of race politics outside its walls, the black college is thoroughly permeated by it. Though the students at New Hope sing songs affirming that their alma mater offers a haven within "sacred walls" whose beauty "shall e'er be on our hearts engraven" (*Stranger* 10), they cannot ignore the fact that their school is run entirely by white administrators and professors, some of whom espouse openly racist doctrines they defend as scientific fact and all of whom have a vested interest in maintaining the status quo. Politically liberal professors, a staple target in satirical academic fiction set on white campuses, are rare and fleeting presences at New Hope, where a young female teacher is fired for remarking that "the yellow peril was the streak up some men's backs" (24). The only black professor at New Hope, Dr. Clarkson, urges Howden to promise "that we will not bring up the race question," which Clarkson considers "a nuisance" (53). But Howden, assigned Madison Grant's *The Passing of the Great Race* by his young white sociology professor, lacks the requisite intellectual position outside the racist economy of the curriculum from which to recognize "the scholarship of prejudice" and engage in the "Socratic dialogue" the professor disingenuously claims to seek as he lectures his class with racist invective (48). Rather, Howden merely determines that "his grim struggle with abstract thought [has] given him a headache" (47–48).

The distance of the black campus novel from its white counterpart is probably clearest in Redding's depiction of the faculty at New Hope. While campus novels set at white colleges could feel free to mock professors' politics and beliefs as out of step with those embraced in the "real" world, *Stranger and Alone* depicts professors as representatives of the dominant social order. The black university presented by Redding is thus an extension of a broader pattern of oppression, not a vantage point from which to critique it. Indeed, the lone student who objects to the professor's lecture is expelled as a result.

The discussion of the role to be played in American society by African Americans after World War II began to take on its now-familiar contours before the war's end was even in sight, and the role of the historically black college was crucial to the debate. The worrisome question was how black colleges, historically aimed at producing undergraduates with "useful" degrees, would be viewed in an environment in which university education was destined to expand to include a broader swath of the American public than ever before, upping the educational ante for participation in the professions across the board. (In 1940, 75 percent of American adults had never finished high school, while only 5 percent had finished college [Mayer 215]; after 1945, the rapid expansion of the system of higher education, coupled with the GI Bill and other Cold War–era federal programs aimed at increasing the number of American students studying math and science at the university level, began the inexorable reversal of those statistics.) In this changing context, would black colleges remain financially viable? Would they continue to function, as many did, with black deans and presidents but boards of trustees made up largely of whites, a situation that inevitably created a power differential and led to mistrust of black educators by precisely the people they sought to teach? Educator Leander L. Boykin articulates both the difficulty of the transition and what was ultimately at stake: "The truth of the matter is," he wrote in 1943, "this is not just another war. It is a social revolution.... If readjustments are to be made peacefully and without a bloody revolution, it is important that we have an integrated and cooperative program of socio-economic-civic education that will supplement our national planning and effort.... The Negro colleges will undoubtedly play a big role in this transition to the new society" (595–96).

Though the questions being asked were propelled by a new urgency, they were certainly not new. African Americans desperate to gain literacy almost universally saw black schools and colleges founded during Reconstruction as an unambiguous good. In addition, the field of black education provided numerous nineteenth-century political leaders (among them Thomas W. Cardozo and James Walker Hood), and teachers were a potent source of community organizing. Yet by the 1920s and 1930s, the enthusiasm of the previous decades had begun to slacken, the logical result, as civil rights historian Adam Fairclough argues, of the observable reality of the decoupling of political progress and economic equality from black education. Though African Americans had for decades believed that increased levels of black literacy and higher education would lead to higher standards of living and more political power, that belief was becoming harder and harder to justify:

> To equate education with black empowerment, however, invites numerous objections. The most obvious is that education did not straightforwardly empower black southerners. For one thing, the development of black education in the south was not characterized by linear progress: it was slow and haphazard, and things sometimes went from bad to worse.... That educational disparities widened after blacks lost the right to vote underlines the point: black political power waned even though black literacy had increased. (Fairclough 67)

According to Fairclough, by the Great Depression, when the action of *Stranger and Alone* begins, "social scientists and black intellectuals" had become "increasingly skeptical about the liberating effects of formal education" (68). At the same time, however, few observers were willing openly to criticize an institution so fraught with historical and political significance. In a lengthy essay, "The Past, Present, and Future of the Negro College" (1933), published on the eve of his retirement, Kelly Miller, dean of Howard University's Arts and Sciences Department and author of a weekly column that appeared in more than one hundred newspapers, addressed the issues most germane to the debate. Although the black college of the 1930s had failed to provide the expected number of leaders in politics and religion and had produced "superficiality, sham and pretense" in some of its graduates and professors, "the Negro college" had proved its value:

> It has for all time expelled the widely entertained doubt of the Negro's educability.... The value of this demonstration is beyond all calculation as concerns the welfare of the Negro as part of the white man's cultural scheme....

Through this educated class the Negro is able to state his own cause, in his own tongue, and plead the just claims of his race before the bar of public opinion.... Try to imagine, if you can, what would now be the fate of the Negro if the influence of the college, during the past seventy years, had been withdrawn. (412, 416)

Miller argues on behalf of a more strategic investment in the black college's purpose, which he sees as being the provision of four-year degrees in fields relevant to African Americans; graduate programs were better provided by white institutions, which had larger endowments and greater resources. That a divide exists between the majority-white attitude and that of blacks toward higher education is obvious to Miller, and he suggests that African American educators do themselves no favors by attempting to mimic white ones, comparing the effort to "catch up" to that of a farmer who attempts to create a straight furrow by lining up his plow with a moving object on the horizon: "Precisely at the time when the [doctoral] degree itself is losing its significance in the estimation of the education world, the Negro seems to be carried away with its talismanic power.... The college world of today is undergoing profound adjustment to meet the shifting demands of the age.... Time wasted in mimicry is lost to effective results" (418). But at no point does Miller intimate that the black college should abandon its position altogether; its work is simply too important. (Miller's view that "it seems the wisest policy that boards of control should be predominantly white and composed of the very best men of the country, North and South, who have a vital interest in the higher development of Negro life" [419] is presented by Redding in *Stranger and Alone* as a hypocritical stance made obsolete by the shift already in evidence toward black boards of trustees.) "Whatever the role of the college for white youth," white social anthropologist Ina Corinne Brown wrote almost a decade later, "the Negro college cannot escape its responsibility" (378). Just months after Pearl Harbor, Brown is already looking ahead to the end of the war, drawing implicit parallels between what she repeatedly calls the "reconstruction" that will follow World War II: "There is no hope of a return to normalcy after this war, even if pre-war conditions were regarded as desirable," writes Brown. "Nor can we hope that the post-war reconstruction will be accomplished in a brief period.... Unless we destroy one another so that the past 300 years are reversed, we must go on toward an interdependent world of cooperation among peoples" (380). Her use of the hortatory voice notwithstanding, Brown neatly elides the obligations of nonblacks in her vision of the race-neutral democracy of the future:

> In the total world population the colored peoples are in the majority, and no peace can be permanent, no world order just or lasting that denies to them freedom to exercise the rights and duties of citizens in whatever political or geographical unit of which they may be members.... Will the American Negroes be prepared to make their contribution to the staggering task that lies ahead? One of the major responsibilities of the Negro college is that of helping Negro youth seek not only advantages for themselves but to gain knowledge, insight and understanding which will enable them to make a contribution to the progressive reconstruction of society not only in this country but throughout the world. (381)

To argue against the purpose of black colleges, then, meant taking a highly unpopular stance. Zora Neale Hurston, for example, was roundly criticized for labeling small black colleges "begging joints" in a brief but pointed 1945 essay in the *American Mercury* in which she argued that such institutions did more harm than good by encouraging the poor to waste their money on a second-rate education with the result that graduates "cannot fit in where they think they belong, but will not adjust themselves to their level of fitness" (941). Hurston notes sardonically that although "Chitterling Switch 'college' in the backwoods of Mississippi" was "a natural part of the times" in the nineteenth century, these schools are "unburied corpses" in the postwar era (942). Hurston exempts such well-known universities as Howard and Fisk from her critique, but she also admonishes her readers that "most all the Northern white colleges" and "the leading universities of Europe, from Scandinavia to Spain" are accessible to black students (942). (In a characteristically iconoclastic move, Hurston vociferously protested the *Brown* decision nine years later.)[11] While Hurston's views were eccentric, her critique struck home; Moon's *Without Magnolias* features a negative portrayal of Laura Burroughs, a character identified by

Charles J. Heglar as clearly representing Hurston. Burroughs appears at a social event at a black college "on the lookout for material to write one of the Menckenlike articles for which she found a fairly steady market among certain pseudo-intellectual magazines" (qtd. in Heglar 390).

Though Redding was an avowed integrationist who saw *Brown* as a victory for African Americans, he, like Hurston, had strong reservations in the 1940s about the value of black colleges in the South. The portraits he gives of black college faculty in *No Day of Triumph* are merciless: "Negro schoolmen," he writes, "are terrific snobs, the true bourgeoisie.... They are a bulwark against positive action, liberal or even independent thought, and spiritual and economic freedom" (119). He discovers "a shocking indecency in their intellectual pretensions"; although "they were an intensely race-conscious lot," they lacked "real pride in it and any real faith in its future" (120). Yet Redding saves his real vitriol for the college's president, characterizing his attitude as "testy captiousness" (121); the president gives an address in which he berates the faculty to the students:

> Surely this was not an institution of learning, of higher learning! No wonder, then, that a terrible apathy, cloaked in job-saving dilettantism, had replaced the enthusiasm of the earliest days of Negro education.... I wondered how I could have forgotten the snobbery and the moral weakness, the paternalism, the downright administrative bullying, and the almost psychopathic hurly-burly of much that passed for education. (123)

As he wrote *Stranger and Alone*, then, Redding was keenly aware of the issues and motivated by an outrage he considered fully justified. In 1945, in his regular column in the *Afro-American*, Redding inveighed against the system as a whole, sounding much like Hurston: "Like it or not, it remains true that, with only the doubtful exception of Howard, there is not a colored liberal arts college in the land" ("Second Look," September 15, 1945, 4). Yet while Redding's views had been received favorably in a work of nonfiction in 1942, they were less palatable to critics in a novel eight years later. *Stranger and Alone* borrows liberally from *No Day of Triumph*, as several reviewers, including Ulysses Lee, John Lovell Jr., and Ralph Ellison, noted at the time. A general consensus held, however, that *Stranger and*

Alone was distinctly overshadowed by the earlier work: Ellison points out that in the novel, Redding's "writing lacks the high quality that marked the autobiographical *No Day of Triumph*" ("Collaborator" BR3), while Lovell remarks that "at no point does" *Stranger and Alone* "rise to the fine exuberance or stern revelation of the best passages of *No Day of Triumph*" (69). Lee articulates most clearly the central complaint: "Through the novel flit familiar images from an earlier book. But though some of the sketches of the latter half of *No Day of Triumph* are extended here, they are merely more detailed, not deepened" (181).

This flattening out of the novel's action is not an artistic failure but a deliberate strategy with a larger purpose, as the earlier manuscripts show. Like Yerby, Redding understood the politics of genre and chose fiction to communicate what he thought might go unread by or be less persuasive to the average reader in a work of history or sociology. Like Yerby, Redding also saw the popular fiction's potential both for harmful reductionism and for revolutionary cultural work. In a column written on the occasion of Thomas Dixon's 1946 death, Redding recalls his first childhood encounter with Dixon's "obscene" novels, which "haunted" Redding's "mind"; though Redding ultimately concludes, in a moment of striking political naïveté, that "nobody now believes that race-hatred can accomplish anything good," he acknowledges that there were once "millions of American whites" who idealized Dixon and would have considered "his passing a calamitous loss" ("Second Look," April 20, 1946, 4). Two decades later, in 1967, Redding became possibly the only black critic in America to review William Styron's *The Confessions of Nat Turner* positively, noting that "facing the reality [of southern history] was a job for the novelist" and that *Confessions* "serves, like all good novels, a social function too" ("Fateful" W18). That "social function" was as obvious to Redding as it was to Yerby: in a society in which, as Redding's contemporary C. Hugh Holman put it in 1950, "the masses . . . for over a century have learned their history from their novelists" (392), fiction could and did remold popular conceptions of historical "fact."

Yet unlike Yerby, Redding opted not to entice the reader to engage with revisionist historiography through exotic characters and overwrought plot devices that, as Yerby straightforwardly notes, drew in the "little blue-haired Southern ladies in tennis shoes" who "went on to find out who Stephen Fox was screwing tonight, which was what interested them" (J. L. Hill, "Interview" 210–11).[12] Nor did he seek to elicit sympathy from his readers for characters trapped in intolerable situations occasioned by their racist surroundings. Instead, the published version of *Stranger and Alone* veered sharply in another direction. Redding's refusal to pander to the reader in search of a heroic, downtrodden character, an exciting plot, or even the folksy "local color" Moon had so faithfully provided in *Without Magnolias* is breathtaking in its strictness. Set almost exclusively on anonymous campuses and in charmless southern towns, the book also offers a protagonist who evokes in the reader little sympathy and only a dispassionate, formal interest in his actions.

More a cipher than a character in his final incarnation, Howden is transmogrified in successive manuscripts into a walking manifestation of the failure of the African American educational system to awaken a sense of higher purpose or appreciation of human commonality. Redding's titles reflect his shifting priorities; the character who inhabits "The Secret Life of Gaynor Howden" exhibits a warmth, curiosity, and imagination entirely absent in the "stranger" of the final novel. Characterized by a pure self-interest entirely unadulterated by reservations or insight, Shelton Howden begins and ends "alone." So does the reader—denied the pleasures of sentimental identification with Howden, the reader must confront his or her expectations for a specifically African American academic novel, a genre caught between competing imperatives that can neither allow itself to laugh nor encourage its readers to cry.

Far from denigrating higher education as irrelevant, then, the novel ultimately demands that learning be considered crucial. Yet the centrality of higher education for African Americans in the struggle for racial equality also demands that it be open to revision and criticism, lest its status as a sacred cow impede its efficacy. Thus, in its rejection of either the pastoral or the satirical comedic form that characterizes the academic novel in its mid-twentieth-century incarnation, Redding's book intervenes politically in the long-standing debate over education for African Americans, which had reached a crisis point by the early 1950s and in which Redding was deeply involved professionally and personally. (While Redding was revising his novel in 1949, his brother, prominent civil rights lawyer Louis L. Redding, had begun work on the landmark *Parker v. University of Delaware* case, which would result in the first legal desegregation of a state university at the undergraduate level and would lead to his arguing the Delaware case decided as part of *Brown*.) Saunders Redding saw, with a clarity he was perhaps uniquely positioned to enjoy, the challenges ahead for black education; he also realized that the African American academic novel could afford neither the luxury of poking fun at its subject nor the risks of boring or alienating its potential readership by indulging in the clichés or sanctimony of the traditional protest novel. The development of *Stranger and Alone* from manuscript to book reveals the process through which Redding determined his approach to the genre and his contribution to the debate unfolding around him. The narrative is flat, the better to delineate the urgency of its central claim—that cherished beliefs about the link between literacy and freedom aside, true progress cannot happen organically given the educational system's inherent constraints. Shelton Howden is no anomaly but rather the natural product of the education available to him.

Redding's intense interest in the depiction of black campus life is evidenced by a review of the manuscript version of the planned sequel to *Stranger and Alone*. The manuscript version of "The Cross and the Crown" begins with Perkins Wimbush's death and Shelton Howden's accession to the presidency of Arcadia College. However, by the time he began writing, Redding had clearly determined that his deliberately distanced approach to his flattened characters had been unsuccessful and needed to be revisited. "The Cross and the Crown," intended to describe the redemption of Shelton Howden, is told not from the dispassionate third-person perspective of *Stranger and Alone* but through a colloquial, even chatty, first-person narrator, Sam (whose name, Redding tells the reader at some length, is a bastardization of his actual name, the British Soame, which no one in the South can pronounce). Sam's/Soame's opening gambit is to address the reader directly: "This is not really my story, but since I'm telling it, you've a right to know, and it's probably my obligation to say, who I am" ("Cross" 6). Sam/Soame offers the rounded portraits of Perkins Wimbush and Howden that were so carefully excised from the earlier book. In the unpublished manuscript, for example, the reader learns more details about Wimbush's heritage as well as his lifelong inner turmoil, which reveals itself as he approaches death in "sudden spells of violence" during which "the obscenities would flow from him in a self-hypnotizing torrent" (1).

While he evidently revisited the success of those choices in the sequel, the style and narrative of *Stranger and Alone* purposefully draw attention to the background conventions of the protest novel—a sympathetic but hapless African American overwhelmed by social forces beyond his control—against which Redding's novel delineates its purpose. In so doing, Redding forces readers to read the story neither as an individual tragedy nor as a universal tale of the perfidy of humankind, pace critic Blyden Jackson, who declared that *Stranger and Alone* was "a study of Uncle Tomism that illuminates *sub specie aeternitatis* the ubiquitous errand-boys for Caesar" ("Essay," 342). Rather, the story emerges as a historically specific indictment of a system too crucial to the lives of millions of people to be abandoned yet too flawed to be allowed to continue as it is. Rejecting the protest genre while simultaneously avoiding the satirical campus novel form then becoming prominent, Redding treads a careful path between competing options, highlighting the fact that the ideological work performed by genre is not only context-specific but also, at least for African American writers in the late 1940s, race-specific. His novel is a generic stranger, positioned alone among the other "lesser lights" of postwar black literature and on the cusp of the successful treatment of many of its themes in *Invisible Man* and contemporaneous with but unable to unreservedly join the 1950s academic satire. The book thus provides a final fascinating testament to the immediate need to return to the writers presented in this volume as we rethink and more fairly evaluate our view of the postwar African American novel.

Conclusion

A representation of the immediate postwar period in African American literature as little more than a series of repetitive protest novels does a disservice to an era that was in fact marked by experimentation and debate. Nevertheless, all of the authors presented here used their postwar debut novels to respond to the protest genre—some defiantly, others obliquely. And the experience of writing these early books and their subsequent reception also clearly marked the remainder of these authors' careers. Chester Himes and Frank Yerby became permanent expatriates in the mid-1950s, preferring to live and work outside the constraints of American society and away from the expectations of American readers and publishers; both developed sizable European audiences, with Himes's work becoming increasingly experimental and Yerby's generally becoming more hackneyed. William Gardner Smith, who also moved permanently overseas in the 1950s, wrote two novels during that time set in his native Philadelphia, with both seeming to respond more directly to the protest imperative than did his first book. *Anger at Innocence* (1950), marks Smith's foray into "raceless" fiction, while *South Street* (1954), in a striking reversal, deals with African American militancy in the face of racially motivated violence. Neither, however, was a success. Saunders Redding remained in the United States but never wrote another novel, opting instead to focus on his academic career and nonfiction.

By the mid-1990s, when most critics agree that contemporary African American novelists had reached a level of prominence previously unknown, Himes, Yerby, Smith, and Redding were dead, and most of their books were out of print. As scholars looked back over the path that had led simultaneously to the enormous popularity of Toni Morrison and Terry McMillan and the postmodern sophistication of Charles Johnson and Trey Ellis, critical evaluations of black literature in the immediate postwar period began to take on their familiar contours. The excitement and intellectual ferment of those years were forgotten as writers and critics alike sought to emphasize the disjuncture between their work and the outmoded Wrightian protest novel, which came to be a pars pro toto signifier of the period between *Native Son* and *Invisible Man*. For example, Ernest Gaines, whose novels are widely read and regularly taught, has emphasized repeatedly in interviews that his influences do not include "any black writers" because "the black writers are so much more interested in content—you know, putting it down like it is—and the style is sort of secondary" (Fitzgerald and Marchant 13–14). "What I've always been saying," he told Mary Ellen Doyle, "is that the blueprint for Black literature is not *Native Son*" (150).

Yet the novel for which Gaines is arguably best known, *A Lesson before Dying*, is most profitably read as a response to *Native Son*, whose central events Gaines's work reflects. The story of Jefferson, an illiterate African American teenager in rural Louisiana who is convicted of having murdered a white man and is subsequently sentenced to death, *A Lesson before Dying* begins where *Native Son* ends, with a courtroom scene in which a defense attorney argues for clemency based on Jefferson's reduced capacity. Jefferson, he argues, could no more act with malice aforethought than could a hog. The local schoolteacher, Grant Wiggins, is persuaded by his aunt and Jefferson's godmother to teach Jefferson to "die like a man," with self-respect and dignity. Initially reluctant, Wiggins ultimately helps Jefferson find his voice, rendered in the penultimate chapter of the book as a journal entry in Jefferson's misspelled and ungrammatical idiom. Though Jefferson is executed, he meets his death with poise and courage; Wiggins, who has previously disdained his community and his profession, is reconciled to his life and future.

The novel is set in 1948—not coincidentally the year in which Gaines, who had moved from a sharecropper's house on a former plantation in Pointe Coupée Parish to Vallejo, California, as a teenager, began to write fiction about African Americans in Louisiana. In this context, the novel's foregrounding of the theme of the redemptive power of the written word makes available a reading of the text as a meditation on precisely the questions explored in this study regarding the position of the protest genre in postwar African American fiction. Grant Wiggins, torn between what he perceives to be his duty to his race and his community and his desire to deny the limitations that duty imposes on him, struggles, like Himes's protagonists, to find a narrative that will enable him to find a way out of his dilemma. In a much-discussed moment in the novel, Wiggins sits in a bar listening to two old men tell stories about and impersonate Jackie Robinson. He realizes that telling stories about black sports heroes provides these men with ways to articulate their thwarted desires in an accessible vernacular. Nevertheless, he rejects such racially specific narratives as fundamentally useless, noting that he also has heard of a condemned man who begged in vain for help from "Mr. Joe Louis" as he was dragged to the electric chair.

At the same time, despite his best efforts, Wiggins is unable to tap into the "universality" of James Joyce's modernism. As he listens to the old men, he also recalls a speaker at his university:

> The little Irishman … this little white man with the thick accent, talking to us about Irish literature. He spoke of Yeats, O'Casey, Joyce—names I had never heard before. I sat there listening, listening, trying to remember everything he said. And a name he repeated over and over was Parnell. And he told us how some Irishmen would weep this day at the mention of the name Parnell. Parnell. Parnell. Parnell. Then he spoke of James Joyce. He told about Joyce's family, his religion, his education, his writing. He spoke of a book called *Dubliners* and a story in the book titled "Ivy Day in the Committee Room." Regardless of race, regardless of class, that story was universal, he said. (*Lesson* 89)

Yet the story's transcendent universality is not available to Wiggins. Instead, he recalls that upon first hearing about Joyce's story and then while reading and rereading it, he was struck by its unfamiliarity, its *lack* of universality, its uncompromising specificity: "I could not find," Grant says, "the universality that the little Irishman had spoken of" (90). His recollection of the racially specific circumstances under which he acquires a copy of the text to read—borrowing it from a black professor at his university who has to borrow the book from a white colleague—marks the turning point in his wavering willingness to help Jefferson. "I was not thinking now about Jackie Robinson, or Joe Louis, or the little Irishman," he thinks as he finishes his reminiscence, "I was thinking about that cold, depressing cell uptown" (90). Unable to reconcile the two competing narrative imperatives—that of the racially specific stories of Jackie Robinson and Joe

Louis that testify to the pressing need for social and political reform and that of the "universal" fiction of Joyce—Wiggins looks to another genre altogether. The result is Jefferson's journal entry, which takes the onus of providing the narrative off Wiggins.

The issues that animated the debates of the late 1940s have not yet been resolved. Sixty years after the publication of the books discussed in the preceding chapters, the protest form continues to cast a long shadow over African American fiction. While African American writers today produce an extraordinary range of work in a stunning array of genres, the novel of social realism, even—perhaps especially—as it shades into ghetto gothic, retains an undeniable fascination for American readers. In 2009, cinemas across the United States hosted sold-out screenings of *Precious*, the film adaptation of Sapphire's award-winning 1996 novel, *Push*. *Precious* tells the story of Clareece "Precious" Jones, an obese African American teenager who is repeatedly raped and impregnated by her father, as a result of which she not only gives birth to a child with Down syndrome but contracts HIV. She subsequently endures physical, psychological, and sexual abuse by her mother, who considers the girl a rival for her father's attention. With the help of a caring social worker and a dedicated teacher, however, the previously illiterate Precious learns to read and write; with literacy comes self-actualization. The horrors of Precious Jones's life obviously dwarf those of Bigger Thomas's, both in the novel and in the film, whose "methodical commitment to abjection," in the words of reviewer Dana Stevens, results in "robbing the audience of all agency." The narrative is, in fact, so extreme a reworking of the Wrightian model that it arguably demands evaluation as satire. Yet critics' response to *Precious* largely echoes the reception of *Native Son* seven decades ago as a harrowing, important work. Given that African American film in many respects enjoys the same dominant cultural position the novel once occupied, it seems worthwhile to ask whether films too will be subjected to critical misapprehension. Perhaps *Precious* will be, in film histories yet to be written, represented as a new peak, with the films that follow inevitably cast as imitators of a successful formula. Alternatively, however, we can hope that literary history is not necessarily doomed to repeat its mistakes and that peaks-and-valleys models for African American cultural production can be discarded in favor of paradigms that do justice to the complexity of their subjects.

Notes

INTRODUCTION

1. I have omitted Chinua Achebe's *Things Fall Apart* (1958) and Lorraine Hansberry's *A Raisin in the Sun* (1959) for geographical and generic reasons.

CHAPTER ONE

1. Wald notes that "*Iron City* was intended in some respects as a corrective" (viii) to the tendency Brown saw in Wright and Himes to portray African American characters as victims. Despite this shift of focus, however, it is hard to see Brown's novel as anything but a protest novel.

2. Werner devotes one chapter to Wright and another to Gwendolyn Brooks; while Werner's readings of their work are original, it would be difficult to argue that either author qualifies as "undervalued."

3. This idea of the centrality of the black experience to an understanding of modernity more generally is, according to Paul Gilroy, an important part of Wright's embrace of existentialism. Gilroy cites C. L. R. James's remark that Wright saw the experience of the black man in 1930s American society as providing "insight into what today is the universal attitude of the *modern* personality" ("Black Atlantic" 159).

4. In addition to James Baldwin's scathing 1961 response to *On the Road* ("Black Boy"), see Mark Richardson's "Peasant Dreams" for a detailed critique that baldly links Kerouac's real-life racist diatribes to his fiction "across a spectrum running from embarrassing, to bad, to abominable" (231).

5. Though it is true that a few publishers, notably Dial Press and Charles Scribner's Sons, issued novels by African American writers without expressly identifying the authors as black, doing so was hardly standard procedure.

CHAPTER TWO

1. Franklin Roosevelt's Executive Order 8802 stipulated that government contractors could not discriminate among workers based on race or national origin; however, the order contained no provision for enforcement.

2. In a move that perfectly illustrates the dominance of the Wright-Ellison pairing at the center of the traditional critical model of the postwar black novel, Dickson-Carr relies only on *Invisible Man* to bolster his thesis that the "inevitable result of

the hegemony maintained by the Wright school of social document fiction was a backlash against its form and content" (88).

3. See Mullen's thought-provoking "Breaking the Signifying Chain" for a fuller discussion of the place of class analysis in African American critical thought; see Breu's "Freudian Knot or Gordian Knot?" for a thorough discussion of Himes's embrace of violence as a "positive" signifier for black masculinity.

4. Much of the pioneering theory in this area has focused on Jewish humor. Martin Grotjahn's summary of the logic behind Jews telling anti-Semitic jokes suggests how the practice strips the racist (or sexist or homophobic) insult of its power: "It is as if the Jew tells his enemies: You do not need to attack us. We can do that ourselves—and even better. But we can take it and we will come out all right" (25).

5. *The End of a Primitive* was published under that title at this time only in France; the edition copyrighted by the New American Library was edited substantially for "obscenity" and retitled *The Primitive*. References here are to the 1990 restored version, which makes Himes's revision of the protest novel form clearer than did previous editions.

6. Bergson's disguise is related to W. E. B. Du Bois's notion of the veil. Du Bois's suggestion that African Americans live "behind the veil" and as such experience a double consciousness that enables them to see themselves both through their own eyes and as they are perceived by others provides one of the main paradigms for understanding black identity.

7. According to Himes's biographers, Edward Margolies and Michel Fabre, Walter and his wife are modeled on Ralph and Rose Ellison (186).

CHAPTER THREE

1. The same anonymous reviewer or reviewers also recommended Adam Clayton Powell Jr.'s *Marching Blacks* and folklorist B. A. Botkin's *Lay My Burden Down*, an anthology of slave narratives, warning readers that the former was "violent and very disturbing" but "important" and reassuring them that not only had the latter been compiled by an eminent scholar but "most of the selections are very short" (427–28).

2. The market for fiction about educated and affluent African Americans remained problematic throughout the decade; nevertheless, as Saunders Redding found, it did exist. For a detailed description of Yerby's experience with the attempted publication of *This Is My Own*, see Gene Jarrett, *Deans* 150–52.

3. For two critical perspectives on the Confederate romance, also called the "plantation novel," see Nichols, "Slave Narratives"; Gates, *Figures*.

4. Like Arceneaux and LeBlanc, the name *Waguespack* belongs to a prominent Louisianan Creole family. The Waguespacks are descended from a German immigrant, Joseph Waguespack, who bought a French Creole owner's plantation after

the Civil War in a sheriff's sale and farmed sugarcane throughout the nineteenth century in the region in which Yerby's novels are set.

5. In an early synopsis of *The Foxes of Harrow* that Yerby apparently submitted to an editor at Dial, Stephen Fox's end remains overdetermined, though somewhat differently, as he becomes a victim less of the changes wrought to the South by the end of the Civil War than of southerners themselves: "Stephen is killed by his own men as he tries to stem the rout before New Orleans as [Admiral David G.] Farragut steams up the river" (Letter to editor 3).

6. Stephen Fox also produces a daughter, Julie, with his second wife, Odalie's sister, Aurore. Largely undeveloped as an individual character, Julie marries a Bostonian and returns north with him, abandoning Harrow.

7. Mitchell's response to critics who noted that she had repeated long-discredited tales of Yankee brutality, such as grave robbing during Sherman's March to the Sea, as if they were truth was to disclose that her "sources" were texts by regional historians unfettered by concerns about accuracy. For more information about Mitchell's research methods and the responses to them, see Chadwick 183–211.

8. The reception of the latter work can perhaps be inferred from the fact that the *American Historical Review* did not mention or review *Black Reconstruction* when it appeared. For a fuller explication of the Dunning School's influence and attempts made to counter it, the standard reference is still John Hope Franklin's *Reconstruction after the Civil War* (1961).

9. Viewers of the film will have a less strong sense of this perspective than readers of the book, largely because, although Mitchell attested to her depiction of the Klan as "common knowledge to every southerner" (qtd. in Chadwick 196), Selznick, troubled by the resurgence of the organization in the 1930s, had no desire to glorify it. As a result, as Thomas Cripps and other film scholars have noted, the film leaves unnamed the vigilante group that retaliates against "Shantytown" after Scarlett is assaulted by a white man (not a black, as in the novel).

10. This stunning lack of skepticism was noted almost immediately by C. Vann Woodward, as it has been in virtually every other subsequent critical treatment of Cash.

11. Buckmaster, like many of her contemporaries, saw in World War II the event that she believed would spur American writers to use historical fiction for progressive ends. "History, as pure history," she writes, "has no value whatever ... except the value of telling us how and why and with what weapons people fought for progress.... Perhaps the value is no more than that of an analogy, but analogies have proved singularly disarming and have made flexible many rigid minds" (170).

12. Discovering Gail naked with a Yankee soldier, her elder brother, Victor, responds with the violent irrationality of a jilted lover, killing the soldier, while her younger, more introspective, brother imagines Gail engaging in sexual intercourse in vivid, erotically charged language: "He realized with a sudden horror that there was a

vicarious pleasure in these mental images. 'God help me!' he murmured. 'God in his mercy, help me!'" ("Ignoble" 300).

13. In *Gone with the Wind*, John Wilkes is the patriarch of the Wilkes clan and the owner of the vast Twelve Oaks plantation.

14. The map is part of the Frank Yerby Papers in the Howard Gotlieb Collection at Boston University.

15. For further reading on the context of the Colfax massacre, see Steven Hahn's *A Nation under Our Feet* and Nicholas Lemann's *Redemption*. For the most recent and most thorough overviews of the Colfax massacre, see Charles Lane's *The Day Freedom Died* and LeeAnna Keith's *The Colfax Massacre*.

16. The description of the massacre survives in *The Vixens* in a somewhat abbreviated form (315–20). Taken out of the context of the other attacks, however, and stripped of the story delineating Isaac's community and Inch's political endeavors, the scene loses much of its impact. In *The Vixens*, the hero, Laird Fournois, tries to stop the massacre and is then attacked by the novel's archvillain, Hugh Duncan, whom Fournois kills. Duncan's death frees his mistress, who is Fournois's erstwhile lover, underscoring the fact that the events at Colfax are less a product of revisionist historiography than a means to effect romantic closure.

17. Although today James is a major figure in postcolonial and cultural studies, his work was largely ignored until the early 1970s, as historian Eugene Genovese notes in *In Red and Black* (155). Indeed, Stuart Hall and others argue that James's early writing, including *The Black Jacobins*, is even today not engaged as often or as critically as his later, more cultural-studies-oriented work.

18. Dunn died abruptly while in office after a brief illness, and there is still no consensus about whether his death was natural. In a detailed account published in *Phylon* in 1945, Marcus Christian lays out a persuasive argument that Dunn was poisoned; Yerby allows Dunn's illness to remain mysterious.

CHAPTER FOUR

1. Two attacks that drew widespread attention were the beating and blinding of veteran Isaac Woodard by police in Aiken, South Carolina, and the Georgia murder of two black veterans and their wives by a mob that dragged them from their car and shot them repeatedly. Smith refers specifically to the Woodard case in *Last of the Conquerors* (72).

2. For an overview of African American contributions to the war novel, see Jennifer C. James, "African American War Literature."

3. For an extensive treatment of films set in Berlin between 1946 and 1949, see Robert R. Shandley's *Rubble Films*. My point here is not that these views of Berlin were not legitimate but that Smith deliberately ignores these available tropes in his depiction of the city.

4. For a useful overview of the historically adversarial relationship between the culture of Berlin and the rest of Germany, see Ronald Taylor's *Berlin and Its Culture*.

5. The civil rights movement is often identified exclusively with the postwar period, especially the 1950s and early 1960s, but as Fehrenbach notes, those years "represented a continuation and intensification of social transformations that began in earnest during World War II" (19).

6. Especially useful examples of work in this field are Posnock's *Color and Culture* and Tania Friedel's *Racial Discourse and Cosmopolitanism in Twentieth-Century African American Writing*, as well as Paul Gilroy's groundbreaking (and controversial) *The Black Atlantic* and *Against Race*.

7. This is one of the objections raised, for example, by Simon Gikandi in his response to Gilroy's work in *The Black Atlantic* and *Against Race*. Gikandi argues that Gilroy "privileges Europe as the crucible of cosmopolitanism" and "represses alternative narratives of a pan-Africanist identity" (600). For my purposes, this is an interesting but not crucial distinction; what matters for Smith is not the Europeanness of Dawkins's encounters but their difference.

8. Possibly the most appropriate symbol of Hitler's intentions in Berlin is the Schwerbelastungskörper, an enormous (18 meters high) and extremely heavy (approximately 12,650 metric tons, or 27.8 million pounds) concrete weight Speer designed to test the Berlin-area marshland for its ability to withstand the pressure of the massive marble buildings he envisaged.

9. Hitler's dislike of Berlin "turned to a lasting hatred in January 1918, when the munitions workers went on strike, demanding an end to the war. 'What was the army fighting for,' he demanded bitterly, 'if the homeland itself no longer wanted victory?'" (Read and Fisher 23).

10. Issues of gender and sexuality received notable attention in general; feminist activity in Berlin was matched by early activism on behalf of homosexuals, much of it centered on the Institut für Sexualwissenschaft (Institute for Sexual Research) founded by Magnus Hirschfeld, who was driven by the Nazis into exile and died in France in 1935.

11. These objections do not argue that military personnel would not harbor anti-Semitic sentiments but rather that Doyle has shown no hint of prejudice before this scene and shows none after, so his comments appear uncharacteristic for him specifically.

12. *Veronika* was a blanket epithet applied to German women who engaged in sexual relationships with American soldiers; such women were also labeled, mostly by other Germans, *Amiliebchen* (roughly "Yank lovers") and "soldiers' brides." The term originated with the army newspaper *Stars and Stripes*, which ran a cartoon strip featuring a character named Veronica Dankeschön (Veronica Thank you very much), a seductive woman intent on spreading both venereal disease and Nazi propaganda.

13. Despite a musical pedigree that included degrees from Juilliard and Columbia University, Dixon was unable to find a permanent position as a conductor in the United States in the 1940s. As a result, he worked in Sweden, Germany, and Australia until 1970. His experience was typical: "'The symphony orchestra, as an institution,

was assumed to be an organization for white people," says Catherine French, president of the American Symphony Orchestra League" (qtd. in Wheeler 44).

14. See Fehrenbach's *Race after Hitler* for a detailed historical explanation of the biracial occupation children who "became a nexus around which social, cultural and scientific debates about the meaning of race—and its implications for postwar German society—whirled" (75).

15. The Hoffmans' house is located in the Tempelhof district, then as now an industrial and working-class section of Berlin.

CHAPTER FIVE

1. Gates persuasively argues that *To Make a Poet Black* establishes the links between individual works in a self-contained African American literary tradition, emphasizing the centrality of the vernacular while avoiding the simple essentialism that characterized earlier studies, such as Benjamin Brawley's *The Negro in Literature and Art in the United States* (1918): "It is this central and original thread of reasoning, valorizing indigenously black forms, which confirms the legacy of *To Make a Poet Black*" ("Introduction" xxiv).

2. It is not clear why Redding never published a second novel. Scholar Faith Berry notes that "had he been offered the choice, he would have devoted his literary career more to writing fiction than scholarly books" (5). He began to think about writing a sequel to *Stranger and Alone* in the early 1950s, and by 1959 he had secured both a Guggenheim Fellowship and a contract with Random House. Nevertheless, the sequel, which he intended to call *The Cross and the Crown*, remained largely unwritten.

3. I am omitting James Weldon Johnson's *The Autobiography of an Ex-Colored Man* and Nella Larsen's *Quicksand* because although they include brief depictions of black college life, they are not set primarily on college campuses.

4. The author of a series of books addressing the literary contributions and political situation of African Americans in the 1940s and widely recognized as, to use Arthur P. Davis's phrase in a 1946 review of Moon's *A Primer for White Folks*, a "man of goodwill," Moon offers a substantially more nuanced portrait of African American life than does Hedden. Nevertheless, *Without Magnolias* ultimately relies for its effect on the imposition of the standard conflict (and dichotomies) of protest fiction onto its narrative.

5. Between 1944 and 1966, when he resigned as the newspaper chain's book review editor, Redding produced well over a thousand book reviews in his weekly column in the *Afro-American*.

6. These reviews can be found in the J. Saunders Redding Papers, Special Collections, John Hay Library, Brown University.

7. It is virtually impossible to determine the precise chronological order of Redding's drafts, but evidence suggests that he initially planned to write the book,

originally titled "Bright Bowl of Brass," from the perspective of a northern activist who, while organizing in the South, meets a former lover who is now married to a traitorous school superintendent, the model for *Stranger and Alone*'s protagonist, Shelton Howden.

8. Redding repeatedly used the phrase "the time on the clock of the world." It is the title both of one of his early columns in the *Afro-American* and of the first chapter of the earliest manuscript version to feature Howden as a protagonist ("Secret Life").

9. Fiedler calls the form "hopelessly middlebrow ... not so much transcendent explorations of the failures of institutions of higher learning as depressing symptoms of the way in which such institutions subserve the flight from excellence" (7).

10. In her widely read study *Killers of the Dream* (1949), Lillian Smith comments that although every historically black college was different, "all of them are alike in that their students and their faculties are cut off from the main-stream of American society ... and all have the certainty that whenever their graduates leave their 'retreat,' they will be thrust into a hostile society" (221).

11. Andrew Delbanco notes that Hurston's political views were "never very coherent" and suggests that "it is a mistake, really, to take her opinions too seriously," especially as she veered in the 1950s further and further toward a "belligerent conservatism" (106).

12. The repackaging of *Stranger and Alone* as a pulp romance for the abridged Popular Library paperback reprint of the novel is fascinating in this context. The cover features a fabricated pull quote ("'I've had a HUNDRED LOVERS!' Gerry Wimbush laughed mockingly behind the wheel of the speeding car") and an image of a dark man embracing a much lighter woman; the overall impression is that the novel's central focus is on their relationship and what the cover calls Howden's "mixed fury of rage and lust."

Works Cited

Agee, James, and Walker Evans. *Let Us Now Praise Famous Men: The American Classic, in Words and Photographs, of Three Tenant Families in the Deep South.* 1941; New York: Mariner, 2001.
Amis, Kingsley. *Lucky Jim.* 1954; New York: Penguin, 1993.
Anderson, Benedict. *From Imagined Communities: Reflections on the Origin and Spread of Nationalism.* London: Verso, 1983.
Anonymous. Review of *The Foxes of Harrow. College English* 7.7 (1946): 426–29.
Anonymous. Review of *If He Hollers Let Him Go. American Mercury* 62:266 (1945): 249.
Appiah, Kwame Anthony. *Cosmopolitanism: Ethics in a World of Strangers.* New York: Norton, 2006.
Baker, Houston. *Blues, Ideology, and Afro-American Fiction.* Chicago: University of Chicago Press, 1987.
Bald, Wambly. "Young Man Tackles Great Irony." *New York Post,* August 23, 1948.
Baldwin, James. "The Black Boy Looks at the White Boy." *Esquire,* May 1961.
Balfour, Alan. *Berlin: The Politics of Order, 1737–1989.* New York: Rizzoli, 1990.
Barkin, Kenneth D. "'Berlin Days' 1892–1894: W. E. B. Du Bois and German Political Economy." *Boundary 2* 27.3 (2000): 79–101.
Barrett, Lindon. "African American Slave Narratives: Literacy, the Body, Authority." *American Literary History* 7.3 (1995): 415–42.
Barton, Rebecca Chalmers. *Witnesses for Freedom: Negro Americans in Autobiography.* New York: Harper, 1948.
Bates, Gerri. "Images of European Women in William Gardner Smith's *Last of the Conquerors* and *The Stone Face.*" *MAWA Review* 6.2 (1991): 1–4.
Beck, Ulrich. *Cosmopolitan Vision.* Cambridge: Polity, 2006.
Bell, Bernard W. *The Contemporary African American Novel: Its Folk Roots and Modern Literary Branches.* Amherst: University of Massachusetts Press, 2004.
Bergson, Henri. *Laughter: An Essay on the Meaning of the Comic.* New York: Macmillan, 1914.
Berry, Faith. *A Scholar's Conscience: Selected Writings of J. Saunders Redding, 1942–1977.* Lexington: University Press of Kentucky, 1992.
"Black Authors Don't Know They Have Entered the Literary Canon until They See a CliffsNotes Version of Their Work." *Journal of Blacks in Higher Education* 32 (Summer 2001): 25.

Bone, Robert. *The Negro Novel in America*. New Haven: Yale University Press, 1958.
Bontemps, Arna. "Tough, Carnal Harlem." *New York Herald Tribune Weekly Book Review*, February 10, 1946.
Boris, Eileen. "'You Wouldn't Want One of 'Em Dancing with Your Wife': Racialized Bodies on the Job in World War II." *American Quarterly* 50.1 (1998): 77–108.
Bowers, Claude. *The Tragic Era: The Revolution after Lincoln*. Cambridge, Mass.: Riverside, 1929.
Boykin, Leander L. "The Survival and Function of the Negro College in a Changing Social Order." *Journal of Negro Education* 12.4 (1943): 589–99.
Branch, William. "Marketing the Products of American Negro Writers." In *The American Negro Writer and His Roots*. New York: American Society of African Culture, 1960.
Brawley, Benjamin. *The Negro in Literature and Art in the United States*. New York: Duffield, 1918.
Breu, Christopher. "Freudian Knot or Gordian Knot?: The Contradictions of Racialized Masculinity in Chester Himes' *If He Hollers Let Him Go*." *Callaloo* 26.3 (2003): 766–95.
Brice, Ashbel G. Unpublished review of *Last of the Conquerors*, August 10, 1948. Farrar, Straus, and Giroux Collection, New York Public Library, New York.
Brooks, Van Wyck. *The Confident Years: 1885–1915*. New York: Dent, 1955.
Brown, Ina Corinne. "The National Survey of Negro Higher Education and Post-War Reconstruction: The Place of the Negro College in Negro Life." *Journal of Negro Education* 11.3 (1942): 375–81.
Brown, Lloyd. *Iron City*. Intro. Alan Wald. 1951; Boston: Northeastern University Press, 1994.
Brown, Sterling A. "Count Us In." In *Primer for White Folks*, ed. Bucklin Moon. Garden City, N.Y.: Doubleday, 1945.
———. "The Negro Author and His Publisher." *Quarterly Review of Higher Education among Negroes* 9.3 (1941): 140–46.
Buckmaster, Henrietta. *Let My People Go: The Story of the Underground Railroad and the Growth of the Abolition Movement*. New York: Beacon, 1941.
Butcher, Margaret Just. *The Negro in American Culture, Based on Materials Left by Alain Locke*. New York: Knopf, 1956.
Cash, W. J. *The Mind of the South*. New York: Vintage, 1941.
Cavendish, Henry. "Negroes All Good ... White Folk All Bad." Review of *Without Magnolias*. *Chicago Daily Tribune*, May 15, 1949.
Chadwick, Bruce. *The Reel Civil War: Mythmaking in American Film*. New York: Knopf, 2001.
Chandler, G. Lewis. "Coming of Age: A Note on American Negro Novelists." *Phylon* 9.1 (1948): 25–29.
Christian, Marcus. "The Theory of the Poisoning of Oscar J. Dunn." *Phylon* 6.3 (1945): 254–66.

Coleman, Robin R. Means. *African American Viewers and the Black Situation Comedy: Situating Racial Humor.* New York: Garland, 1998.

Conrad, Earl. "The Blues School of Literature." *Chicago Defender,* December 22, 1945.

Coulter, E. Merton. *The South during Reconstruction.* Baton Rouge: Louisiana State University Press and Littlefield Fund for Southern History of the University of Texas, 1947.

Cripps, Thomas. "Winds of Change: *Gone with the Wind* and Racism as a National Issue." In *Recasting: Gone With the Wind in American Culture,* ed. Darden Asbury Pyron. Miami: University Presses of Florida, 1983.

Crouch, William Terry, ed. *What the Negro Wants.* Ed. Rayford W. Logan. Chapel Hill: University of North Carolina Press, 1944.

Crowther, Bosley. "'Foxes of Harrow,' Fox Film, Starring Rex Harrison and Maureen O'Hara, Bill at Roxy—'Desert Fury' at Paramount." Review of *The Foxes of Harrow. New York Times,* September 25, 1947.

Daly, Victor. *Not Only War: A Story of Two Great Conflicts.* 1932; New York: AMS, 1970.

Davis, Arthur P. *From the Dark Tower: Afro-American Writers, 1900–1960.* Washington, D.C.: Howard University Press, 1974.

———. "Men of Goodwill." Review of *A Primer for White Folks,* by Bucklin Moon. *Journal of Negro Education* 15.2 (1946): 201–4.

Dearborn, Mary V. *Mailer: A Biography.* New York: Mariner, 2001.

Delbanco, Andrew. "The Mark of Zora." *New Republic* 213.1 (1995): 30–35.

Demby, William. *Beetlecreek.* Intro. James C. Hall. Jackson: University Press of Mississippi, 1998.

Dickson-Carr, Darryl. *African American Satire: The Sacredly Profane Novel.* Columbia: University of Missouri Press, 2001.

Doyle, Mary Ellen. "A *MELUS* Interview: Ernest J. Gaines—'Other Things to Write About.'" *MELUS* 11 (1984): 59–81. Reprinted in *Conversations with Ernest Gaines,* ed. John Lowe. Jackson: University Press of Mississippi, 1994.

Du Bois, W. E. B. *Black Reconstruction in America.* 1935; New York: Free Press, 1998.

———. *Dusk of Dawn: An Essay toward an Autobiography of a Race Concept.* 1940; Franklin Center, Pa.: Franklin Library, 1980.

———. *The Philadelphia Negro: A Social Study.* 1899; New York: Oxford University Press, 2007.

———. "Reconstruction and Its Benefits." *American Historical Review* 15.4 (1910): 781–99.

Edgerton, Robert B. *Hidden Heroism: Black Soldiers in America's Wars.* Boulder, Colo.: Westview, 2002.

Ehrenreich, Barbara. *The Hearts of Men: American Dreams and the Flight from Commitment.* New York: Anchor, 1987.

Ellison, Ralph. "Collaborator with His Own Enemy." *New York Times Book Review,* February 19, 1950.

———. *Invisible Man.* 1952; New York: Vintage, 1995.

———. "The World and the Jug." In *Shadow and Act*. New York: Signet, 1967.
English, Daylanne K. "Selecting the Harlem Renaissance." *Critical Inquiry* 24.4 (1994): 807–22.
Fabre, Michel. "Interview with Chester Himes." In *Conversations with Chester Himes*, ed. Michel Fabre and Robert Skinner. Jackson: University Press of Mississippi, 1995.
Fabre, Michel, and Robert Skinner, eds. *Conversations with Chester Himes*. Jackson: University Press of Mississippi, 1995.
Fairclough, Adam. "Being in the Field of Education and Also Being Negro ... Seems ... Tragic": Black Teachers in the Jim Crow South." *Journal of American History* 87.1 (2000): 65–91.
Farred, Grant. "'Victorian with the Rebel Seed': C. L. R. James, Postcolonial Intellectual." *Social Text* 38 (Spring 1994): 21–38.
Fast, Howard. *Freedom Road*. 1944; Armonk, N.Y.: Sharpe, 1995.
Favor, J. Martin. *Authentic Blackness: The Folk in the New Negro Renaissance*. Durham: Duke University Press, 1999.
Fehrenbach, Heide. *Race after Hitler*. Princeton: Princeton University Press, 2005.
Fiedler, Leslie A. *Love and Death in the American Novel*. New York: Criterion, 1960.
———. "The War against the Academy." *Wisconsin Studies in Contemporary Literature* 5.1 (1964): 5–17.
Fitzgerald, Gregory, and Peter Marchant. "An Interview: Ernest J. Gaines." *New Orleans Review* 1 (1969): 331–35. Reprinted in *Conversations with Ernest Gaines*, ed. John Lowe. Jackson: University Press of Mississippi, 1994.
Foley, Barbara. "From Communism to Brotherhood: The Drafts of Invisible Man." In *Left of the Color Line: Race, Radicalism, and Twentieth-Century Literature of the United States*, ed. Bill V. Mullen and James Smethurst. Chapel Hill: University of North Carolina Press, 2003.
———. *Telling the Truth: The Theory and Practice of Documentary Fiction*. Ithaca: Cornell University Press, 1986.
Fontaine, William T. "The Mind and the Thought of the Negro of the United States as Revealed in Imaginative Literature, 1876–1940." *Southern University Bulletin* 28.3 (1942): 5–50.
Ford, Nick Aaron. "Blueprint for Negro Authors." *Phylon* 11.4 (1950): 374–77.
Franklin, John Hope. *Reconstruction after the Civil War*. Chicago: University of Chicago Press, 1961.
Friedel, Tania. *Racial Discourse and Cosmopolitanism in Twentieth-Century African American Literature*. New York: Routledge, 2007.
Gates, Henry Louis, Jr. *Figures in Black: Words, Signs and the "Racial" Self*. London: Oxford University Press, 1987.
———. "Harlem on Our Minds" *Critical Inquiry* 24.1 (1997): 1–12.
———. "Introduction: '... and Bid Him Sing': J. Saunders Redding and the Criticism of American Negro Literature." In *To Make a Poet Black*. Ithaca: Cornell University Press, 1988.

Works Cited

Genovese, Eugene. *In Red and Black: Marxian Explorations in Southern and Afro-American History*. London: Pantheon, 1971.
Gikandi, Simon. "Race and Cosmopolitanism." *American Literary History* 14.3 (2002): 593–615.
Gillmore, F. Grant. *The Problem: A Military Novel*. Rochester, N.Y.: Connolly, 1915.
Gilroy, Paul. *Against Race: Imagining Political Color beyond the Color Line*. Cambridge: Harvard University Press, 2000.
———. *The Black Atlantic: Modernity and Double Consciousness*. Cambridge: Harvard University Press, 1993.
———. *Postcolonial Melancholia*. New York: Columbia University Press, 2005.
Gloster, Hugh. *Negro Voices in American Fiction*. Chapel Hill: University of North Carolina Press, 1948.
———. "The Significance of Frank Yerby." *The Crisis*, January 1948, 12–13.
Goedde, Petra. *GIs and Germans: Culture, Gender and Foreign Relations, 1945–1949*. New Haven: Yale University Press, 2003.
Graham, Maryemma. "Frank Yerby, King of the Costume Novel." *Essence*, October 1975.
Grant, Madison. *The Passing of the Great Race*. New York: Scribner's, 1916.
Grotjahn, Martin. *Beyond Laughter: Humor and the Subconscious*. New York: McGraw-Hill, 1957.
Hahn, Steven. *A Nation under Our Feet: Black Political Struggles in the Rural South from Slavery to the Great Migration*. Cambridge: Harvard University Press, 2003.
Hall, Stuart. "Breaking Bread with History: C. L. R. James and *The Black Jacobins*: Stuart Hall interviewed by Bill Schwarz." *History Workshop Journal* 46 (Autumn 1998): 17–32.
Halsey, Margaret. *Color Blind: The White Woman Looks at the Negro*. New York: Simon and Schuster, 1946.
Harrington, Michael. *The Other America*. New York: Macmillan, 1962.
Hedden, Worth Tuttle. *The Other Room*. New York: Crown, 1947.
Heglar, Charles. "Literary Portraits of Zora Neale Hurston and the Forgotten Image of Laura Burroughs in Bucklin Moon's *Without Magnolias*." *CLA Journal* 50.4 (2007): 379–94.
Hemenway, Robert. *Zora Neale Hurston: A Literary Biography*. Urbana: University of Illinois Press, 1980.
Hill, Herbert, ed. *Anger, and Beyond: The Negro Writer in the United States*. New York: Harper and Row, 1966.
Hill, James L. "The Anti-Heroic Hero in Frank Yerby's Historical Novels." In *Perspectives of Black Popular Culture*, ed. Harry B. Shaw. Bowling Green, Ohio: Bowling Green State University Popular Press, 1990.
———. "Interview with Frank Garvin Yerby." *Resources for American Literary Study* 21.2 (1995): 206–39.
Himes, Chester. "All He Needs Is Feet." In *The Collected Stories of Chester Himes*. New York: Da Capo, 2000.

———. *Cast the First Stone*. New York: Coward-McCann, 1952.
———. *Collected Stories*. New York: Da Capo, 2000.
———. "Democracy Is for the Unafraid." In *Primer for White Folks*, ed. Bucklin Moon. Garden City, N.Y.: Doubleday, 1945.
———. *The End of a Primitive*. 1956; London: Allison and Busby, 2000.
———. "Heaven's Changed." In *The Collected Stories of Chester Himes*. New York: Da Capo, 2000.
———. "He Seen It in the Stars." In *The Collected Stories of Chester Himes*. New York: Da Capo, 2000.
———. *If He Hollers Let Him Go*. 1945; New York: Thunder's Mouth, 1986.
———. Letter to Richard Wright, n.d. [1945]. Richard Wright Papers, Beinecke Rare Book and Manuscript Library, Yale University, New Haven, Connecticut.
———. *Lonely Crusade*. New York: Knopf, 1947.
———. "Make with the Shape." In *The Collected Stories of Chester Himes*. New York: Da Capo, 2000.
———. *Plan B*. Jackson: University Press of Mississippi, 1993.
———. *The Quality of Hurt: The Early Years*. New York: Thunder's Mouth, 1995.
———. "Second Guesses for First Novelists." *Saturday Review of Literature*, February 16, 1946.
———. *The Third Generation*. Cleveland: World, 1954.
Hine, Darlene Clark. *Hine Sight: Black Women and the Reconstruction of American History*. Bloomington: Indiana University Press, 1997.
Hodges, LeRoy S., Jr. *Portrait of an Expatriate: William Gardner Smith, Writer*. Westport, Conn.: Greenwood, 1985.
Höhn, Maria. "*Heimat* in Turmoil: African-American GIs in 1950s West Germany." In *The Miracle Years: A Cultural History of West Germany, 1949–1968*, ed. Hanna Schissler. Princeton: Princeton University Press, 2001.
Holman, C. Hugh. Review of *The American Historical Novel*. *Journal of Southern History* 16.3 (1950): 392–94.
Hughes, Carl Milton. *The Negro Novelist, 1940–1950*. New York: Citadel, 1953.
Hurston, Zora Neale. "The Rise of the Begging Joints." *American Mercury* 60 (March 1945): 288–94.
———. *Zora Neale Hurston: A Life in Letters*. Ed. Carla Kaplan. New York: Doubleday, 2002.
Jablon, Madelyn. *Black Metafiction: Self-Consciousness in African American Literature*. Iowa City: University of Iowa Press, 1997.
Jackson, Blyden. "An Essay in Criticism." *Phylon* 11.4 (1950): 338–43.
———. "Full Circle." *Phylon* 9.1 (1948): 30–35.
———. "Silver Foxes." Review of *The Foxes of Harrow*. *Journal of Negro Education* 15.4 (1946): 649–52.
Jackson, Lawrence. "Irredeemable Promise: J. Saunders Redding and Negro New Liberalism." *American Literary History* 19.3 (2007): 712–44.

———. "Ralph Ellison's Politics of Integration." In *A Historical Guide to Ralph Ellison*, ed. Steven C. Tracy. Oxford: Oxford University Press, 2004.

James, C. L. R. *The Black Jacobins: Toussaint L'Ouverture and the San Domingo Rebellion*. 1938; New York: Vintage, 1989.

James, Jennifer C. "African American War Literature." In *The Encyclopedia of American War Literature*, ed. Philip K. Jason and Mark A. Graves. Westport, Conn.: Greenwood, 2000.

Janoff, Bruce. "Black Humor: Beyond Satire." *Ohio Review* 14.1 (1972): 5–20.

Jarrett, Gene, ed. *African American Literature beyond Race: An Alternative Reader*. New York: New York University Press, 2006.

———. *Deans and Truants: Race and Realism in African American Literature*. Philadelphia: University of Pennsylvania Press, 2007.

———. "'For Endless Generations': Myth, Dynasty, and Frank Yerby's *The Foxes of Harrow*." *Southern Literary Journal* 34.1 (2006): 54–70.

Jarrett, Thomas D. "Toward Unfettered Creativity: A Note on the Negro Novelist's Coming of Age." *Phylon* 11.4 (1950): 313–17.

Johnson, James Weldon. *The Autobiography of an Ex-Colored Man*. Boston: Sherman, French, 1912.

Kant, Immanuel. *Toward Perpetual Peace (1795)*. In *Practical Philosophy*, ed. Mary J. Gregor. Cambridge: Cambridge University Press, 1996.

Karem, Jeff. *The Romance of Authenticity: The Cultural Politics of Regional and Ethnic Literatures*. Charlottesville: University of Virginia Press, 2004.

Kazin, Alfred. "The Alone Generation: A Comment on the Fiction of the Fifties." *Harper's Magazine* 219 (October 1959): 127–31.

———. *On Native Grounds: An Interpretation of Modern American Prose Literature*. New York: Reynal and Hitchcock, 1942.

Keith, LeeAnna. *The Colfax Massacre: The Untold Story of Black Power, White Terror, and the Death of Reconstruction*. New York: Oxford University Press, 2008.

Kerouac, Jack. *On the Road*. New York: Viking, 1957.

Klotman, Phyllis. "A Harrowing Experience: Frank Yerby's First Novel to Film." *CLA Journal* 31.2 (1987): 210–22.

Kostelantz, Richard. *Politics in the African American Novel: James Weldon Johnson, W. E. B. Du Bois, Richard Wright, and Ralph Ellison*. Westport, Conn.: Greenwood, 1991.

Kramer, John E., Jr. *The American College Novel: An Annotated Bibliography*. New York: Garland, 1981.

Lane, Charles. *The Day Freedom Died*. New York: Holt, 2008.

Larsen, Nella. *Quicksand; and Passing*. Ed. and intro. Deborah E. McDowell. New Brunswick: Rutgers University Press, 1986.

Lash, John S. "The Race Consciousness of the American Negro Author: Toward a Reexamination of an Orthodox Critical Concept." *Social Forces* 28.1 (1949): 24–34.

Lee, Ulysses. "Hatred and Betrayal." Review of *Stranger and Alone*. *Phylon* 11.2 (1950): 180–81.
Lemann, Nicholas. *Redemption: The Last Battle of the Civil War*. New York: Farrar, Straus, and Giroux, 2006.
Levine, Lawrence. *Black Culture and Black Consciousness: Afro-American Folk Thought from Slavery to Freedom*. New York: Oxford University Press, 1978.
Lhamon, W. T. *Deliberate Speed: The Origins of a Cultural Style in the American 1950s*. 1990; Washington, D.C.: Smithsonian Institution Press, 2002.
Locke, Alain. "From *Native Son* to *Invisible Man*: A Review of the Literature of the Negro for 1952." *Phylon* 14.1 (1953): 34–44.
———. "Reason and Race: A Review of the Literature of the Negro for 1946." *Phylon* 8.1 (1947): 17–27.
Lodge, David. "The Campus Novel." *New Republic* 186.10 (1982): 34–36.
Logan, Rayford Whittingham. *The Negro in the Post-War World: A Primer*. Washington, D.C.: Minorities, 1945.
Lovell, John, Jr. "The Strange and the Lonely." Review of *Stranger and Alone*. *Journal of Negro Education* 20.1 (1951): 67–69.
Lubin, Alex. *Romance and Rights: The Politics of Interracial Intimacy, 1945–1954*. Jackson: University Press of Mississippi, 2005.
Lukin, Joshua. "Under Gray Flannel: Introduction to 'Fifties Fiction.'" *Paradoxa* 18 (2003): 1–7.
Lyons, John O. *The College Novel in America*. Carbondale: Southern Illinois University Press, 1962.
MacGregor, Morris J., Jr. *Integration of the Armed Forces, 1940–1965*. Washington, D.C.: U.S. Government Printing Office, 1981.
Mailer, Norman. *The Naked and the Dead*. New York: Rinehart, 1948.
———. "The White Negro: Superficial Reflections of the Hipster." In *Advertisements for Myself*. 1957; Cambridge: Harvard University Press, 1992.
Margolies, Edward. *Native Sons: A Critical Study of Twentieth Century Negro American Authors*. Philadelphia: Lippincott, 1968.
Match, Richard. "The Vulpine Master of Harrow." Review of *The Foxes of Harrow*. *New York Times*, February 10, 1946.
May, Lary. *Recasting America: Culture and Politics in the Age of Cold War*. Chicago: University of Chicago Press, 1989.
Mayer, William G. *The Changing American Mind: How and Why American Public Opinion Changed between 1960 and 1988*. Ann Arbor: University of Michigan Press, 1993.
Mayfield, Julian. "Challenge to Negro Leadership." *Commentary* 31.4 (1961): 297–305.
———. "Into the Mainstream and Oblivion." In *The American Negro Writer and His Roots*. New York: American Society of African Culture, 1960.
Mayne, Richard. *The Recovery of Europe: From Devastation to Unity*. New York: Harper and Row, 1970.

Works Cited

McCarthy, Mary. *The Groves of Academe*. New York: Harcourt, Brace, 1952.
McKay, Claude. *Home to Harlem*. New York: Harper, 1928.
McLendon, Jacquelyn. *The Politics of Color in the Fiction of Jessie Fauset and Nella Larsen*. Charlottesville: University of Virginia Press, 1995.
———. "'A Round, Unvarnished Tale': (Mis)Reading Othello or African American Strategies of Dissent." In *Othello: New Essays by Black Writers*, ed. Mythili Kaul. Washington, D.C.: Howard University Press, 1996.
Michener, James. Letter to John Farrar and Roger Straus, August 1, 1948. Farrar, Straus, and Giroux Collection, New York Public Library, New York.
Miller, Kelly. "The Past, Present, and Future of the Negro College." *Journal of Negro Education* 2.3 (1933): 411–22.
Mitchell, Margaret. *Gone with the Wind*. New York: Macmillan, 1936.
Moon, Bucklin, ed. *Primer for White Folks*. Garden City, N.Y.: Doubleday, 1945.
———. *Without Magnolias*. Garden City, N.Y.: Doubleday, 1949.
Moore, Jack B. "The Guilt of the Victim: Racial Themes in Some Frank Yerby Novels." *Journal of Popular Culture* 8.4 (1975): 746–56.
Morgan, Stacy I. *Rethinking Social Realism: African American Art and Literature, 1930–1953*. Athens: University of Georgia Press, 2004.
Morrison, Toni. *Playing in the Dark: Whiteness and the Literary Imagination*. New York: Vintage, 1993.
Motley, Willard. *Knock on Any Door*. New York: Appleton-Century, 1947.
———. "Let No Man Write Epitaph of Hate for His Chicago." *Chicago Sunday Sun-Times*, August 11, 1963.
Mullen, Bill V. "The African American Literary Response to World War II." *African American Review* 30.1 (1996): 5–15.
———. "Breaking the Signifying Chain: A New Blueprint for African American Literary Studies." *MFS* 47.1 (2001): 145–63.
———. "Popular Fronts: *Negro Story* Magazine and the African American Literary Response to World War II." *African American Review* 30.1 (1996): 5–15.
Mullen, Bill V., and James Smethurst, eds. *Left of the Color Line: Race, Radicalism, and Twentieth-Century Literature of the United States*. Chapel Hill: University of North Carolina Press, 2003.
Nadel, Alan. *Containment Culture: American Narrative, Postmodernism and the Atomic Age*. Lexington: University Press of Kentucky, 2002.
Nelson, Cary. "What Happens When We Put the Left at the Center?" *American Literature* 66.4 (1994): 771–79.
Nichols, Charles H. "The Forties: A Decade of Growth." *Phylon* 11.4 (1950): 377–80.
———. "Slave Narratives and the Plantation Legend." *Phylon* 10.3 (1949): 201–10.
Nussbaum, Martha. "Patriotism and Cosmopolitanism." In *For Love of Country: Debating the Limits of Patriotism*. Ed. Joshua Cohen. New York: Beacon, 1996.
O'Meally, Robert. Introduction to *New Essays on Invisible Man*. London: Cambridge University Press, 1988.

Orvell, Miles. *The Real Thing: Imitation and Authenticity in American Culture, 1880–1940*. Chapel Hill: University of North Carolina Press, 1989.
Ottley, Roi. *New World A-Coming: Inside Black America*. New York: Houghton Mifflin, 1943.
———. *No Green Pastures: The Negro in Europe Today*. New York: Houghton Mifflin, 1952.
Park, Robert. "Negro Race Consciousness as Reflected in Race Literature." In *The Collected Papers of Robert Ezra Park*, vol. 1, *Race and Culture*, ed. Everett Cherrington Hughes et al. Glencoe, Ill.: Free Press, 1950.
Pine, Hester. *Beer for the Kitten: A Heady Brew in Which to Toast the Pedagogues, Their Wives; in Which to Taste the Seductions of Higher Learning. Ladies and Gentlemen! The Faculty! Seen Through a Glass but Not Darkly*. New York: Farrar and Rinehart, 1939.
Poiger, Uta G. *Jazz, Rock, and Rebels: Cold War Politics and American Culture in a Divided Germany*. Berkeley: University of California Press, 2000.
Pollock, James K. "An Areal Study of the German Electorate, 1930–1933." *American Political Science Review* 38.1 (1944): 89–95.
Posnock, Ross. *Color and Culture: Black Writers and the Making of the Modern Intellectual*. Cambridge: Harvard University Press, 1998.
———. "The Dream of Deracination: The Uses of Cosmopolitanism." *American Literary History* 12.4 (2000): 802–18.
Randall, Alice. *The Wind Done Gone*. Boston: Houghton Mifflin, 2001.
Rankin, David C. "The Origin of Black Leadership in New Orleans during Reconstruction." *Journal of Southern History* 40.3 (1974): 417–40.
Ransom, John Crowe. "Reconstructed but Unregenerate." In *I'll Take My Stand: The South and the Agrarian Tradition*. 1930; Baton Rouge: Louisiana State University Press, 1977.
Read, Anthony, and David Fisher. *The Fall of Berlin*. New York: Da Capo, 1995.
Redding, J. Saunders. *An American in India: A Personal Report of the Indian Dilemma and the Nature of Her Conflicts*. Indianapolis: Bobbs-Merrill, 1954.
———. "The Black Man's Burden." *Antioch Review* 3 (Winter 1943): 587–95.
———. "The Cross and the Crown." Unpublished manuscript. J. Saunders Redding Papers, John Hay Library, Brown University, Providence, Rhode Island.
———. "A Fateful Lightning." Review of *The Confessions of Nat Turner*, by William Styron. J. Saunders Redding Collection, Brown University, Providence, Rhode Island.
———. "If There Be Any Praise." Unpublished manuscript. J. Saunders Redding Papers, John Hay Library, Brown University, Providence, Rhode Island.
———. *The Lonesome Road: The Story of the Negro's Part in America*. 1950; New York: Doubleday, 1958.
———. *The Negro*. Washington, D.C.: Potomac, 1967.

———. "The Negro Writer and American Literature." In *Anger, and Beyond: The Negro Writer in the United States*, ed. Herbert Hill. New York: Harper and Row, 1966.
———. "The Negro Writer and His Relationship to His Roots." In *The American Negro Writer and His Roots*. New York: American Society of African Culture, 1960.
———. *No Day of Triumph*. 1942; New York: Harper, 1968.
———. *On Being Negro in America*. Indianapolis: Bobbs-Merrill, 1951.
———. Review of *The Negro Novelist*, by Carl Milton Hughes. *Afro Magazine*, November 30, 1953: 11.
———. Review of *Without Magnolias*, by Bucklin Moon. *Afro Magazine*, May 5, 1949: 9.
———. Review of *Youth of Color*, by Caroline Wasson Thomason. *Afro Magazine*, February 7, 1952: 10.
———. "A Second Look." *Afro-American*, September 15, 1945.
———. "A Second Look." *Afro-American*, April 20, 1946.
———. "A Second Look." *Afro-American*, May 18, 1946.
———. "A Second Look." Review of *If He Hollers Let Him Go*. *Afro-American*, June 1, 1946.
———. "The Secret Life of Gaynor Howden" (early manuscript of *Stranger and Alone*). J. Saunders Redding Papers, Brown University, Providence, Rhode Island.
———. *Stranger and Alone*. New York: Harcourt, Brace, 1950.
———. *They Came in Chains: Americans from Africa*. 1950; Philadelphia: Lippincott, 1973.
———. *To Make a Poet Black*. 1939; Ithaca: Cornell University Press, 1988.
Richardson, Mark. "Peasant Dreams: Reading *On the Road*." *Texas Studies in Literature and Language* 43.2 (Summer 2001): 218–42.
Riesman, David, in collaboration with Reuel Denney and Nathan Glazer. *The Lonely Crowd*. New Haven: Yale University Press, 1950.
Ro, Sigmund. *Rage and Celebration: Essays on Contemporary Afro-American Writing*. Atlantic Highlands, N.J.: Humanities, 1984.
Robinson, C. Kelly. *Between Brothers: A Novel*. New York: Random House, 2001.
Rolo, Charles J. Review of *Last of the Conquerors*. *Atlantic Monthly*, October 1948.
Ross, Andrew. "Hip and the Long Front of Color." In *No Respect: Intellectuals and Popular Culture*. New York: Routledge, 1989.
Savery, Pancho. Introduction to *Stranger and Alone*, by J. Saunders Redding. Boston: Northeastern University Press, 1989.
"Scarlet Splash." Review of *The Vixens*. *Time*, May 5, 1947, 113.
Schraufnagel, Noel. *From Apology to Protest: The Black American Novel*. Deland, Fla.: Everett/Edwards, 1973.
Scott, Robert F. "It's a Small World, after All: Assessing the Contemporary Campus Novel." *Journal of the Midwest Modern Language Association* 37.1 (2004): 81–87.

Scott, W. T. "Saunders Redding's Novel of a Heel." *Providence Sunday Journal*, February 19, 1950.

Scruggs, Charles. *Sweet Home: Invisible Cities in the Afro-American Novel*. Baltimore: Johns Hopkins University Press, 1993.

Shandley, Robert R. *Rubble Films: German Cinema in the Shadow of the Third Reich*. Philadelphia: Temple University Press, 2001.

Shelby, Tommie. "Cosmopolitanism, Blackness, and Utopia: A Conversation with Paul Gilroy." *Transition* 98 (2008): 116–35.

Smethurst, James. *The New Red Negro*. New York: Oxford University Press, 1999.

Smith, Barbara Herrnstein. *Contingencies of Value: Alternative Perspectives for Critical Theory*. Cambridge: Cambridge University Press, 1988.

Smith, Lillian. *Killers of the Dream*. 1949; New York: Norton, 1994.

Smith, Valerie. *Self-Discovery and Authority in the Afro-American Narrative*. Cambridge: Harvard University Press, 1987.

Smith, William Gardner. *Anger at Innocence*. New York: Signet, 1950.

———. *Last of the Conquerors*. New York: Signet, 1948.

———. Letter to Carolyn Wolfe, April 8, 1949. Farrar, Straus, and Giroux Collection, New York Public Library, New York.

———. "The Negro Writer: Pitfalls and Compensations." In *Remembering the Harlem Renaissance*, ed. Cary D. Wintz. New York: Garland, 1996.

———. *Return to Black America*. Englewood Cliffs, N.J.: Prentice Hall, 1970.

———. *South Street*. New York: Farrar, Straus, and Young, 1954.

Sommer, Doris. *Proceed with Caution When Engaged by Minority Writing in the Americas*. Cambridge: Harvard University Press, 1999.

Stepto, Robert. *From behind the Veil: A Study of Afro-American Narrative*. Urbana: University of Illinois Press, 1979.

Stevens, Dana. "Sorry, I Didn't Like This Movie." Review of *Precious*. *Slate*, November 5, 2009.

Stovall, Eugene. "Why Frank Yerby Costumed His Novels: A Critical Essay." Frank Yerby Renaissance Project. www.frankyerby.com. March 12, 2009.

Susman, Warren. "Did Success Spoil the United States?" In *Recasting America: Culture and Politics in the Cold War*, ed. Lary May. Chicago: University of Chicago Press, 1989.

Taylor, Helen. *Scarlett's Women: Gone with the Wind and Its Female Fans*. New Brunswick: Rutgers University Press, 1989.

Taylor, Ronald. *Berlin and Its Culture: A Historical Portrait*. New Haven: Yale University Press, 1997.

Thompson, Era Bell. "Negro Publications and the Writer." *Phylon* 11.4 (1950): 304–6.

Tidwell, John Edgar, and John S. Wright. "Steady and Unaccusing: An Interview with Sterling Brown." *Callaloo* 21.4 (1998): 811–21.

Tillman, N. P. "The Threshold of Maturity." *Phylon* 11.4 (1950): 387–88.

Toomer, Jean. *Cane*. New York: Boni and Liveright, 1923.
Tracy, Henry. "Answered in Fiction." Review of *If He Hollers Let Him Go*. *Common Ground*, Summer 1946, 109–10.
Turner, Darwin. "Frank Yerby as Debunker." *Massachusetts Review* 20 (Summer 1968): 569–77.
———. "Introductory Remarks about the Black Literary Tradition in the United States of America." *Black American Literature Forum* 12.4 (1978): 140–47.
Tyree, Omar. *College Boy*. New York: Simon and Schuster, 2003.
Vassilowitch, John, Jr. "Ellison's Dr. Bledsoe: Two Literary Sources." *Essays in Literature* 8 (Spring 1981): 109–13.
Wald, Alan. *Exiles from a Future Time: The Forging of the Mid-Twentieth-Century Literary Left*. Chapel Hill: University of North Carolina Press, 2002.
Walker, Alice. *Meridian*. New York: Harcourt, 1976.
Warren, Kenneth. *Black and White Strangers: Race and American Literary Realism*. Chicago: University of Chicago Press, 1993.
———. "The End(s) of African-American Studies." *American Literary History* 12.3 (2000): 637–55.
Washington, Mary Helen. "'Disturbing the Peace: What Happens to American Studies If You Put African American Studies at the Center?': Presidential Address to the American Studies Association, October 29, 1997." *American Quarterly* 50.1 (1998): 1–23.
Watkins, Mel. *On the Real Side: A History of African American Comedy*. New York: Hill, 1999.
Weber, Donald. "Memory and Repression in Early Ethnic Television." In *The Other Fifties*, ed. Joel Foreman. Urbana: University of Illinois Press, 1997.
Weik, Alexa. "The Uses and Hazards of Expatriation: Richard Wright's Cosmopolitanism in Process." *African American Review* 41.3 (2007): 459–75.
Weisenburger, Steven. *Fables of Subversion: Satire and the American Novel, 1930–1980*. Athens: University of Georgia Press, 1995.
Werner, Craig Hansen. *Playing the Changes: From Afro-Modernism to the Jazz Impulse*. Urbana: University of Illinois Press, 1994.
Wheeler, Robyn E. "Making Classical History." *American Visions* 8.1 (1993): 44–45.
White, Walter. *The Fire in the Flint*. New York: Knopf, 1924.
Whitfield, Stephen J. *The Culture of the Cold War*. Baltimore: Johns Hopkins University Press, 1991.
Williams, John A. "My Man Himes." In *Conversations with Chester Himes*, ed. Michel Fabre and Robert Skinner. Jackson: University Press of Mississippi, 1995.
Williams, John A., and Lori Williams. *Dear Chester, Dear John: Letters between Chester Himes and John A. Williams*. Detroit: Wayne State University Press, 2008.
Williamson, Joel. *A Rage for Order: Black-White Relations in the American South since Emancipation*. New York: Oxford University Press, 1986.

Winsor, Kathleen. *Forever Amber*. New York: Macmillan, 1944.
Woodson, Carter G. Review of *The Foxes of Harrow*. *Journal of Negro History* 31.3 (1946): 353–54.
Woodward, C. Vann. *Origins of the New South, 1877–1913*. Baton Rouge: Louisiana State University Press, 1951.
Wright, Richard. "Blueprint for Negro Writing" (1937). In *The Portable Harlem Renaissance Reader*, ed. David Levering Lewis. New York: Penguin, 1995.
———. "How Bigger Was Born." Introduction to *Native Son*. New York: Harper, 1940.
———. *Uncle Tom's Children: Four Novellas*. New York: Harper, 1938.
———. *White Man, Listen!* 1957; New York: HarperCollins, 1995.
Yerby, Frank. *The Foxes of Harrow*. New York: Dial, 1946.
———. *The Golden Hawk*. New York: Dial, 1948.
———. "Health Card." *Harper's*, May 1944, 548–53.
———. "How and Why I Write the Costume Novel." *Harper's Magazine*, October 1959.
———. "Ignoble Victory" (manuscript). Frank Yerby Collection, Howard Gotlieb Archival Research Center, Boston University, Boston.
———. Letter to editor, n.d. Frank Yerby Collection, Howard Gotlieb Archival Research Center, Boston University, Boston.
———. *The Vixens*. New York: Dial, 1947.
Zijderveld, Anton C. "Jokes and Their Relation to Social Reality." *Social Research* 35.2 (1968): 186–311.

Index

academic novel, African American, 135, 158, 159
African American Viewers and the Black Situation Comedy (Coleman), 26
Afro-American, 156
Agee, James, 25–26
Algren, Nelson, 37
Ali, Muhammad, 73
"All He Needs Is Feet" (Himes), 53
American College Novel, The (Kramer), 135
American Historical Review, 167n8
American in India, An (Redding), 132
American Mercury, 155
Amis, Kingsley, 135
Anderson, Benedict, 4
Anger, and Beyond (Hill), 12
Anger at Innocence (W. G. Smith), 22, 161
Appiah, Kwame Anthony, 109–10
Aswell, Edward, 71
Attaway, William, 39

Baker, Houston, 35
Baldwin, James, 28
Balfour, Alan, 113
Barkin, Kenneth D., 107
Barrett, Lindon, 148
Barton, Rebecca Chalmers, 38
Bates, Gerri, 116
Beck, Ulrich, 130
Beer for the Kitten (Pine), 150
Beetlecreek (Demby), 10
Bell, Bernard W., 12

Bergson, Henri, 59
Berlin, 104–5, 107, 109–10, 111, 112–15, 116–17, 121–24, 125–27
Berry, Faith, 134, 170n2
Bibb, J., 27
biraciality, 125–27
Black Arts movement, 4, 12, 14
Black Boy (Wright), 11
"Black Boy Looks at the White Boy, The" (Baldwin), 28
Black Culture and Black Consciousness (Levine), 59
Black Jacobins, The (James), 95, 96, 168n17
Black Reconstruction in America (Du Bois), 82, 83, 95, 167n8
"Blueprint for Negro Authors, A" (Ford), 38
"Blueprint for Negro Writing" (Wright), 17
Bogart, Humphrey, 37
Bone, Robert, 23, 38, 41, 68, 116
Bontemps, Arna, 22, 39
Boris, Eileen, 49
Botkin, B. A., 166n1
Bowers, Claude, 83
Boykin, Leander L., 152
Bradley, Omar, 102
Branch, William, 35–36
Breu, Christopher, 49
Brice, Ashbel G., 120
Brooks, Van Wyck, 47
Brown, Ina Corinne, 154–55

Index

Brown, Lloyd, 9
Brown, Sterling, 19, 34–35, 36, 37
Brown v. Board of Education, 101, 134, 156
Buckmaster, Henrietta, 86, 167n11
Butcher, Margaret Just, 24

campus novel, 134–35, 140, 149, 151
Cane (Toomer), 14
Cash, W. J., 84, 85–86
Cast the First Stone (Himes), 22, 56
Cavendish, Henry, 136
Chadwick, Bruce, 82
Chandler, G. Lewis, 8, 16
Charles, Louis, 94
Chicago Defender, 48
Chicago Sun-Times, 37
Chicago Tribune, 137
Coleman, Robin R. Means, 26, 27
Colfax, La., massacre at, 92–93, 98
College English, 67
college novel, 134
Color Blind (Halsey), 20
"Coming of Age: A Note on Negro American Novelists" (Chandler), 16
Compromise of 1877, 89
Confessions of Nat Turner, The (Styron), 157
Conrad, Earl, 48
Containment Culture (Nadel), 7
Contemporary African American Novel, The (Bell), 12
Contemporary Negro Novel, The (Ford), 39
Cook, Fannie, 137
costume novel, 68, 71, 89, 97, 98. *See also* historical romance
Coulter, E. Merton, 83
Country Place, A (Petry), 22
Crisis, The, 53
"Cross and the Crown, The" (Redding), 159

Crouch, William Terry, 19
Culture of the Cold War, The (Whitfield), 7

Daly, Victor, 103
Davis, Arthur P., 133
Dearborn, Mary V., 28
Delbanco, Andrew, 171n11
Deliberate Speed (Lhamon), 7
Demby, William, 10
Derek, John, 37
desegregation, 101
Dickson-Carr, Darryl, 41, 165n2
Dixon, Dean, 123, 169n13
Dixon, Thomas, 82, 157
Döblin, Alfred, 105
Douglass, Frederick, 3
Doyle, Mary Ellen, 162
Du Bois, Shirley Graham, 108
Du Bois, W. E. B., 11, 73, 82, 83, 86, 95, 106, 107–8, 132, 166n6
Dumas, Francis E., 94
Dunn, Oscar J., 86, 94, 95, 96, 97, 168n18
Dunning, William Archibald, 82
Dusk of Dawn (Du Bois), 107

Edgerton, Robert B., 100
Ehrenreich, Barbara, 136
Eisenhower, Dwight D., 102
Ellis, Trey, 161
Ellison, Ralph, 3, 7, 13, 33, 59, 135, 142, 156, 157; *Invisible Man*, 4, 7, 10–11, 14, 30
End of a Primitive, The (Himes), 45, 57, 58, 59, 60–66, 166n5; Jesse Robinson, 58, 60–65, 66; Kriss Cummings, 60, 61, 63–65; Pope, 62–63; Walter, 64, 65
English, Daylanne, 13
Evans, Walker, 25–26

Fabre, Michel, 44, 45, 47, 49, 57
Fairclough, Adam, 153
Farred, Grant, 96

Farrell, James T., 37
Fast, Howard, 73
Faulkner, William, 45, 84
Favor, J. Martin, 8
Fehrenbach, Heide, 101, 103, 105, 109, 118, 126, 169n5, 170n14
Fiedler, Leslie, 33, 149, 171n9
Fire in the Flint, The (White), 104
Fisher, David, 113–14, 169n9
Fisher, Rudolph, 41
Fitzgerald, Gregory, 162
Fleming, Robert, 37
Foley, Barbara, 10, 11, 31–32
Fontaine, William T., 32
Ford, Nick Aaron, 38–39
Forever Amber (Winsor), 73
Foxes of Harrow, The (Yerby), 37, 67–72, 74–82, 92, 99; Aupre, 80; blackness and whiteness in, 75; Caleen, 78–80; Ceclie, 74; Cyrus, 81; Desiree, 80, 81; Etienne Fox, 74, 77, 79, 80–81; Hugo Waguespack, 75; Inch, 78, 79, 81; Odalie Arceneaux, 75, 78, 79, 80; Stephen Fox, 67, 75, 76–78, 79, 80, 81, 92
Franklin, John Hope, 82
Freedom Road (Fast), 73
French, Catherine, 169n13
Friedel, Tania, 108
From Apology to Protest (Schraufnagel), 12
From behind the Veil (Stepto), 148
"From *Native Son* to *Invisible Man*" (Locke), 14

Gadamer, Hans-George, 124
Gaines, Ernest, 3, 5, 31, 162
Gates, Henry Louis, Jr., 12, 32, 33, 132, 170n1
Genovese, Eugene, 168n17
Gikandi, Simon, 169n7
Gillmore, F. Frank, 103

Gilroy, Paul, 80, 107, 119, 165n3, 169n7
Gloster, Hugh, 14–15, 68, 75
Goedde, Petra, 103, 105, 116, 117
Golden Hawk, The (Yerby), 37, 68
Gone with the Wind (Mitchell), 72, 75–76, 81, 82–83, 84, 88, 89
Graham, Maryemma, 70
Grotjahn, Martin, 166n4
Groves of Academe, The (McCarthy), 135

Haitian Revolution, 94–96
Hall, James C., 10
Hall, Stuart, 168n17
Halsey, Margaret, 20, 28–29
"Harlem on Our Minds" (Gates), 12
Harlem Renaissance, 12, 13, 14
Harrington, Michael, 25
Harris, Joel Chandler, 82
Hayes, Rutherford B., 89
"He Seen It in the Stars" (Himes), 54
"Health Card" (Yerby), 70
"Heaven's Changed" (Himes), 54
Hedden, Worth Tuttle, 136, 137, 138
Heglar, Charles J., 156
Heller, Joseph, 58
Hemingway, Ernest, 100
Highet, Gilbert, 66
Hill, Herbert, 12
Hill, James L., 70, 71, 73, 83
Himes, Chester, 5, 22, 41–44, 53–54, 56–60, 62–63, 149, 161; *The End of a Primitive*, 45, 57, 58, 59, 60–66; and humor, 58, 59, 62; *If He Hollers Let Him Go*, 5, 19–20, 41–58, 67, 133, 135; and protest novel, 41–44, 48, 56, 57–58, 60, 61, 63, 66; and satire, 66; and Richard Wright, 41, 44, 47
Hine, Darlene Clark, 85
historical romance, 5, 72, 73, 74, 81, 86
historiography, 5, 73, 82, 83–85, 90, 91, 93, 96, 97
Hitler, Adolf, 111–12, 113–14, 169n8, 169n9

Hodges, LeRoy S., Jr., 99, 100
Höhn, Maria, 103
Holman, C. Hugh, 157
Home to Harlem (McKay), 104
"How and Why I Write the Costume Novel" (Yerby), 70, 87
Hughes, Carl Milton, 21–22, 29, 32, 38, 47, 48, 58, 61, 137
Hughes, Langston, 36
humor, African American, 58–59, 66
Hurston, Zora Neale, 22, 155, 156

If He Hollers Let Him Go (Himes), 5, 19, 41–58, 60, 67, 133, 135; Alice, 46, 50, 53, 55; "Arky Jill," 54; Bob Jones, 45–48, 50–56; Don, 54; Madge, 46, 51, 54–56
"Ignoble Victory" (Yerby), 73–74, 82, 83, 85, 86–98; Cyrus Inchcliff, 87, 91–93, 95, 96, 97, 98; Desiree, 87; Etienne Fox, 87, 90, 92; Gail Fox, 87, 88; Hope Varrick, 86, 87, 88, 92; Hugh Duncan, 87, 90; Isaac Robinson, 87, 88, 91, 96–97, 98; Land Moreau, 86, 87, 88, 89, 92; Sabrina Duncan, 87, 88; Tennessee Rhodes, 86
integration, 102
Invisible Man (Ellison), 4, 7, 10–11, 12, 14, 30, 135
Iron City (Brown), 9
Isherwood, Christopher, 105

Jablon, Madelyn, 23
Jackson, Blyden, 68, 160
Jackson, Lawrence, 133
James, C. L. R., 95, 96, 165n3, 168n17
Janoff, Bruce, 58
Jarrett, Gene, 69
Jarrett, Thomas D., 15
jazz, 27, 30
Joel, George, 73
Johnson, Charles, 5, 161
Johnson, James Weldon, 11

Journal of Blacks in Higher Education, 3
Joyce, James, 163

Karem, Jeff, 8
Kazin, Alfred, 47, 71
Kerouac, Jack, 26, 27, 28, 29, 30
Klotman, Phyllis, 72
Knock on Any Door (Motley), 37, 99
Kostelantz, Richard, 11
Kramer, John E., 135
Ku Klux Klan, 10, 80, 83

Larsen, Nella, 120
Lash, John S., 39
Last of the Conquerors (Smith), 99–107, 109–13, 115–17, 119–30; Captain Doyle, 115, 117; Captain Johnny Polke, 111, 112, 113, 129; Charles Henry (the Professor), 110, 112, 115; Corporal Stevenson, 111; Frau Hoffman, 126, 127; Hayes Dawkins, 104, 105–6, 107, 109, 110–11, 112–13, 115–16, 117, 119–24, 127–30; Homo, 115, 117; Ilse, 104, 105–6, 111, 115–16, 117, 119–20, 125, 127–28, 129; Lela, 127; Randy, 110, 112, 115; Sergeant Brink, 111, 112, 113; Sergeant Murdock, 115, 116, 129; Sonny, 124, 125, 126–28
Lay My Burden Down (Botkin), 166n1
Lee, Ulysses, 156, 157
Lesson Before Dying, A (Gaines), 3, 162–63
Let Us Now Praise Famous Men (Agee and Evans), 26
Levine, Lawrence, 59, 61
Lhamon, W. T., Jr., 7, 26
Light in August (Faulkner), 45
Locke, Alain, 14, 68
Lodge, David, 150
Logan, Rayford Whittingham, 20, 131
Lonely Crusade (Himes), 56
Lonesome Road, The (Redding), 132

Lovell, John, Jr., 156, 157
Lubin, Alex, 103, 105, 118
Lucky Jim (Amis), 135
Lukin, Josh, 3
Lyons, John O., 150

MacGregor, Morris J., Jr., 101
Mailer, Norman, 27, 28–30, 103
"Make with the Shape" (Himes), 53
Marchant, Peter, 162
Marching Blacks (Powell), 166n1
Margolies, Edward, 12, 23, 24, 49
Match, Richard, 70
May, Lary, 7
Mayer, William G., 152
Mayfield, Julian, 24
Mayne, Richard, 105
McCarthy, Mary, 135
McKay, Claude, 104
McLendon, Jacquelyn, 63
McMillan, Terry, 161
Meridian (Walker), 135
Michener, James, 102
Miller, Flontina, 44
Miller, Kelly, 153–54
Mind of the South, The (Cash), 84, 88
miscegenation, 75, 80, 118
Mitchell, Margaret, 72, 82–83, 84, 167n7, 167n9
Moon, Bucklin, 19, 46, 136, 137, 138, 155
Moore, Jack B., 69, 70
Morgan, Stacy I., 8
Morrison, Toni, 33, 80, 161
Motley, Willard, 5, 16, 22, 37, 39, 99
Mrs. Palmer's Honey (Cook), 137
Mullen, Bill V., 9, 49, 53

Nadel, Alan, 7, 30, 34
Naked and the Dead, The (Mailer), 103
Narrative of the Life of Frederick Douglass (Douglass), 3
Nash, Christopher Columbus, 93

Native Son (Wright), 4, 8, 10–11, 12, 16, 43, 44, 162; and *The End of a Primitive*, 63, 65; and *If He Hollers Let Him Go*, 47, 57
Native Sons: A Critical Study of Twentieth Century Negro Authors (Margolies), 12
Negro, The (Redding), 132
Negro in American Culture, The (Butcher), 24
Negro in the Post-War World, The (Logan), 131
Negro Novelist: 1940–1950 (Hughes), 21, 137
Negro Story, 53
Negro Voices in American Fiction (Gloster), 15
"Negro Writer: Pitfalls and Compensations" (W. G. Smith), 16
Nelson, Cary, 9
New Criticism, 11, 30
New Orleans, La., 76, 78
New Orleans Tribune, 86, 94
New South, 84
New York Times, 70
Nichols, Charles H., 16
"Nigger, A" (Himes), 49
Nixon, Richard, 25
No Day of Triumph (Redding), 132, 134, 135, 156, 157
Not Only War (Daly), 103
Nussbaum, Martha, 108

O'Meally, Robert, 62
On Being Negro in America (Redding), 18, 132
On the Road (Kerouac), 27, 29
Orvell, Miles, 25
Othello (Shakespeare), 57, 63
Other America, The (Harrington), 25
Other Room, The (Hedden), 136
Ottley, Roi, 20, 102, 109

Page, Thomas Nelson, 82
Pamela (Richardson), 12
Park, Robert, 32
Parker v. University of Delaware, 158
"Past, Present, and Future of the Negro College, The" (Miller), 153
Petry, Ann, 5, 22, 39
Philadelphia Negro, The (Du Bois), 107
Phylon, 15, 21
Pinchback, Pinckney Benton Stewart, 94
Pine, Hester, 150
Pittsburgh Courier, 27, 102, 110
Plan B (Himes), 59–60
Playing the Changes (Werner), 13
Poiger, Uta G., 118
Politics in the African American Novel (Kostelantz), 11
Pollock, James K., 111–12
Posnock, Ross, 106, 107, 108
Powell, Adam Clayton, Jr., 166n1
Precious, 164
Primer for White Folks (Moon), 19, 46
Problem: A Military Novel, The (Gillmore), 103
protest novel, 5, 11, 12, 21, 22, 30–31; and Himes, 41–44, 45, 48, 56, 57–58, 60, 61, 63, 66; and Redding, 133, 134, 138, 139–40, 160; and Yerby, 74, 98
Push (Sapphire), 164
Pynchon, Thomas, 58

Quality of Hurt, The (Himes), 49
Quicksand (Larsen), 120

"Race Consciousness of the American Negro Author, The" (Lash), 39
racism, 101; and Himes, 43, 45, 46, 47, 48; and Yerby, 98
Randall, Alice, 76
Rankin, David C., 86
Ransom, John Crowe, 84
Ray, Nicholas, 37

Read, Anthony, 113–14, 169n9
Recasting America (May), 7
Reconstruction, 6, 73, 76, 82; and Cash, 84, 85, 88; and Yerby, 72, 83–84, 85, 86, 88, 89, 90, 91, 93, 94, 97
"Reconstruction and Its Benefits" (Du Bois), 82
Redding, J. Saunders, 5, 6, 18, 39, 42, 132–33, 137–40, 156, 161; and campus novel, 134–35, 140, 151; and college novel, 134, 135; and higher education, 148–49, 150, 151, 156, 158–59; and protest fiction, 133, 134, 138, 139–40, 160; *Stranger and Alone*, 131, 133–51, 154, 156–60
Redding, Louis L., 158
Reed, Ishmael, 58
Reel Civil War, The (Chadwick), 82
Rethinking Social Realism (Morgan), 8
Return to Black America (Smith), 122
Richardson, Mark, 165n4
Richardson, Samuel, 12
Riesman, David, 29
Ro, Sigmund, 17
Robinson, C. Kelly, 135
Rolo, Charles J., 106
Romance of Authenticity, The (Karem), 8
Roosevelt, Eleanor, 43
Roosevelt, Franklin, 165n1
Ross, Andrew, 25
Roudanez, Jean Baptiste, 94

Sapphire, 162
Saturday Review of Literature, 49
Savery, Pancho, 147
Schmoller, Gustav, 107
Schraufnagel, Noel, 12
Scott, Robert F., 149
Scott, W. T., 142
Scruggs, Charles, 122
segregation, 19
Selznick, David, 83, 167n9

Seraph on the Suwanee (Hurston), 22
Shelby, Tommie, 108
Skinner, Robert, 44, 45, 47
slavery, 78, 96
Smethurst, James, 9, 34
Smith, Barbara Herrnstein, 5
Smith, Lillian, 171n10
Smith, Valerie, 148
Smith, William Gardner, 5, 6, 16–17, 22, 39, 99–100, 108, 122, 131, 161; and biraciality, 125–27; and interracial relationships, 106; *Last of the Conquerors*, 99–107, 109–13, 115–17, 119–30; in the military, 100, 102; and war novel, 103, 133
Sommer, Doris, 43
Souls of Black Folk, The (Du Bois), 107
South during Reconstruction, The (Coulter), 83
South Street (Smith), 161
Speer, Albert, 113
Stepto, Robert, 148
Stevens, Dana, 164
Stovall, Eugene, 70
Stowe, Harriet Beecher, 31
Stranger and Alone (Redding), 18, 131, 133–51, 154, 156–60, 171n12; Curtis Flack, 139; Edward Pettijohn, 139; Fred Thompson, 142–43; Gerry Wimbush, 146–47; Nan, 146, 147; Perkins Wimbush, 139, 140, 141, 148; Professor Clarkson, 143, 151; Shelton Howden, 139, 140–48, 151, 158, 159; Spurgeon Kelly, 139; Valrie Tillet, 144–45
Street (Petry), 22
Styron, William, 157
Supreme Court, U.S., 101, 134
Susman, Warren, 25

Taylor, Helen, 82
Taylor, Ronald, 110

television, 26
Telling the Truth (Foley), 31
They Came in Chains (Redding), 132
Third Generation, The (Himes), 56, 57
This Is My Own (Yerby), 71
Thomason, Caroline Wasson, 137
Thompson, Era Bell, 36
Tidwell, John Edgar, 35
Tilden, Samuel, 89
Tillman, N. P., 15, 36, 37
Time, 68
To Make a Poet Black (Redding), 133, 170n1
Toomer, Jean, 14
Tracy, Henry, 47
Tragic Era, The (Bowers), 83
Treitschke, Heinrich von, 107
Trevigne, Paul, 94–95, 96
Truman, Harry S., 102
Turchock, Wanda, 72
Turner, Darwin, 70, 72, 74
Tyree, Omar, 135

Uncle Tom's Children (Wright), 8, 43
University of Berlin, 114
University of North Carolina Press, 84

Vassilowitch, John, Jr., 135
Vixens, The (Yerby), 37, 69, 71–74, 80, 89, 92, 93, 98; original manuscript, 71, 72, 73–74. *See also* "Ignoble Victory"
Vonnegut, Kurt, 58

Wagner, Adolf, 107
Wald, Alan, 9, 165n1
Walker, Alice, 7, 135
Warmoth, Henry C., 94, 97
Warren, Kenneth, 32
Washington, Mary Helen, 9
Watkins, Mel, 59
Weber, Donald, 26
Weik, Alexa, 124–25, 128

Weisenburger, Steven, 58, 66
Werner, Craig Hansen, 13, 165n2
West, Nathanael, 58
What the Negro Wants (Crouch), 19
Wheeler, Robyn E., 170n13
White, Walter, 104
"White Negro, The" (Mailer), 27
Whitfield, Stephen J., 7
Williams, John A., 7, 43, 45, 57
Williamson, Joel, 44
Wind Done Gone, The (Randall), 76
Winsor, Kathleen, 73
Without Magnolias (Moon), 136, 137, 155, 170n4
Witnesses for Freedom (Barton), 38
Wolfe, Carolyn, 99, 100, 108
Wolfe, Thomas, 84
Woodson, Carter G., 68
Woodward, C. Vann, 167n10
Woodward, Isaac, 168n1
World War II, 46
Wright, John S., 35
Wright, Richard, 3, 10, 11, 12, 13, 14, 16, 22, 30, 33, 44, 47–48, 109, 121, 165n3; blueprint, 17, 23, 33, 66, 67, 99; *Native Son*, 4, 8, 10–11, 43; *Uncle Tom's Children*, 8

Yerby, Frank, 5, 16, 22, 37, 38, 73, 75, 99, 161; and Confederate romance, 87–88, 90, 91, 97; and costume novel, 68, 71, 89, 97, 98; *The Foxes of Harrow*, 67–72, 74–82; and historical romance, 72, 73, 86, 133; and historiography, 73, 82, 83–85, 90, 91, 93, 96, 97; "Ignoble Victory," 73–74, 82, 83, 85, 86–98; and miscegenation/interraciality, 75, 80, 81, 82, 97; and protest novel, 74, 98; *The Vixens*, 37, 69, 71–74, 80, 89, 92, 93, 98; as Wright's equal, 39
Youth of Color (Thomason), 137

Zijderveld, Anton, 59
Zuckmayer, Carl, 110

www.ingramcontent.com/pod-product-compliance
Lightning Source LLC
Chambersburg PA
CBHW022021220426
43663CB00007B/1162